Jesus As Brother

Jesus As Brother

What Christianity Owes America

Phillip Griffin, Ph.D.

2001
Galde Press, Inc.
Lakeville, Minnesota, U.S.A.

Jesus As Brother
© Copyright 2001 by Phillip Griffin
All rights reserved.
Printed in the United States of America
No part of this book may be used or reproduced in any manner whatsoever without written permission from the publishers except in the case of brief quotations embodied in critical articles and reviews.

First Edition
First Printing, 2001

Library of Congress Cataloging-in-Publication Data
Griffin, Phillip, 1925–
   Jesus as brother: what christianity owes america / Phillip Griffin.—1st ed.
    p. cm.
   Includes bibliographical information (p. 221).
   ISBN 1–880090–90–2 (pbk.)
    1. Christianity and politics—United States. 2. Liberalism—Religious aspects—Christianity. I. Title.
   BR115.P7 G737 2000
   261.7'0973—dc21   00–057647

Galde Press, Inc.
PO Box 460
Lakeville, Minnesota 55044–0460

This book is dedicated to my grandchildren: Chris, Mandy and Robin Kintner, Daniel Tarver, Abby and Adam Sterne, Shelby, Emma and Jordan Griffin, and to three young people who have been my foster-grandchildren, Luke, Katherine and Tanya. Their generation will live and work in a future that I believe will see rich opportunities for a world in which the human values of justice, equality and respect are the legacy of them and all their world neighbors. My deepest wish is that this book will challenge them to the realization of that legacy.

Contents

	Acknowledgments	xi
	Introduction	xiii
1	Jesus and the Quality of American Public Life	1
2	Origins of American Triumphalism	17
3	Morality and Triumphalism	31
4	Many Things Are Known, But All Incompletely	57
5	Religion and Community	81
6	Organic and Atomistic Individuals and Society	101
7	Religion As Relationship	123
8	Religion and Race	139
9	Religion, Politics, and Economics	163
10	America's Next Religion	189
	Reference Notes	217
	Bibliography	221

Acknowledgments

ONLY AN UNKNOWN and previously unpublished teacher-turned-writer can appreciate the value of a publisher such as Galde Press. This process of cooperative and generous effort has made this book possible, and Phyllis Galde and David Godwin have my heartfelt thanks for all they have done. The skill and patience of my editor at Galde Press, Barbara Bergstrom, has saved a passable teacher from being a miserable writer. Due to the work of all at Galde Press, I can hope that this book will be readable to those concerned about their beliefs and relationships.

My heart's devotion and appreciation go to my sweet and lovely wife, Muriel W. Sterne, whose passion for clear and direct language has enabled me to avoid many unfortunate meanderings.

By its very nature, this book is uniquely personal in its content and expression. Any inadequacy or awkwardness is entirely the responsibility of the person whose name is on the cover.

Introduction

THE CHRISTIAN SOLDIERS are marching on. The wars against abortion, homosexuality, and evolution are being waged in churches, voting booths, and worldwide media coverage. The foot soldiers are mustered for battle in mammoth gatherings that rival rock concerts in volume and hysteria. Patriotism and holiness are displayed in light and sound spectacles that rival Mardi Gras. Each ministry has to outdo the others to attract the crowds and offerings. The prosperity preachers offer an outpouring of financial blessings in exchange for the money that their followers send them. The bigger the offerings, the bigger the returns in blessings.

American Christianity has mastered the production of modern spectacles which put the ministries on the level of the television extravaganzas. If people will send in enough money, they are assured that they will get as much and more money by divine contract. There is no question but that American Christianity is building bigger followings, more famous personalities, and more expensive buildings than ever before in history.

Christianity seems intent upon a return to a male-dominated, wealth-powered, and white-controlled America. The masses of fundamentalist Christians not only tolerate but vigorously support the sharp divisions of Americans into the power status of male and female, rich and poor, white and nonwhite. Rule by authoritarian institutions and elite coalitions is projected by the predominant churches as preferable over democracy and freedom of conscience. This kind of mentality is sometimes called "Triumphalism." Briefly, triumphalism is the attitude or belief that one's own religion or way of life is superior to all others, and will eventually supercede all others. This attitude or belief has an affinity for indoctrination instead of education, intimidation instead of persuasion, and dogmatism instead of candor. But triumphalism is not the only face of Christianity.

What Christianity owes America is its other face, which makes reconciliation its primary purpose. While triumphalism preaches that some of us are "saved" and the rest "lost," some of us are right and the rest wrong, some of us worthy and the rest unworthy, reconciliation shows us the equality of all of us in our intrinsic humanity. We are different one from the other, as we have every right to be, but we are not divided from each other in our essential worth. The message of reconciliation is the core of the teachings and example of Jesus, and the religion that bears his name has the ability to inspire and motivate us to recognize our equal worth and to reconcile our divisions that arise from mistaken beliefs that the triumphalists advocate.

Mounting disparity between the rich and the poor in America shows more vividly how mistaken the triumphalist message is. It is not just the poor adults who are enmeshed in hereditary poverty, but also their children, who grow up with inferior housing, schools, nutrition, and health care who will be left out of future job opportunities, with the next generation to repeat the cycle. The hunger and homelessness of families and children is the shame of our country. We need the reconciling message of Jesus to hold up before us the image of the suffering of the innocent who are left behind in our rush to wealth and overconsumption. Christianity owes it to our nation to convict us of the outrage of greed and avarice which corrupt our public life.

Triumphalism is not the only mistaken belief that plagues us. Racism, homophobia, and dogmatism are all associated with it. In these pages I will attempt to portray coherently how religious triumphalism is allied with these and other noxious beliefs that have crippled our social conscience. If I overdraw some of the social evils that I see, it will be in the conviction that to understate them would be the same as complicity with them. I endeavor to state fairly the views that I criticize, since I recognize so many of them from my own misguided past. So when some reader feels that I have been harsh in my criticism of cherished beliefs, let him and her consider that it is the mistaken belief that I mean to criticize, and not the person who believes it.

1

Jesus and the Quality of American Public Life

THE CHASM THAT EXISTS between the races today in American culture exemplifies how far we have yet to go before we realize the meaning and benefits of our ideal of a public. We are so accustomed to segmenting ourselves into "interest groups," or blocs of "special interests" that we have not yet listened to those three words that stand like jewels at the beginning of the Constitution: We The People. Is there a "public"? Is there a "We" who constitute the "People of the United States of America"? Or are there only individuals who loosely assemble into groups that gather and dissolve capriciously? This is not just a political question; it is also a moral and religious one. This issue gets to the question of our essential concept of ourselves and the value and respect due to our humanity itself. It is a moral question because it gets to the heart of how we treat each other and how we expect others to treat us. These issues are the basic stuff of this book. I hope that my treatment of them will start some arguments and raise some dust, especially among the schoolrooms of the nation.

What does Jesus have to do with the quality of American public life? It depends on whom you ask. If you ask a Neo-Puritan from the fundamentalist core of the Evangelical churches, he would tell you that Jesus is the only answer to the spiritual and moral death of the lost souls of American men, women, and children. All of these people, he would tell you, are sinners, except for those who have been born again according to the evangelical formula. Jesus, the Neo-Puritans say, offers the only hope of escaping the consequences of their sins on earth and hell in eternity. But when the evangelicals say, "Jesus," they mean to identify Jesus the teacher as the eternal Son of God, the second person of their triune God. This tradition of Christendom was constituted and defined centuries after the life of Jesus the teacher. Through the culture of Christendom the Christian church gave shape and meaning to the familiar view of earth and heaven, sin and salvation, and nature, humanity, and God.

The Christian Coalition and its fellow-travelers currently conduct crusades against contraception, abortion, homosexuality, the public schools, and support for poor mothers and children. Are the campaigns really a valid representation of the teachings and example of Jesus? This little-noticed issue in the current maze of

"Christian Coalition" and "people of faith" crusades and causes demands scrutiny. For these people, the self-defined keepers of morality and godliness, hold that the teachings of Jesus Christ are expressed in the activities of those who want to define and restore the Puritan ideal of a "New Jerusalem" in the New World. The loudest and most opinionated voices, feeding on the strength of mass mailings and television entertainment evangelism, have expressed their puritanical condemnation of all efforts to amend and refine the public policies and practices that would make America more truly a land of compassion and fairness. This reactionary condemnation passes for public morality, while programs intended to reduce poverty, hunger, and degradation are allowed to wither and public policies expanding wealth and privilege for those who "have it made" are supported by the Christian Coalition.

The members of the Neo-Puritan Christian Coalition are correct when they claim to speak for a version of traditional Christian theology and morality. They are clearly in step with their ideological ancestors who hanged Quakers on Boston Common and killed suspected witches in Salem. The Neo-Puritans demonstrate uncritical loyalty to the very best thinking of those seventeenth-century ministers and governors whose excesses of fanaticism finally turned the stomachs of their British rulers and their New World neighbors. But those in the Christian Coalition are incorrect to associate their deadly thinking with the name of Jesus. Scholarly work has discovered a new role played by Jesus in the saga of the early church. In this role he is a teacher and exemplar of compassion and respect for people of all sorts and stations in life. Jesus opposed those Jews who set themselves up as protectors of privilege and power and scorned the poor and powerless among them. He opposed the Romans who cruelly and arrogantly dominated the lives and freedom of their subject people. He showed concern for what happened to individuals in the world, whoever they were. He identified his own concerns with those of all needy and suffering people.

Jesus shone like a bright light in a dark world. He had no access to the knowledge of humanity that has come to us in an age of discovery, education and communication. His light emanated from a heart open to the richness of human relationships and to the creativity of moral imagination. He spoke to people who believed themselves to be inimical to each other, but who really needed to learn to respect each other, so that they could give and receive the good life that they all deserved. Jesus spoke to diverse sorts of people who heard him gladly. Inevitably, some of the people he cared for would now be called handicapped, sexually deviant, and culturally alien to himself. In the darkness that characterized his time, Jesus was determined to respect all who heard him.

In his universal respect for humanity Jesus touches most vitally on what we now call "the public." The Neo-Puritans declare some of the American public to be beyond respect. Those who do not conform to the Neo-Puritan image of standard economic and moral virtue, and who are not ready to renounce their differences are not considered humanity worthy of public interest. In their division of the American public along the lines of religious doctrines, the Neo-Puritans desert Jesus. Instead of following his teachings and example, they choose to march in their Christian crusades for a "Nation under God." They translate godliness into a morality that gives priority to separation, isolation, and greed in our economic and cultural life. This morality becomes " virtues," or "family values" that exclude fairness, tolerance, and respect for all people. William Bennett's best-selling book, *A Book of Virtues*, does not have the word "justice" in its index. This book recounts the traditional virtues that are supposed to undergird our national life, yet the author does not consider the public virtue of justice important enough to include in the index. Instead, he treats "justice" as only an individual virtue. Bennett cites Socrates' dialogue on the just soul, but omits Plato's extension of that idea to its corollary, the concept of the just state. Bennett reduces the scope of moral virtue from the model of a well-taught and well-socialized individual to a model of a sinful individual who needs to be indoctrinated into the conventional morality of the currently predominant religious institution. This presents not only a travesty of Plato, but also a misreading of Jesus.

The Christ Problem and the Jesus Answer

Christian tradition and current usage so completely conjoin the words "Jesus" and "Christ" as to make them inseparable. The long and complex history of that conjunction has occupied scholars and advocates over the centuries. As we examine this issue, little risk of controversy will attend a few general statements. The personal name "Jesus" belongs to the Jewish teacher who became identified as the Christian savior and lord. During the time the "Jesus Christ" identity developed, the title "Christ" was widely applied to men who were considered especially anointed or chosen and empowered by deity to rule over a nation or race of people. Over time in Western culture, the term "Christ" became exclusively associated with the Church teaching that God made Jesus the teacher both the Savior of humanity and also the unique and exclusive Son of God. Thus "Jesus Christ" virtually became the full name of the principal object of Christian worship, in whose name all the power and truth of God were held to be expressed and employed. It is not compatible with the creeds and practices of Christendom that Jesus could be identified as other than Christ, or that Christ could refer to anyone except Jesus.

While this "name," Jesus Christ, does not appear in the canonical records of the experiences of the followers of Jesus during his lifetime, later founders of the Christian tradition worked laboriously to make it the formal designation of their institutional Lord and Savior, their God. This book attempts to unravel that assumption and restate a better understanding of the meaning of Jesus' teachings and their application to our common public life. as well as to our personal relationships. It is my conviction that the two words "Jesus" and "Christ" do not constitute a valid expression of either who Jesus was or what he believed and taught about humanity and God. This conviction cuts across the traditional foundation of Christendom and will be condemned by many followers of that tradition. I would have condemned it so myself in an earlier period of my life. Since then, what I have learned about humanity and the world we collectively inhabit has brought me to affirm different assumptions and beliefs. I found that if I were going to take my beliefs seriously, I had to open myself to the possibility that there was more to know than I had learned so far. Such openness is still the best stand I can take and advise for others.

The Christ problem has arisen because it implies the concept of a nonhuman source of help that deters personal and social responsibility and growth. This concept places the causes of human good and evil beyond the reach of credible understanding and alteration. I am reminded of a story told to me by a colleague from Texas. A father watched as a number of brave men heroically saved his little daughter from a flooded river. A bystander said to him, "Thank the Lord that your daughter got out alive." The father responded, "I thank the men who went into the river at the risk of their own lives. I won't mention the Lord who let her get swept away in the flood if you won't steal the credit from the men who saved her."

The "Christ problem" appears not only in the religious elements of our public culture, but also in many elements—secular, philosophical, and historical—that our American public life has inherited from Christendom. Christendom has served as a powerful determinant of the way we see ourselves and our world, giving us assumptions of supernaturalism, male dominance, and white supremacy. But it also seeps into secular elements of our culture, such as radical individualism and a narrow view of economic rights. These are not specifically religious concepts, but our Western world-view has so assimilated them that they now stand as correlative elements with the religious "Christ" view of the world.

The "Jesus Solution" that I will propose is also a complex world-view composed of several compatible secular elements. Among those elements are universal human kinship, creative morality, and mutual responsibility of and for all people of the nation. Partnership and cooperation are also generally consistent with the teachings and example of Jesus.

But the "Jesus Solution" is not derived from just one historic person, although its principles are well exemplified by the Jewish teacher of that name. Jesus typically called himself "the son of man," and he asked his followers to address God as "Our Father," implying that those who would join him in prayer are brothers and kinfolk of each other. Jesus' caring spans the chasms of human alienation and embraces all persons as worthy of respect, even when they might set themselves apart as enemies. He reserved his praise for those people who met adversity with courage, hope, and good will. To him, healing human relationships was more virtuous than ritual obedience. He told us that the real source of human misery is the greed with which people accumulate wealth, privilege and power to dominate others. The demands Jesus placed upon himself and his followers to recognize the value of every person have challenged us down through the years to see beyond the superficial superiorities and inferiorities that we impose upon ourselves. Jesus represents the reconciliation that resolves the problem of exclusion engendered by the Christ problem.

The Christ problem expresses concepts of exclusion and superiority that have plagued America from its beginnings. Our European ancestors considered their "civilization" superior to that of any other people on earth, and they identified genuine civilization only with their own system of religious and economic beliefs. They brought to America their belief that their own god was the only true supernatural deity, and that their own system of land-holding and commerce, even though it had developed only recently, gave them license to take over the earth, dispossessing whoever stood in their way. Eventually, these assumptions became the basis for unlimited competition and individualism. Thus, we have inherited a threadbare and sterile conception of a common good. Our rampant and radical individualism has made it all but impossible for us to help ourselves by helping one another. The European economic model and our Christ-type of religion have sanctioned the degradation of humanity and nature whenever it suits the purposes of an individual or a separate group. Now, we require a new Jesus-type of religion that will support the worthy needs of our inclusive community of people and inspire us to enhance that community for everyone.

America's Present and Future Religions

America will give rise to another religion. There have been several in the past, and there will be another one in the future.

A new messiah will not necessarily appear to lead an entirely new kind of religion. The world's cultures, including our religions, are always evolving. Likewise, we will have some assimilation of various elements of the old religion and new cultural elements, so that what emerges can be called "new religion." This has happened more than once in the past. For instance, the religion of the theocratic church state of the early colonial period, typified by the Puritans, gave way fairly rapidly to the more tolerant climate of the Jeffersonian period. In the past four hundred years, many elements, some specifically religious and others more generally cultural, have combined into our present-day religious pluralism.

A historically new factor will inevitably emerge in the new century and the new millennium as we recognize the human dynamics involved in all cultural developments, including religions. We are just now becoming aware of ourselves as making conscious decisions about our religion and, even more crucially, as recognizing its implications for what is really sacred. Some of us will recognize our responsibility for the outcomes of our religious beliefs.

In our next American religion, many believers will feel more comfortable saying, "Brother Jesus," instead of "Lord Jesus." This will be a difference not only of terminology but also of conception. We will largely outgrow the authoritarian aspects of Christianity and other religions as well. Although Christianity will continue to be a major religion, it will also become more inclusive of all humanity. This means an adjustment in Christian thinking about who Jesus was and what his own vision of God was. Because I am neither a prophet nor a theologian, I will not try to predict the contours and dimensions of those concepts and visions, but their shaping will be an exciting and invigorating process.

The present predominant American religion is a version of Protestant Christianity that can best be described as "triumphant." Triumphalism has held sway since Puritan times, and this public consensus in the mainstream continued virtually unchallenged until approximately the First World War. It crystallized in the declared purpose for Americans' entering that conflict: "To make the world safe for democracy." This phrase expresses the belief that America has a divinely appointed destiny to lead the rest of the world to a civilization on the order of Christendom, with the added feature of Enlightenment egalitarianism. Its underlying ideal suggests that we in the United States have a system of government that sets the standard by which all other governments should be judged. The religious culture of this "world safe for democracy" would also be modeled after the traditional Protestant culture amended as necessary for modern life.

Harold Bloom, one of the outstanding literary critics in America and the Sterling Professor of Humanities at Yale, says in his 1992 book, *The American Religion,* "The American religion moves toward the twenty-first century with an unrestrained triumphalism." Although it is necessary to take his assessment seriously, it is also necessary to explore the assertion to see what might substantiate his claim and what might be grounds to question it.

Bloom does not define his use of the word "triumphalism," but the dictionary might help us understand this awkward-sounding term. *Merriam-Webster's Collegiate Dictionary* defines triumphalism as "The doctrine, attitude or belief that one religious creed is superior to all others." Christianity has traditionally held that the Christian system of dogma is superior to all others, and that Christianity is divinely destined to supersede all other religious traditions and institutions. Christianity shares this self-aggrandizing belief with the other Western monotheistic religions, Judaism and Islam. Monotheistic religion provides a powerful agency for dividing humanity into separate factions, as well as for strengthening the inner unity of those factions.

Triumphalism divides humanity into discrete but fictitiously separate kinds of persons. The triumphalist and the anointed stand on one side of the chasm, and everyone else on the other side. No matter how few there are on the triumphalist's side, and how many on the other side, the triumphalist remains certain that his side is the right side. A triumphalist religion involves the image of a divinely chosen people set against the rest of humanity. Early in the course of its history, Judaism conceived of itself as made up of such a chosen people. In time, the Christians came to see themselves as a new chosen people: chosen by the same God, to be sure, but replacing the Jews as God's anointed. This concept of humanity divided between two kinds of people, with whom the same God deals in two different ways, has become less and less credible. Some Christians have even begun to question not just who the chosen people are, but whether there are any chosen people at all. Not all Christians fit the triumphalist mold.

The term "triumphalism" first came to my attention in a book about the First Baptist Church of Dallas, Texas. This church is legendary in American Protestantism, and especially in the South, where Southern Baptists outnumber all other religious groups. It was a megachurch before we knew megachurches could exist. The Dallas church— known to other Southern Baptists as simply the "First"—has a congregation whose members number in the thousands. The First has an accrued wealth in the millions and owns many square blocks in downtown Dallas. Dr. Joel Gregory, who served briefly and sadly as pastor of that church, wrote the book *Too Great a Temptation*. Dr. Gregory had been selected to succeed Dr. W. A. Criswell, pastor for nearly fifty years, who had become a demigod to the church, the city, and the denomination. However, the spirit of "triumphalism" that infected the First affected the transition from the old warhorse to the young go-getter.

Dr. Gregory's experience with the megachurch proved disastrous for his ministerial career. In his book, he reflects:

> There are qualities in the reign of God through His church that cannot be measured. The real danger of our addiction to bigness is that we will forget this vital warning and give way to triumphalism, believing our own press notices about being "the greatest church in the world." Beware of a triumphalism that contradicts the message.

The same spirit of triumphalism that corrupted the megachurch in Dallas can also corrupt a small village-crossroads Quaker meeting. Size alone does not make the triumphalism contradictory to the Christian message. Dr. Gregory remains loyal to the Baptist vision of aggressive and authoritarian pastor-church combinations, but I believe the whole premise of divine ordination of human institutions has fatal flaws. Although I still value human institutions, I believe only in humanly guided institutions, not in heaven-sent organizations that speak for an absolute deity who commands humanity through some supernatural power.

"Triumphalism" seems an appropriate characterization for the general spirit of American religion and its heritage from Christendom. Triumphalism is a better term than any official or ideological designation. It does not specify "liberal," "conservative," "evangelical," "fundamentalist," "mainstream," or "charismatic" ideology. "Triumphalism" or derivatives of the term leaves open other theological and ethnic characteristics and focuses on a shared trait that is sometimes overlooked and may be absent from almost any of the designated groups. One aspect of "triumphalism" involves the spirit of "hubris," the pride of standing superior to lesser competitors in religious values, and that is the primary focus in my attribution of the term.

We have learned that all segments of humanity have worth. No one deserves bad treatment from a God who could treat him or her better if he so chose. Nor can we find anything unique about any particular people—ourselves included—that would make them deserve to be treated especially well. All of us have potentially valuable characteristics, even though these qualities may differ. But, after we live together for awhile, the elements seem to merge and assimilate among us, so that we naturally become more alike and less different. We are all both good and bad.

Not only have we discovered that humanity is a unified species, but we have also learned that humanity is the source and creator of knowledge and truth. For thousands of years we have been told that the gods bestow knowledge and truth on those people who are divinely favored. Some people seem to be naturally gifted with great intuitive powers that enable them to earn knowledge, but even these individuals follow the natural process by which all people everywhere have gained insights and wisdom. As part of the commonplace activities of life, we gather experience from trial and error, successfully adjust our activities to the demands of nature, and through this accretion of understanding learn how the world works, within us and around us. This wisdom does not come from "up there" or "out there" but from the here and now, in all times and in all places. The revelations presented to us as true, absolute, and unchanging inevitably disagree with each other in important concepts and in definitive details. They cannot all be true, and so we still have to act as mere human beings and decide which is right and which is wrong. Those who claim to decide for us revert to a revelation as their justification.

This kind of discussion always takes on an adversarial tone. I am opposed to triumphalism as a set of beliefs and attitudes, but I am also committed to acting with respect for those who I am opposing. I realize at the outset that I am contradicting positions that I also once held, but I still do not consider those positions to be without merit and foolish. I have fond memories of the years that I spent trying to convert other people to those positions and failing more than succeeding. But, I remember that those who instructed me in that way of thinking did not admonish me to respect those who disagreed with me. To the contrary, the acrimony that accompanied their advocacy offended me, even while I sought to carry out their program. It has taken me a long time to understand how and why I believed what I did, and I have found a better way of opposing ideas that I find unacceptable.

How do you respect an adversary? It is important to listen to him to find out what he is saying, not just what he is reported to have said. One listens to learn what his assumptions are and to discover what leads him to his position, and not just the *ad hominem* factors underlying his argument, such as whether he is rebelling against his father's beliefs. Give an opponent credit for having good reasons for saying what he does. Then examine whether or not your disagreement is real or just rhetorical. Identify his context, his hopes, and his fears; see what makes him tick. Then, if you can, offer alternatives to those assumptions that you find faulty and say why your suggestions are preferable to your opponent's assumptions. At that point you and he are in the same situation. Neither you nor he can determine what other people will make of the controversy. You will not defeat him by your argument, but your listeners will assess both arguments and pass judgment on their validity. My responsibility is to give my adversary a fair hearing and, when representing his thinking, to do it as accurately as I can. I further need to remember that we all learn more from those who disagree with us than from those who agree with us.

Most people in the triumphalist group listen only to themselves and to each other. They seldom admit that someone who disagrees with them has anything valuable to say. I will try to show why this is, in the context of their own claims, self-defeating.

It is a frightful thing to try to decide for yourself the answers to questions that others have told you are answerable only by God's chosen spokespersons. But it is also frightening to learn that your son or daughter has a serious, life-changing decision to make and wants your advice. The "revealed truth books" have no unambiguous answers to such questions. "Authorities" might help you but you will still get only recommendations. You and you alone must decide what advice you will take and give. This is a time when you must look within your own mind and heart and find or, should I say, create something that will reflect the best that you know and you care most about. So, we face frightening junctures in life that call upon us to decide what we mean when we say "Good" or "True." In these intriguing predicaments we find what it means to be human, whether we like it or not.

A Personal Note

As a serious-minded youth, I felt strongly that I was being divinely directed in the steps that I was taking in my education, marriage, and career. In reflecting on those steps and where they led, as well as the influences that led to my taking them, I am now aware that I was not following God's direction as I thought I was. I can see now that I was propelled along a path forged by a number of influences, among them rising ego, late-adolescent romantic confusion, and bad advice from well-meaning friends. There were even some mild elements of exploitation that were both aimed at me and aimed by me. These motivations were not unusual, except that piety had so well disguised them that they were more harmful than they would have been if I had known better their root causes. I realize now that the overt or covert decisions I was making were just as binding on my future as if I had been fully aware that they were my own choices. Instead, I was impressed with what had the appearance of powerful collective piety. Everyone, friends and myself, insisted that "This is the will of God," and I knew no better.

It is a seductive idea to think that God has a special plan for your life, which is also part of the cosmic plan that includes the lives of other people and the global events that affect everyone. This divine plan—a supposedly all-inclusive blueprint—coordinates your life with the lives of other people, so that all kinds of circumstances magically coalesce to bring people to do what is essentially God's will. All of your youthful confusions and frustrations are removed and replaced by a certainty that is shared by many admirable people. The feeling of resolution and connection is so strong that almost anything is believable. Any event that offers the slightest evidence of confirmation that you are now in the absolutely right place, time, and circumstance gives a new cause for celebration. Small miracles seem to come daily from nowhere, proving God's immediate confirmation of your new path. The late D. Elton Trueblood called this exciting experience, "The explosive power of a new affection."

Although this idea is seductive and quite plausible to the naive mind, the plain fact is that the will of God simply does not work in this way. People who have lived a lifetime with this belief have learned to rationalize the gaps and lapses in God's benevolence that happen to them and other people. Some people just stop talking about "God's plan," rather than admit to an embarrassing case of childishness. Others have invested so much in the whole bundle of beliefs that accompanies the idea of God's will that they continue to twist and bend their explanations for whatever happens. Still others—and no one ever records their numbers—simply give up on the idea of the will of God and more or less on the religion that goes with it.

The magic behind the idea of "God's will" is, of course, that coincidences or random occurrences are directly caused by God. However, good things and bad things happen to everybody. When bad things happen to people who are "in God's will," they attribute it to some beneficial purpose of God's design. He is teaching or punishing or testing or otherwise working out some secret plan entirely beyond human understanding. The pious person will defend his submission to God's will against all evidence to the contrary. But, if he will look critically, he will also see that the world works for him in the same way as if there were no "God's will" at all.

The failure of God's will to make a critical difference would indeed be of little consequence if this belief in a miraculous world were simply a private and personal fixation. Error and regret may be part of all decisions, but we are told that we can avoid these unfortunate results if only we trust God. But this is not so, because many people suffer unnecessarily tragic results of decisions that are made in accordance with this belief, results that might have been avoided with the exercise of more reasonable caution. There is also a terrible price to pay when people begin to define God's will for other people. Some leaders of suicidal cults have convinced their followers that death is the only course open to them, in accordance with God's will. We know about the tragic consequences that befell otherwise ordinary people who placed too much confidence in fallible leaders. If you are committed to following God's will, it is easy to overlook the obvious differences in human powers that people possess. Some people with enormous talents or abilities for persuasion may also deny that their power is simply a human power. Such leaders may really believe that their powers are divinely bestowed on them, and that they are carrying out God's will when they use those powers.

When a person of impressive and intense powers presents and reiterates widely held and deeply felt religious beliefs, the will of God can become alive and compelling for even intelligent and serious-minded people. The more conscientious person listening to such a presentation often has a stronger likelihood for persuasion and obedience. The very strength of a person's sensitivity to ideals of duty and compassion can be the persuader's best ally. The responsible, empathic person will feel the greatest attraction to calls for dedication and sacrifice. The more extraordinary the behavior called for, the more the conscientious person will attempt to comply with the demand. The same dynamics that work in political or commercial persuasion also apply to religious persuasion. The person with persuasive power can use it for furthering either God's will or patriotism, or personal profit.

The influence of a powerful personality can be dangerous. Although such power may be liberating, inspiring, or empowering, it can also be misleading and destructive. As a teacher I wanted to impress on my students that they should not simply take my word in critical matters. The classroom situation obliges me to hold myself open to questions, and I take this to be a natural responsibility for anyone who has any semblance of authority, whether teacher or parent or judge or minister. My realization of the inherent dangers in pulpit preaching made it impossible to contemplate such a career. I have bitter memories of what can happen when powerful but arrogant or malicious personalities exercise authority. The injuries I have suffered from those authoritarian sources have passed into memories, but when I see so many of the same abuses happening to other people, I must advise skepticism as a general practice.

A segment of our present American religious society has become most involved in invoking its version of the will of God for its own institutional or personal purposes. This authoritarian tradition flourishes in situations of stress and change.

People grow restless when they fear what the future may hold for them and their families. Religions can use this uneasiness to gain access to the fearful and the decisions that they make in anticipation of trouble. Today, we are uncertain about the global standing of the United States in the future, as well as our own positions in our work and home life. Thus, we are ready targets for those with easy solutions to our concerns, no matter how far those explanations are from reality.

The religion we need to develop in the future will provide more compassion and less judgment. Humanity itself will take higher priority than abstract ideological absolutes. The rise of reason has so far failed to make this distinction in importance. Empirical intelligence has opened culture to the resources of human potential for goodness, truth, and beauty that far outweigh the resources of the supernaturalist past. But nothing in the "scientific," political, and philosophical progress of Euro-America kept it from replicating the genocides of the medieval world. "Reason" did not prevent the Stalinists from sacrificing millions of Russians for their collective state. "Logic" did not keep Hitler from massacring the Jews and other "subhuman" ethnic groups. Neither science nor faith deterred the Allies from fire-bombing Dresden, Tokyo, and Hiroshima. People who carried out all these atrocities against humanity were basically ideological absolutists. They killed people in the name of their state, their culture, or their economy, not because they were employing reason but because they were misusing faith.

Triumphalist Christianity has not been able to extend the teachings and example of Jesus to include the respect and compassion for humanity that he embodied. Quibbling about differences in theology or doctrines, or over the practices of celibacy or male dominance, accomplishes nothing other than putting Jesus' message aside for the sake of institutional survival. If we look critically at the record of Euro-American Christianity, with its colonialism, slavery, and willingness to use technological means of mass killing, we have a hard time making a concrete case that this Christian civilization has been good for humanity. Do our successes in medicine and materialism really outweigh the pollution and greed we practice domestically and globally? No! Reason alone cannot restore the feeling for others taken away by ideologies. We need a core of beliefs about the value of humanity for its own sake, so that the dispossessed and the disadvantaged will become the focus of our attention rather than remain at the periphery. Jesus has already embodied these beliefs, but we have hidden them under a mass of self-serving talk and self-indulgence.

From "Lord Jesus" Back to "Brother Jesus"

Having lived for many years within the world and fellowship of traditional and evangelical Christians, I am keenly aware of the vast distance that is involved in the spiritual and intellectual journey from "Lord Jesus" to "Brother Jesus." The warmth and comradeship of that Christian world can hold a person in that fellowship, but a wrenching of conscience can also accompany attempts to move out of that fellowship. Such a move cannot be made quickly or casually, but only with great consideration and hesitation, if at all. For many earnest believers, the price of saying "Brother Jesus" instead of "Lord Jesus" may be too great in the loss of personal and social identity. I did not choose this long and arduous process at the beginning, but I pursued it gladly once I realized what was in prospect. I would not return to the kind of belief system necessary for the "Lord Jesus" concept. Instead, I am continually more and more satisfied to be free and open to say "Brother Jesus," just as I do "Sister Helen" (Keller), or "Brother Frederick" (Douglass), or "Brother Martin" (Buber), or "Brother Mohandas" (Ghandi). I consider all these people my secular patron saints; I am honored to share the identity and role of human individual with them, and I desire to learn better from them how to be human. I do not think that I have denigrated Jesus by calling him "brother" but rather have found in him, my brother, a person from whom I can draw beautiful, creative strength and a fuller understanding of human life.

The difference between "Brother Jesus" and "Lord Jesus Christ" emerges not just in the beliefs and behavior of Christians. A system of belief that does not align with "Brother" is imbedded in the title "Lord," and I will identify that system as "Christendom," the prevailing religious system in the Western world for fifteen hundred years. Christendom arose in the declining years of the Roman Empire, with 315 C.E. as a convenient marker. In that year the Roman Emperor Constantine made Christianity an official state religion. Remnants of other religions survived for some years in various parts of the empire, but Christianity no longer faced constant persecution and restraint and could be freely proselytized throughout the remaining imperial Roman world. Constantine needed a well-ordered institutional religion to solidify his reorganized regime, and so he called the Council of Nicea in 325 to settle some of the more troublesome doctrinal quarrels in the Church. During the next hundred years, the Roman Catholic Church received its lasting charter for domination and authority, culminating in the work of Augustine, Bishop of Hippo. Since then, Christendom has supported self-perpetuating and self-authenticating institutions that have spread their rule as far as they could, under prevailing cultural and political circumstances. These institutions are the Roman Catholic and Protestant churches and their tributaries and splinters. As they follow apostolic tradition, they claim to speak for God Almighty in the name of the Lord Jesus Christ.

The concept of Jesus as brother-in-humanity differs radically from the several versions of a trinity concept in the traditional theology. This "brother" theology supports a number of beliefs in the meaning of deity and of humanity, which various Christians have held down through the centuries. However, traditional Christian theology generally holds a very unnatural concept of the human Jesus. This unnatural concept calls for worship and submission and is reserved for the one and only God, but somehow it also applies to Jesus. Theology systematically brings that concept into the institution of the church with every item of liturgy and practice that tells us that Jesus is not human but supernatural. Trinitarian theologians take a different approach to Jesus from the approach taken in this book. Their system starts with the concept of God as the one and only final authority in the universe, while I seek to understand the human world on the basis of what we can learn about it as we live in it. The concept of "Brother Jesus" is a very important part of that world of human experience.

In years past, I would never have been able to make the distinction between "Brother Jesus" and "Lord Jesus." The culture of the Bible Belt, that most heavily pious part of America where I was born and grew to adulthood, had no place for Jesus as anything but Lord. Early in my childhood, I learned to fear dying in sin or, worse, being caught in sin at the Second Coming of Christ. My maternal grandmother had planted this fear in my mind and nourished it with earnest ministrations. She had brought this fear with her when she came to live with us from her old home in the Blue Ridge Mountains. Although nearly illiterate, she compensated for her inability to read easily by regularly leafing through a marvelous book of pictures with Bible quotations for captions. Many of these gruesome and fancifully detailed illustrations depicted how sinners, including children, would be poured into the mouth of hell. Grandma could recite the scriptural admonitions as though she were reading. As she turned the pages, I looked on in horror. That book might have shown the love and mercy of God, but I was not aware of it. Perhaps Grandma herself had only been shown the hell part. As the youngest member of the household, and her only available auditor, I was a captive audience for her Christian mission.

Many of us have personally experienced something like that instilling of fear, but more importantly, that fear has become part of our culture. This fear of God loads us with an unnatural and unnecessary burden. It endangers our survival and growth as persons. We do not need to know in detail who produced this image of humanity under the judgment of an angry God, but we do need to understand something of its consequences for our world. I will attempt to show the consequences of this kind of religion in the creation of social divisions in humanity. I will also attempt to offer a source of hope to remedy those divisions. That hope centers on the rehumanized concept of Jesus, whose name is still the most powerful one in our language.

2

Origins of American Triumphalism

CHRISTIANITY AS WE KNOW IT, with its creeds, scriptures, and institutions did not begin with Jesus, but with the Apostles, Jesus' original disciples according to the canonical texts. Triumphalism was a hallmark of Christianity from its beginning. The earliest writings that we have, those of the Apostle Paul, date from 53 C.E., and define the "gospel" as it emerged from the Jewish communities of Palestine and other centers of the Jewish Diaspora. Early Christianity faced a major problem in establishing what relationship existed between the new "chosen people," the followers of the Messiah-Jesus, and the old "chosen people," the descendants of the covenanted Israelites. Out of the convoluted arguments and resolutions that the church debated internally, the prevailing Pauline position verifies that the faithful of the Apostolic church had replaced the children of Israel as the "chosen people." The Apostles and the later Church Fathers, eclipsing the "old testament," the Jewish canon, designated the Christian canon as the "new testament." Paradoxically, the "old testament" was considered to be an indispensable part of the "new," so that nothing in the "old testament" could be disregarded by followers of the "new." Christians believed their God to be the same as the God of Abraham, Isaac, and Jacob, but that their new revelation superseded the old. So, the Christian gospel denied the finality of the religion of the Jews, but selectively incorporated elements from it. The Christian tradition retained, but exaggerated, the triumphalism of the God of the Jews that is based on the mythic covenants between Yahweh and the Israelites.

Covenants of the "Chosen People"

Triumphalism grows out of a series of covenants ostensibly made between Yahweh, Abraham's God, and humanity, or a part thereof. In temporal order, these are the Noahic, the Abrahamic, and the Mosaic covenants. Seen in that order, the covenants reveal a narrowing in how God values humanity universally, and a sharpening of the demands he places on the recipients. This tells us that earlier, God was believed to be concerned with more of humanity than just one race or nation, but that later his promises were believed to be focused on divine sponsorship of a particular "chosen people."

After the flood, Noah received the most general and inclusive of the covenants. Yahweh is quoted as saying:

> I establish my covenant with you, that never again shall all flesh be cut off by the waters of a flood and never again shall there be a flood to destroy the earth....I set my bow in the cloud...When the bow is in the clouds, I will look upon it and remember the everlasting covenant between God and every living creature of all flesh that is upon the earth. (Gen. 9:11-16)

This story might be suitable to answer a child who asks about the origin of that beautiful and brief but perfect vision of color and order arcing through the sky, connecting the recent rain with a show of natural grace. We notice that God requires nothing of Noah or "every living creature of all flesh" in exchange for God's promise. We also see that the promise affects all of humanity, not just a few who are singled out.

The story of the next covenant is not so generous or inclusive. In it God calls Abram and designates him as the father of a special people. Yahweh says:

> No longer shall your name be Abram, but your name shall be Abraham; for I have made you the father of a multitude of nations....And I will establish my covenant between me and you and your descendants after you throughout their generations for an everlasting covenant...And I will give unto you, and to your descendants after you, the land of your sojourning, all the land of Canaan, for an everlasting possession....And you shall be circumcised in the flesh of your foreskins, and it shall be a sign of the covenant between me and you. (Gen. 17:5-11)

The Abrahamic covenant differs from the previous one in several specific elements. The intended recipients of benefits narrow from "all flesh" to the children of Abraham. A clear distinction is made between a "chosen" group of people and the rest of humanity. Scholars have found that a group's identity —whether based on racial, national, or class categories—can be reinforced in its collective memory by adding the special power of divine favor for those under that identity. The reinforcement increases if an endowment of a special territorial right is part of the divine show of favor. When Yahweh promises Abraham that his children will possess the land of Caanan, even though that land is inhabited by another group of people, Yahweh gives tacit divine approval for the invasion of that land and the decimation and later domination of its inhabitants.

This reference to the triumph of God's chosen group over their enemies is especially pertinent to the religion of America. It was enough to provide the justification for another self-anointed people of God, predominantly English Christians, to later invade, decimate, and dominate the native people of the New World. The wrath of God was destined to fall on those inhabitants of America whose only crime was residing in their own homeland, in the same way that the wrath of Abraham's God fell on the Canaanites centuries before.

At one point in their trek to Canaan, the Hebrews confronted a native king with a request for passage through his land. The Book of Numbers describes the conquest by the Hebrews as they moved under Moses' leadership from Egypt into the Promised Land:

> But the Lord said to Moses, "Do not fear him; for I have given him into your hand, and all his people and his land; and you shall do to him as you did to Sihon king of the Amorites, who dwelt at Heshbon." So they slew him, and his sons, and all his people, until there was not one survivor left to him; and they possessed his land. (Num. 21:34-35)

This and other texts like it portray the way in which the triumphant chosen people of Yahweh were said to have carried out their divine mandate to possess the land that had been promised to Abraham and his descendants. It may be that "This is the way everyone did it in those days." Perhaps so, but we need to see and understand how this attitude toward the various peoples of the world allowed some "chosen people" to believe that they had a divine mandate to annihilate other people in taking their land. This is a source of the triumphalism that has characterized the behavior of European Christians toward other people who stood in their way.

The triumphalist attitude became particularly evident in the treatment of the native inhabitants of America by invading Europeans. It had its parallel in the forced importation of Africans from their homelands, to provide slave labor for the United States. In narrow economic interests, this conquest by annihilation may be simply explained as the most practical way of dealing with the problem of native inhabitants. But for those Christians who have been the leaders of America, this attitude slanders the teachings of Jesus and the ideals of democracy.

The English Puritans and Pilgrims who emigrated to the New World had descended from several generations of self-selected Christians who believed that God had commissioned them to reinvent their religion. They opposed Roman Catholicism, the Church of England, and the Calvinist Dutch with unwavering vigor. The king of England granted them a charter to settle a colony in New England; they saw it as the hand of God giving them a new Canaan all of their own. When the native inhabitants of that land became an obstacle to the mission, the settlers proceeded to decimate them as the children of Abraham had decimated the old Canaanites. Recent archeological finds have cast some doubt on the credibility of this account of how the Israelites came to be in modern Palestine. But, what is important here is how Christians have modeled their behavior on a mythic pattern of conquest and extermination.

The descendants of Abraham saw their primary benefit of conquest as the divine gift of the land of Caanan, which involved dispossessing the Canaanites of their homes. Such a division of people between the divinely favored and the divinely disregarded has come to be a strong element of triumphalism, as it relates to the Jews and their relations with the people of the land, and to Christians and the inhabitants of the Americas. The "Promised Land" that a newly immigrating group sings of and strives for turns out to be already the cherished home of another group of people. This does not discourage those who believe themselves to be divinely assured of a triumphant destiny. How much moral myopia must nowadays affect the "triumphant" Christians so that they do not see the contradictions between their own actions and the words and actions of Jesus? How much does this moral myopia distort their internal relationships, such as the customary male domination of wives as property, and exploitation of the poor by the greedy wealthy?

The descendants of Abraham who conquered Caanan eventually came to include not only the people we call the Jews, but also those who are called the Muslims. The Jews descended from Abraham through his son Isaac, born to his wife, Sarah. The Muslims descended from the Patriarch through Ishmael, Abraham's son by his Egyptian concubine Hagar, who was also a handmaiden to Sarah.

An impressive footnote to the main story of Abraham's covenant needs to be mentioned here. According to the story told in the Book of Genesis, Abraham's wife, Sarah, grew jealous of Hagar's son, Ishmael, who was actually Abraham's firstborn son and so might inherit the promise made to his father. Sarah persuaded her husband to cast Hagar and Ishmael out, presumably to perish in the desert. But the ancient story says that Yahweh intervened and sent angels to provide for them. Yahweh renewed his promise to Hagar: her son also would be the father of a great nation of the seed of Abraham, in spite of Sarah's hatred and Abraham's callousness. The account of Ishmael and Hagar ends here in the Hebrew bible, but Jews have read and pondered its meaning down through the centuries. The Hebraic story of how God provided for the mythic descendants of Abraham through the castoff son is also recorded in Muslim scripture.

How many of the world's sacred storybooks preserve an account of their own God blessing the ancestor of their mortal enemies? Why did not some unknown Jewish scribe or editor simply omit from his new copy of this text any reference to the Hagar story? Why not just indicate that Isaac was born to Abraham and Sarah, and thus was the ancestor of the Jews? Why preserve a story so antagonistic to their own identity? The followers of Abraham's God merit credit for telling the patriarch's story and recounting the divine compassion bestowed on an unfortunate victim of class and racial degradation, even if the same God was complicit in the victimization. The story of Hagar and Ishmael stands as a flower of compassion in the desert of otherwise moral poverty that accompanied belief in the covenant-promising Hebrew deity.

The Triumphalist Tradition

History has seen the rise of a predominantly European group of Jews who became culturally modern Europeans, and the mainly Mideastern Ishmaelites who became Arabs. We read the histories of those peoples through the prism of triumphalism that the Jewish sages and prophets and rabbis have drawn from their God's covenants with Abraham and Moses. Although the Noahic covenant extended to "all flesh," the covenants with Abraham excluded every people except those who practice sabbath-keeping, male circumcision, and the Levitical Law. The "Children of Israel," the descendants of Isaac, have received the promises of land possession. Many Orthodox Jews as well as other Zionists base their claim to Palestinian soil upon their triumphal belief in the power of those promises. However, some ultra-orthodox Jews refuse to regard the state of Israel as the fulfillment of God's covenant promise, because the Zionist model of Jewish power in the promised land rests upon human efforts and not on an overt divine intervention. They do not reject triumphalism, but rather insist that only an undeniable, supernatural miracle of triumph over Yahweh's enemies will truly fulfill God's covenant. They believe that God will restore them to the land under the Messiah in his own good time. Those pious Jews stand in the same relationship to their version of triumphalism as many followers of the Christian Coalition do to their own belief in triumphalism. That belief in triumphalism is eroding beneath the feet of Jews and Christians alike, at different rates and by different means. The erosion stems not only from their moral repugnance at the sorry fates that they wish upon their enemies, but also from the fading value they place in divine promises as such. Moral myopia provides pious and fearful souls with a strong shield against the unwelcome and dreadful suspicion that the world is moving against them.

The Mosaic covenant is essentially embodied in the gift of the Law, which is epitomized as the Ten Commandments, and is elaborated in the books of Exodus and Leviticus. Where the covenants with Noah and Abraham are general in their requirements and benefits, the Mosaic covenant specifically confers divine favor on the children of Isaac and Jacob—the Israelites—and imposes on them their duty to keep the detailed laws. The Mosaic covenant is given while the people are in extremity in the barren wilderness of Sinai, after having been delivered from bondage in Egypt, and on the threshold of attaining their promised land. This dramatic scene emphasizes how the people depend daily on Yahweh for their food and water and illustrates how fragile is their faith and their devotion to Yahweh. They repeatedly backslide into idolatry and complain against Moses. It is all Moses can do to keep them within the bounds of even lax obedience, and to keep Yahweh from abandoning them to the wilderness. But Moses perseveres and manages to keep them within a covenant relationship with their divine law-giver and liberator. Through all this Yahweh is portrayed as growing more and more arbitrary, and Moses, Yahweh's Leading Man, as becoming more authoritative and accessible. Finally, Yahweh bestows triumph through Moses, and triumph assumes the character of reward for obedience to ordained authority. From the canonical account, participation in the triumph clearly requires total obedience to the leader and repentance for sins against the Law.

The notion of a covenant implies two-sidedness, a voluntary agreement between two or more parties. In these instances of covenants between Yahweh and the Israelites, the human advantage from the covenant came primarily from the triumph over the inhabitants of the "promised land," and then the continuing prosperity of the victorious settlers. Yahweh fulfilled his divine obligation by becoming a war god who would lead and empower this people in struggles with their human enemies and natural hardships. In exchange, this people would declare their allegiance to Yahweh and to his surrogates, and obey the complex laws that had been divinely given. By this transaction, Yahweh presumably would be provided with a supplicant and cowed people, who could be controlled in war and peace through ordained surrogates. The history of the Jews and their survival down to Roman times became one powerful source of Christian triumphalism.

During the last two centuries of the era we call B.C.E. (Before the Common Era), the Roman Empire ruled Palestine. The Romans took the territory by default when the Persian and Egyptian sides of the Ptolemaic Empire failed to settle their quarrels. The "Pax Romana" settled over the Mediterranean world and endured in some fashion for several centuries.

Beginning in the second century B.C.E., the brief but intense struggle known as the Macabbean Revolt rekindled in Judea zeal for the ancient religion of Yahweh. Since their conquest by the Babylonians three centuries earlier, the Jews had no temple and no properly accredited priesthood, and Hellenic culture had spread throughout the upper classes and the corrupt priesthood. The clan of the Macabbees sought to restore a replica of the Davidic Kingdom but failed militarily. This militant effort promoted a splintering of Jewish sectarian leadership, from guerrilla hill fighters to the Pharisees and the Saducees, and on to the mystic desert hermits. The permanent product of this militancy was the concept of a Jewish Messiah or "Anointed One."

Interpretations of vaguely appropriate passages of Hebrew Scripture provided a prophetic credential for this Great Leader who would secure a final triumph for the Children of Israel through the defeat of the enemies of Yahweh. These bits and pieces of writings originated in the prophets' attempts to bolster the courage of Jews undergoing centuries of trials and torments and have prompted succeeding generations of Jews and then Christians to identify and authorize a Great Leader. Some Jews still look for him to appear, and some Christians believe that he appeared as Jesus, and that this same Jesus will come again in the future. His "second coming" will mark the culmination of human history, although just how the prophecies will work out is in dispute. The Maccabees and their warrior-prophets are the historical link between the covenants and Christendom. In all the covenants with Abraham and Moses, we find the same belief in triumph and all its concomitants: divine help in conquering and occupying a promised land, the forceful overthrow of inhabitants or rulers of that land, and divine command to decimate the foes of God's will.

The Roman Empire ruled its multi-ethnic peoples all across the world with a deceptively simple system: Power descends from above, and submission arises from below. No matter who the ruled people might be, or what their prior governing system might have been, once they were part of the Empire, this plain and rigid dictum afforded no exception. The Empire might allow wide latitude in carrying out local affairs, and a few subjects might attain wealth and status as Roman citizens. But it was a certainty that a portion of the area's wealth would find its way to Rome, and that any person's status would hold only as long as it served the purposes of Rome and its agent. Rebellion against Rome was met with swift and sure punishment: Jesus' crucifixion shows how swift and sure that punishment would be. In the time that Jesus and Paul lived under Roman domination, no individual, sect, or group raised an effective challenge to the empire. No living Roman had any reason to believe that the empire would ever suffer defeat. The Roman system had weathered many threats from within and from without, but no one had seen it change, except toward more authoritarian control. The pyramid of authority had at its pinnacle the soon-to-be-deified emperor, who combined the power of man and god in one person. Such a system was bound to impress a person of genius such as the Apostle Paul. The Roman system provided him with the model of a self-perpetuating authority for Christendom, beginning with himself, and continuing with those who reflected his passion for the triumph of Christ, the Anointed One.

The Apostle of Triumphalism

Christianity became a viable religious force under the leadership of the Apostle Paul. The canonical account first mentions Paul as a fervent Jewish opponent of the original followers of Jesus. However, soon after the death of Jesus, Paul had an ecstatic experience that transformed him into the chief architect of the young and growing church. A native of the city of Tarsus and also a Roman citizen, Paul as a Christian missionary naturally turned westward toward the center of Roman imperial power, rather than eastward into the deserts and backwaters of his own ancestral Asiatic world. In proselytizing for the cause of Jesus, who had been killed for opposing the Roman rule of Palestine, Paul also connected Jesus and his religious mission with the fulfillment of the Jewish role of Messiah, which brought to Jesus the title, "Christ." Paul's "gospel," which he claimed to have received directly from God by inspiration, depicted the man Jesus as a person of lesser interest. Instead, Jesus became a cosmic figure who was actually destined to become the supernatural conqueror of all secular and religious powers, and to establish the eternal rule of the God of Abraham, Isaac, and Jacob over all the earth. In Paul's rendering, Jesus and his anointed apostles had been divinely empowered to set up the superracial, supernational, and supernatural Church that superseded the Jewish people as the chosen triumphant instrument of God.

Paul wanted more than the addition of his gospel to the traditional prophetic links in the chain that was Jewish wisdom. He called for the most radical discontinuity between the earthly meaning of the patriarchs and prophets of old and the identity of his new Messiah, Jesus. Paul demanded that the meaning of all prior Jewish and gentile beliefs and practices be set aside, and regarded as only preliminary to the final truth, which he was eager to proclaim.

Paul wrote to his converts in Philippi:

> ...At the name of Jesus every knee should bow,...every tongue should confess that Jesus Christ is Lord, to the glory of God the Father. (Phil.2:10-11)

This is "triumphalism," the conviction that the believer possesses a religious truth that in effect neutralizes or nullifies every other claim to such truth. This belief does not depend upon any consensus of believers for justification of the claim, which might make it persuasive to any who do not already believe it. Paul did not defer to the judgment of the original Apostles for his tacit nullification of the Mosaic Law. There seems to have been little precedent for such a claim in the words of Jesus. By means of a long and torturous path the gospel of Paul became incorporated into a powerful and extensive imperial ecclesiastical institution, and in subsequent centuries into the operational basis of western civilization. This path does not concern us here; instead, we can discern the bold presence of triumphalism in varied forms that has characterized Christendom through the centuries, and is now fading before our eyes.

The single most important historical event in western history since the lifetime of Jesus occurred with the conversion of Saul of Tarsus, who thereby became Paul the Apostle. Had this man not been converted, it is unlikely that Christendom would have become what we have seen it to be. The contours and substance of Christianity would surely have followed a different path of development. Christian scholars tend to see Paul through the viewpoint of the second and third centuries. By that time, the early church had divided into different factions, some to become parts of history, and others to fade into obscurity. Our current record is essentially the account written by those who survived the struggles over the interpretation of Paul's legacy. Subsequent scholars have made this "canonical" version of Paul their own esoterica. What might other "lost" interpretations have given us if some of the non-canonical authors' points of view had been preserved? Are there somewhere, yet to be discovered, a cache of ancient documents that would open new vistas of Pauline scholarship? Is there a repository of historical significance waiting to tell us the story of a different Paul, as the Dead Sea Scrolls and Nag Hamadi findings have told us a different story of Jesus? How much might such findings change our views of the early centuries of Christianity?

Paul's belief in absolute truth matches that of the ancient Hellenistic thinkers. Plato and Aristotle, the great powers of Greek philosophy, believed in absolute truth, however differently they conceived it in their systems. It was also the belief of Philo, the Alexandrian Jew who influenced Paul's world more than any other Jew of his time. I will discuss Paul's suggestion of cognitive relativism at length in a later chapter, but at this point, a brief mention of the problem is in order. Paul displays a disproportionality between his dogmatism, on one hand, and his admission of the limitation of his knowledge on the other.

What I call cognitive relativism is present in the well-known "Love Hymn" in First Corinthians. Praising love, Paul points out its superiority to prophecy, tongues, and knowledge. Prophecy has two functions, i.e., prediction of future events, and pointed application of a general rule to a specific case. Tongues refers to glossolalia, the gift by which a believer uses a language that is not native or acquired, or makes ecstatic utterances that can be interpreted by a witness who also shares the gift. Knowledge is described in the hymn according to its present limitation and its future fulfillment in perfection. Knowledge, Paul claims, will pass away because it is now imperfect, while love endures through time and eternity. His portrayal of knowledge is very close to the contemporary concept of cognitive relativism, which is out of favor with pious believers in traditional Christianity and other revealed religions.

The scientific method tells us knowledge is cumulative, moving from the early suggestion of various hypotheses to confirmation by experiment of one or another of the candidates for proof. Philosophically, according to the concept of cognitive relativism, all knowledge is tentative and situational, being limited at any time to the evidence available to the knower. What I know now is not necessarily false, but it will change and become more nearly true as I progress with more complete awareness of the subject at hand. Cognitive perfection is an illusion, unless we recognize it as an ideal only, and not an accomplishment. We cannot know now what tomorrow may bring of fresh evidence and insight that will transform what I know now into something very different.

Paradoxically, in his "Love Hymn," Paul seems to agree with cognitive relativism. He says the knowledge we have in the "now" world is imperfect, incomplete, tentative, and time-bound. He claims that we see "in a mirror dimly," admitting that "now I know in part." But, in a future time, which he calls "then," we shall see "face to face," and "shall understand fully." Does he mean that in this "then" time, we will be relieved of the limitations to which our "now" knowledge is subject? If so, is he not taking a position like that of the scientist or philosopher who says that although his knowledge is limited by present evidence and experience, that knowledge will expand and become more comprehensive in the future when we have accumulated more evidence and experience? It is necessary to point out that there is a vast difference between the concept of knowledge of Paul and the scientist or philosopher. Paul holds to the existence of an absolute, eternal, and fixed knowledge of truth, while many others hold to knowledge as a product of human experience. Surely, we surmise, this mystically minded Paul is thinking of the contrast between his present, limited bodily state and the post-historical, eternal state in which Paul, the "glorified saint," will have perfect and absolute knowledge in heaven.

That qualification does not answer the question: Did Paul at the time of his writing think that he had a "now" kind of knowledge or a "then" kind? Or did he mean to convey to his converts in Corinth that they had "now" knowledge only, but that he had "then" knowledge as well? A cryptic account in the Second Epistle to the Corinthians may help with this question. Paul refers to his own out-of-body experience of revelation, in which he was

> Caught up into Paradise…and he heard things that cannot be told, which man may not utter….if I wish to boast, I will not be a fool, for I shall be speaking the truth. But I refrain from it, so that no one may think more of me than he sees in me or hears from me. (2 Cor. 12:3-6)

The whole point of the tirade in which this passage is found is the reinforcement of Paul's final and complete apostolic authority in the churches he has founded. Pauline scholars agree that he goes to great lengths to protect his absolute authority. He does not use poetry or metaphors to denounce his detractors. In other instances, his pointedly precise theological teachings often risk incoherence because of some other correlative but contrary statements, such as those concerning the Mosaic law. However, he was clear in his representations of his own "revelations" as superior to anything that the mere "new creatures in Christ" could know for themselves. This bears a strong likeness to the doctrine given by the "elect" of the gnostic movements that were contemporary with the early church. The gnostic teachers, who considered themselves recipients of a superior class of revelation, gave their hearers a version of "knowledge" sufficiently diluted that the lower orders of followers could believe in it. Joseph Smith used this stratagem of "privileged information" when he claimed to have received the "Golden Plates" that bore the text of the Book of Mormon. Likewise, Mohammed claimed that an angel had dictated the Koran to the prophet. Similarly, in a more modern example, a seminary teacher, answering a difficult question, responded, "The answer to that question is in an ancient language that you do not know, so I will not waste time trying to make you understand it." Unfortunately, this appeal to occult sources is not the worst problem implicit in Paul's "Love Hymn." I refer to the problem of the cursing of fellow believers.

Absolutized dogmatism, and the cursing of dissidents, has come down through American religion, which supported the killing of "witches," dissidents such as Mary Dyer, and other Quaker martyrs. The church's claims of certainty, correctness, and finality echo Paul's personal triumphalistic intonations. This attitude has justified the division of humanity into worthy and unworthy segments according to race, gender, or other superficial characteristics. The faith of the slaveholders and Indian fighters in America told them they were carrying out God's divine plan when they dealt death and degradation to the unworthy people they dominated.

We must return to the praise Paul gives to love, in the light of his damning of his supposedly Christian opponents. Let us reconsider Paul's praise to love. Does his love for his Christian brethren in the Lord depend upon their abject submission to his self-certified authority? Does he respect their judgment "as new creatures in Christ" enough to allow voices different from his own to be heard? From his own words, Paul seems to have had only a small reserve of regard for his fellow apostles and preachers. Are we expecting too much of Paul's "love"? Is this an example of the "love" that "is patient and kind; is not envious or boastful or arrogant; does not insist on its own way"? The veneer of piety covers a mansion of deep, malignant insecurity and pride, both in the author of those words of love and in those who repeat Paul's words and deeds today.

The centuries-long train of imitators of Paul's doctrines has brought blood, tears, and degradation to others of his followers. Some in authority have expelled others from the community of believers, and the hurt is deep. But even to witness such expulsion from fellowship of loving companions because of differences in beliefs is itself brutal torture. Paul's contrariness has given birth to a demand for unity of belief that tends to culminate in either forced acquiescence or grudging separation. Bitter sectarianism has become the norm of church membership identification, even when the differences run to the ridiculous. Consider the following case.

A student in a philosophy of religion class told me that he wanted to write his term paper on mixed marriage. In discussing the topic with him, I mentioned the spousal mixtures with which I was familiar, black-white, Protestant-Catholic, Jew-gentile. He shook his head sadly and said, "It's none of those. She belongs to a Missouri Synod Lutheran Church, and I belong to an Evangelical Lutheran Church. Her pastor won't marry us in her church unless I join it first." I agreed that he had good reason to study the problem in some depth and suggested that he invite his intended wife to help him with the research. Later, when I told a Lutheran faculty colleague about the conversation, he introduced me to some of the exquisite doctrinal distinctions commonly made by Lutherans in small-town Wisconsin.

The triumphalist attitude is vitally important to thoughtful Americans because it has seeped down from Christendom into the general culture of the society. It colors secular as well as religious thinking, having been particularly apparent in the Euro-American attitude of superiority toward the native inhabitants of America and toward the Africans who were enslaved to build much of the new nation. When the Puritans gained royal permission to settle a colony in Massachusetts, they saw the hand of God giving them a new Canaan all of their own. They considered the indigenous people and later the enslaved Africans as subhuman, fit only to be tortured and killed for insubordination. The settlers claimed that these alien peoples were an inferior breed that most likely lacked souls that could be converted to Christ. They were, therefore, to be dealt with just as the Canaanites had been dealt with by the Israelites, with subjugation or annihilation as the practical task. The attitudes and practices of the avowed Christians who ruled America slandered the teachings of Jesus and violated the ideals of human rights in a democracy.

Triumphalism is woven into the fabric of Christendom, but it is virtually invisible to those who believe in it and practice it. Our familiarity with triumphalism masks its pervasiveness. Our language conveys it in our mother's home, in the market, and in the schoolhouse. Our present general expectations would be barren if we excluded triumphalism from commonplace life. But, if we consider our experience of the natural world, with our humanity as part of it, we can see how vacuous triumphalism really is. From the act of conception onward, every human individual is the product of personal interaction. All through life, we survive and are nurtured through the cooperation of other persons. If members of a family tried to dominate each other through sheer competitive struggle, the family unit would be in danger of destroying itself. The young cannot survive to reproduce living bodies and minds without the support of some others who are willing to provide that help.

Do we urgently and persuasively see and feel this vital nurturing of individuals by individuals so that the family survives into another generation? Probably not, if we rest with the unquestioned predominance of competition for supremacy that is so prevalent in our culture. If left unexamined, the murky assumption of triumphalism will be transparent to us and only lead us down its sorry path to mutual degradation. Against this tragic outcome, the example and teachings of Jesus offer a truly credible hope for a better future.

3

Morality and Triumphalism
Religious Beliefs and Morality

MORALITY CONCERNS US more than any other aspect of religion. We believe that being religious makes someone a better, more moral person. Thus, people often say that in their opinion living according to Jesus' teachings, rather than according to theology or ritual, is the most important part of Christianity. Non-triumphal Christians feel less concerned about whether their children remain loyal to their own denominations or sectarian affiliations, or whether their grandchildren are baptized in the same rite as their own children were, and are more concerned about whether their children and grandchildren are kind and helpful to their neighbors. Despite the pressures exerted on church members to maintain consensus on issues of sexual behavior, such as prohibitions against premarital sex, abortion, or homosexuality, most Christians have a persistent, enduring sense that the important moral issues involve personal behavior toward other people.

This viewpoint reflects the emphasis that Americans generally have placed on religious practice over theological inquiry. Good intentions and avoiding abuse of other people take priority (over argument about the number of angels that can dance on the head of a pin). People prefer the company of a "good-hearted person" to one who is just successful or popular. If you asked parents if they would prefer their son be a dedicated Boy Scout and a mediocre athlete or a star athlete who sometimes cheated in a game, I still want to believe that their overwhelming choice would be the good scout. In spite of the enthusiasm for "winning" and "success" that has swept through our triumphalist culture in the recent past, people still retain a solid core of respect for the person who puts moral behavior above celebrity. The erosion of the moral stature of our celebrities is a sad result of the rise of the worship of "winning" in our religion and culture generally.

Nearly everyone looks down on the abusive person, especially one whose abuse involves a marked use of greater power. The greater the difference in physical strength, as between an adult and a child, or a strong adult and a weaker one, the more reprehensible, the more immoral the abuse. Domination, whether primarily religious, national, or personal, is a key ingredient in triumphalism. To believe that one individual or group is anointed by God to be the authority on the exact details of His will ignites the enforcement of certain kinds of behavior and the prohibition of others. This attitude is implicit in the covenants of Yahweh with the Israelites and defined their morality. But this is a markedly different morality from the kind that led the Hebrew Prophet Nathan to say to a wanton King David, "Thou art the man," that prompted Jesus to say to those eager to punish the adulterous woman, "Let him among you who is without sin throw the first stone at her." The triumphalist attitude did not provide an adequate basis for morality in ancient times, in Jesus' time, nor does it in our time.

The triumphalist cannot temper morality to make allowance for the changeable situations in which people of good intentions find themselves. In my childhood, it was unusual for a mother to work outside her home. Custom required a woman to do the domestic work in a world of heavy human labor and scarce hired or mechanical labor substitutes. But now, in my grandchildren's world, mothers usually work outside their homes at paying jobs. A mother's intentions to care for her family are likely to be the same whether or not she stays home. Mothers still do as they did years ago, so that the financial situation of the family and the mother's need for varied activity will determine whether she works outside her home. If the mother follows current custom and works outside the home, then all the interpersonal dynamics in the home change: parental nurturing, sibling relationships, and certainly the intimate relations of the wife and husband—all will be affected. Can we impose nineteenth-century-style obligations and expectations on each member of that family without regard for how the times have changed?

If, on the other hand, we ask members of a family to respect one another, to tolerate each other's needs and desires, and to act fairly in their mutual responsibilities, whatever the situation or custom, then they can find creative ways to make their home strong in morality and in happiness. They learn to place more importance on relationships than customs or commandments.

Stories that portray the development of moral insight abound in Hebrew scripture. The story of King David, Bathsheba, and Uriah is memorable and forceful because of the dynamic interplay of values and choices in the tragic events that it recounts. Inspired by the sight of the lovely woman, David acted on the impulse to seize the pleasure of her intimate company. To accommodate his indulgence, he then plotted to make any resulting pregnancy appear to be the work of her husband. When Uriah's nobility prevented that ruse, David arranged to kill her husband. Empowered by his royal prerogatives, David acted and his choices were carried through to accomplish the seduction and murder.

After the deeds of passion and intrigue had been done, the Prophet Nathan came to David to settle God's score with him. Nathan did not chastise David by referring to the Commandments "Thou shalt not kill," or "Thou shalt not covet thy neighbor's wife." Instead, he related a parable:

> There were two men in a certain city, the one rich and the other poor. The rich man had very many flocks and herds; but the poor man had but one little ewe lamb, which he had bought. And he brought it up, and it grew up with him and with his children; it used to eat of his morsel, and drink of his cup, and lie in his bosom, and it was like a daughter to him. Now there came a traveler to the rich man, and he was unwilling to take one of his own flock or herd to prepare for the wayfarer who had come to him, but he took the poor man's lamb, and prepared it for the man who had come to him." Then David's anger was greatly kindled against the man; and he said to Nathan, "As the Lord lives, the man who has done this deserves to die; and he shall restore the lamb fourfold, because he did this thing, and because he had no pity." Nathan said to David, "You are the man." (2 Sam. 12:1-7)

This literary gem shines brilliantly amidst the authoritarian morality of the Israelite legal system. David, the man of many passions and sins, is not simply disobedient. As the parable indicates, David has acted with scorn and brutality against a noble man and his innocent wife. No mere charge of childishly breaking a rule can express the enormity of his wrong and guilt. David had betrayed the rich bounty of his own situation by misusing his power against the weakness and loyalty of those who were powerless to protect themselves and their home against him.

Jesus stood on this same high moral level as Nathan had when he insisted that the Law is not fulfilled by superficial and literal obedience. In Jesus' teaching, if a law-observing Israelite comes to the Temple to make an offering and, while there, remembers a rift in his relationship with his brother, he should leave the gift and become reconciled with his brother before making his offering (Matt. 5:23-24). Jesus teaches that individuals must move away from simple obedience to the Law to follow whatever imperatives he or she assumes upon his or her own responsibility. The personal relationship between individuals has higher moral value than ritual obedience. These two biblical citations should silence the claim that the morality of personal values is merely a recent addition to secular moral laws, and is not a comprehensive religious criterion. In these two instances, the keepers of Hebrew teachings and the preservers of the Christian canon together bear witness that religion was not, and is not, simply or primarily a matter of abiding by some particular rules, as the triumphalists would have it. Mere triumphalism stops far short of the morality of personal responsibility for choices made; it offers no assurance that the mere observance of a legal requirement can fit an ambiguous and complex situation. David's brutal treatment of Bathsheba and Uriah probably lay within the conventions of the times, which were tacitly supported by the attitude of triumphalism that David and all Israelites held. But, as the story tells us, when the king realized what he had done, and recognized the moral repugnance of his treatment of these, his subjects, David was held accountable for abuse and misuse of others, and not for mere disobedience.

The Prophet Nathan and Jesus boldly pronounced behavioral priorities that were based on the responsibilities that people had to each other, as kinsfolk, as neighbors. Both the intentions and results of action are crucial. No matter how good our intentions, if other people are hurt instead of helped as a result of our behavior, we have a moral obligation to change our behavior. Similarly, no matter what positive outcomes we seek, if our effort to achieve those ends results in the denigration of another person or his efforts, then we are morally obliged to change our behavior.

How much latitude do we allow in common situations? A few generations ago divorce and remarriage disqualified individuals from serving as ministers, as officers in many churches, and in some cases as teachers. Now it is fairly commonplace to find divorced or remarried persons occupying such positions. Society once frowned upon common-law marriage, or simply being secretly unmarried; now we see it frequently, especially among older couples with separate financial commitments. Is this "living in sin," as we used to say?

Many attitudes surrounding sexuality are rapidly changing. The old stereotype of the "unfaithful" spouse—the one who violates the exclusive sexual rights in a marriage—is also fading. I knew of one couple whose differences along these lines led to a divorce. She insisted that she was a faithful wife because she had never indulged in sex with anyone but her husband. He said that she was not faithful to him because she had never shown any confidence in him or respect for him as a person. Although neither of them had engaged in sexual promiscuity, each felt betrayed. Because they talked past each other, he never realized that for her, faithfulness meant literal adherence to the terms of the marriage contract; for him, marital fidelity involved the presence of a warm, trusting, and loving companion. I doubt that either ever understood their situation, because neither seemed to see the issue in the terms of the other.

Religious beliefs intermingle with all such customary factors. Triumphalism emphasizes division, domination, and exploitation in all situations. A religion that becomes dogmatic and promulgates teachings that lay claim to absolute certainty, as did the faith of the Apostle Paul and later of Christendom, will eventually cease to respect persons and their relationships. The gospel of God's care for humanity, as Jesus proclaimed, gives those relationships the highest priority. A morality based on that highest priority applies to all levels of human life, and I will attempt to demonstrate some of those applications in the pages to follow.

Triumphalism and the Will of God

Triumphalism claims to be a special way of thinking about the will of God in which God designs earthly events so as to make things morally good in God's eyes. When triumphalist believers assume that they and they alone know the will of God, they are likely to think that they are ordained to bring the rest of humanity into conformity with this highly specific plan. God is supposed to be intimately involved in the affairs of all people, but especially in the lives of the triumphalists and their fellow believers. God's relationship to humanity includes a personal level: it is assumed that the "Plan of Salvation" encompasses all individuals who are predestined to be saved from Hell, and that God has also crafted a specific plan for the daily life of each individual. Therefore, pursuing God's plan is the goal of the morally good life for each and every individual. The morally good life for the individual is believed to be consistent with God's will for the moral good of families and other groups of people: friends, communities, and nations. The "cosmic" level of this plan relates to the "chosen people," to whom God has promised success in battle and security from threats of enemies. According to the basic assumptions of Christendom, triumphalist Christians have superseded the original chosen people, the Children of Israel. This general framework gives rise to other moral decisions, many of them based directly on the assumptions that the chosen people are superior to all other people, and that their advantages in life are part of God's plan for the world. As do many other religiously based moral systems, Christian triumphalism covers its own customs and conventions with a divine veneer and seeks to impose those customs and conventions on everyone it can.

For instance, some Christians—mostly Northern Europeans and Americans—would say that when a storm ravaged the Spanish Armada as it approached the coast of England in 1588, the will of God was preventing Roman Catholicism from dominating the modern world, the way that the primarily Protestant European empires did until recently. Whether or not that is a good reading of the historical situation, it connects conventional ethnic triumphalism with events that might be called morally "good" by those who benefit from them.

Historically, western civilization and especially European empires have operated on triumphalist assumptions. The American colonies and states inherited this model from Europe and have expanded upon it. We are now in a desperate race to out-triumph the older European and rising Asian nations. But triumphalism is not inevitable. Other negative attitudes have faded as we have increased our understanding of human commonality and diversity. We can live well without both triumphalism and the superiority of whiteness; together we can rise above them.

Both triumphalism and the superiority of whiteness are part of our past, and they grew out of the world of monarchy and colonialism. Prior to 1776, colonial Americans had no more lived within a democratic society than had any other Europeans. The ideals of equality, freedom, and government by consent of the governed were just that, ideals. We had no more experience living on an equal footing with the nonwhite people of the world than any other Europeans—-and they had practically none. Colonial thinkers and activists were people of their times and not of ours. Today, we have a broader viewpoint than our ancestors, along with the advantage of living in a diverse, pluralistic public. A bright grade-school pupil can know more about the way foreigners live than our better-educated ancestors could ever have learned. Despite our limited (individual) knowledge, we have an immense advantage over the great minds of the past. Our scholars and adventurers have gone to the ends of earth and beyond, and have discovered intimate secrets of life unimaginable to those great minds of the past. So, can we not rise to a higher plateau of responsibility, transcend the thinking of the past, and embrace a concept of humanity in its unity, diversity, and richness?

Like a stone wall, triumphalism blocks the way to future reconciliation of America's social classes and our cooperation with the nations of the world. Our society cannot thrive if it operates under the assumption that its people are all subordinate to the interests of a particular segment of the public, such as the commercial enterprises. In spite of this, the commercialization of all our needs and functions has subordinated non-economic values. We are enticed into making Social Security a commercial system in which individuals will compete for higher individual benefits, instead of keeping the present system in which cooperative efforts and contributions provide benefits to everyone. This is only one method by which those with economic advantages distance themselves from those who have historically been economically disadvantaged. Today, triumphalist Christians mute these issues of economic justice by insisting that morality is a matter of individual abstinence from "sin" issues, such as abortion, extramarital sex, and homosexuality.

Economic achievement has become the primary focus of all our interests, because in our present world the economic values are the key to all others. In the best of all possible worlds, all interests—economic, political, religious, and familial—will be coordinated so that life as a whole can prosper. Human values of life, liberty, and the pursuit of happiness still remain the birthright of people everywhere. Our economic values of greed and immediate indulgence have become walls that separate us and swords that hang over our heads. A new conception of the public itself as a partnership of people can give us a sound basis for restructuring our values and open the way for economic democracy as well as opportunity. This new conception of the public relies less on knowledge of God and more on a new and better knowledge of humanity. One of the keys to this knowledge, I believe, is learning to call Jesus, "Brother."

This "new" conception of society, of the "public" as a partnership, is really not new at all. It reflects an ancient religious teaching that includes all members of the public in economic policies. Although Hebrew Scriptures assume a primarily command-obedience model of morality, and social policies of that time and people reflect the gradients in class distinctions between rich and poor, these facts do not tell the whole story. Another factor in the Hebrew texts deserves to be considered as a valid part of the Hebrew consciousness of people and their ideas of God and his will for them.

One text in particular illuminates the concern for economic justice and reflects the essential equal worth of individuals in the ethnically and economically diverse community. It is called the "Law of the Gleaners," which appears in the twenty-third chapter of Leviticus:

> And when you reap the harvest of your land, you shall not reap your field to its very border, nor shall you gather the gleanings after your harvest; you shall leave them for the poor and for the stranger; I am the Lord your God.(Lev. 23:22)

This verse enjoins a landowner from harvesting his fields bare, which we might think it is his right to do, and which we would expect any farmer to do today. But, the audience for this law does not represent just a commercial public that values individual profit above all else. This society recognizes everyone's right to share in the benefits of productive processes.

The Old Testament Book of Ruth has a beautiful example of the possible meaning and application of the Law of Gleaners. In this story, a woman is gleaning in the fields of a wealthy landowner, and he arranges for her to find generous gleanings, as he hopes she might remain in the vicinity before moving on. In making his exaggerated observance of the Law of Gleaners, he also wins her love in marriage. The story portrays the natural way that this humanistic economic principle coalesces with a romantic human relationship.

I like to think that in those days, God's prophet would stand in the midst of a field ripe for the harvest and say to the landowner and all others: "Do your work diligently and with thanks for the fruit of the earth. But remember, the fruit of all the fields is God's fruit, and all the people who are here to eat of it are God's people. These gleaners who will come after the harvesters are God's gleaners, and what they gather from the corners of the fields and from that which falls to the ground is theirs by the same right as those who reap the harvest."

Perhaps the time has come for all people who revere the Hebrew Scriptures to attend to the principles of social justice that are an integral part of the teachings that Jesus knew so well.

I have less concern for what the triumphalists will do to thwart this new conception of the public, but greater concern for what other, less intensely motivated Christians will neglect to do to promote it. When we only listlessly oppose politicians who are willing to abandon the poor, the disadvantaged, the newly emigrated—and especially those with growing children—and instead work for lower taxes for the wealthy, whence will come the positive message of compassion and community? American religion has the potential to convey these ideas if it catches the vision of Brother Jesus.

Triumphalism offers another version of morality in the idea that simple obedience to God's laws is the same thing as morality. Thus, a morally good person obeys God's laws and promotes that obedience on the part of others. My objection to this position has nothing to do with God, God's laws, or the validity of His laws. Rather, I object to triumphalism's assumption that morality is reducible to obedience and disobedience.

Morality and Obedience

Our human world does not operate on the basis of simple repetition of simple moral answers that outward authority has provided for repeated, verbatim use as the occasions arise. If I have told my child not to steal, and that child someday finds a wallet in a neighbor's driveway, my rule about stealing may or may not answer the question of what to do with the wallet. However, if I have tried to show concern for helping people in a variety of situations, that object lesson applied to helping our neighbor may inspire the child to decide on the appropriate action. Obedience by itself has limited value, because obedience is the beginning, and not the end, of the progression of moral obligation.

Obedience to authority itself is grounded in the most natural of human relationships, that of the parent and the child. We universally experience this relationship: every adult once started as a child with parents, and almost every child will become an adult with a child. Recognition of this situation comes about not in childhood, which is not quite the time to think so very imaginatively, but in adulthood. The better parent will reflect on the limitations of obedience as a way of meeting problematic situations. If a parent regards morality only as a matter of obedience, that parent will stunt the moral development of his or her child. Morality needs to mature along with intelligence and imagination. A nursery-rhyme example of morality might be appropriate for a preschool child, but it is woefully inadequate for a teenager with hormonal urges that the preschooler never experiences and the nursery rhymes never depict.

Parents will not always be on the scene to serve as the moral authority who must be obeyed. The child will become an adult who must come to decisions independently of parental orders. It behooves the parent, therefore, to attempt to bring the child through the level of simple obedience to the level of moral choice. Choices are based on values that are shaped by experience in everyday life. Children need to have values as internal resources by which the adult-to-be can make wholesome choices and that will also provide the potential for developing better values in future choices. Thus, freedom and responsibility are conjoined qualities for developing the individual's moral life. In summary, this analysis of morality asserts two levels or strata of morality: outer morality, which consists of commands obeyed out of conformity, and inner morality, which consists of conscience applied to personal relations.

This is essentially what Jesus implied when, in the Sermon on the Mount, he repeatedly said, "You have heard that it was said to men of old, 'Thou shall not…', but I say unto you…" He was contrasting the levels of a moral system based on covenanted law with a moral system based on choices that involve values, motives and purposes. This is not just a contrast in times, eras, or "dispensations." Morality was never a case of simply obeying laws; a situation involving moral value always requires some freedom. People have always had some degree of responsibility for considering the values, motives, and purposes entailed in their activities, as well as obedience to laws.

The Morality of Responsibility

Obedience to authority does not equate with moral responsibility. In our "Declaration of Independence" Jefferson states: " We hold these truths to be self-evident...that governments are instituted among men, deriving their just powers from the consent of the governed." Those who are thus governed must be free and equal in weighing their individual and common consent. Jefferson's powerful eighteenth-century rhetoric placed the basis of legitimate government outside any claim of divine right of kings or aristocracy or priesthood. No longer does any moral value inhere in the commands of good kings or bad kings. After this, no government could be called just unless it rested on the "consent of the governed." If George III had been the most benevolent king in history, his government could still not have been called just, because it did not meet this "consent" test. This position had not previously been part of common law, so Jefferson's words, "When in the course of human events," ushered in a new era: the time had come to right the ancient wrong of tyranny, and it should be done without apology to the past. Merely deposing a tyrant results in anarchy, because the people are not necessarily ready for self-government. But, when the time is right, justice requires that people take responsibility for being self-governing. Jefferson and his colleagues not only recognized the appropriateness of the historical moment, but also realized the correctness of laboring for the primacy of consent—the exercise of responsible choices by those who will be affected by the outcomes of those choices.

What a sea-change in the European world! A set of colonists are prepared to cut their ties with their colonial sponsors—those investors and owners of property in the colony—and with the government of the colonial empire, even breaking their various oaths to serve the Crown and honor its laws. Accused of treason, treachery, sedition, and larceny, the former subjects became instant outlaws. They did indeed "Pledge to each other our lives, our fortunes and our sacred honor," not under duress, but freely and with all deliberate intention. Jefferson's words led to the all-out war, and all could have been lost. The British Empire held on in India, for instance, for another century and a half. The American Colonies could have lost their war of independence, but the principle for which it had been fought would not have perished. Henceforth, governments that ignored the consent of the governed could not be called just. The era that identified morality with mere obedience to authority has passed. The course of human events demanded a morality based on freedom of choice, the people's ability to choose how to enact their values as they see fit, with paramount respect for the common good.

Thoreau on the Morality of Responsibility

Henry David Thoreau (1817–1862) stands out among the radical critics of the old order of religion and morality, with its dedication to the ancient past and the indefinite future. Thoreau was an American original. If he heard that a typical well-placed American had agreed with him, Thoreau would have assumed that he had been either mistaken or misunderstood and would have immediately written an essay to accommodate both possibilities. Perhaps not since Socrates has a prolific person given his critics such sharp tools with which to attack him.

Thoreau held the principle of personal responsibility as his abiding polestar, his moral compass. If he ever needed to save himself from drowning by clinging to a plank, he first wanted to be sure that no one else had already trusted his life to it. This abstraction expresses a principle in final terms, but is so unlikely as to be largely irrelevant. Even taken as metaphor—a plank actually stolen, the bereft man about to drown, and then the possibility of Thoreau's rescuing the drowning man by the sacrifice of the essayist's own life—it does not make a compelling argument for small, commonplace acts of justice under ambiguous circumstances. However, the principle of moral debt still holds. Our typical American does not think morality entails an obligation to repay a debt that is not legally binding. The give-and-take of commerce encourages him to forsake any debt that he is not forced to repay. If I owe a small balance to a local merchant, and he goes out of business, am I obligated to pay someone? If so, whom do I pay? Why not just wait until someone sends me a bill, we might ask.

But moral debt is only part of the issue here. Thoreau's hypothetical case of the drowning man and the plank addresses the dilemma of the person in mortal danger who might save himself only by imposing his own danger on an innocent second party. This is the larger problem that confronts so many of us in our complex and interconnected, but competitive, world. For instance, if a public official has made a decision that threatens to cost him his position, will he manipulate the records to suggest that a subordinate was responsible for the mistake? Does a person's superior power give him the moral right to treat a less powerful person unjustly, even to the point of jeopardizing his status or endangering his life? Thoreau pursues this question to a higher level of moral priority: a position of power entails the duty to forego that same power when its exercise would hurt an innocent person.

So many of us are in comfortable, if not elegant, circumstances, and so many others are in such meager situations that we experience nearly constant moral pressure to try to correct the imbalance. But how are we to do this, with all the ambiguities present in our personal, social, and political obligations? How often do we simply give in to a sophistic conclusion that it is just too much to figure out, so we will go along doing nothing, or almost nothing? Thoreau's drowning man goads our easy consciences.

Thoreau raises the question of economic justice. How much excess material wealth do we obtain at the expense of someone else's necessity? Aside from the material things, how many emotional and mental resources that someone else sorely lacks do we thoughtlessly lavish on those who need it so little? Money is reward enough by itself, yet we still mechanically heap credit and praise on those who get the most money for the slightest efforts. The wealthy are blessed by our congratulations that they deserve it all. Meanwhile, many of those who produce the most are depreciated not only by their meager monetary rewards, but also by their lowered self-esteem, resulting from our social judgment that they deserve their poverty, in comparison with the riches of the wealthy. Our culture has moved so far toward the sanctification of material success that anything that does not put it first is considered unnatural.

Our popular standards often encourage those who do not possess conspicuous wealth to try to appear to be allied with the wealthy. We reason that one who cannot enjoy wealth firsthand can at least think himself elevated in status if he can only approve and imitate those who possess it. Remarkably, often the wealthy person rides on the shoulders of the one who mindlessly praises him. Many owners of capitalist enterprises express the universal belief that they are only simple people who derive their satisfaction from knowing that they have given jobs to their workers, who would otherwise starve and freeze without the property owners and their talented efforts.

Many American citizens of the nineteenth century shared Thoreau's belief, if not his dedication. The moral claims of injustice against slavery fueled the agitation that hurled the country toward sectional war. Thoreau spoke for the latent, if not active, moral outrage against slavery felt by many European immigrants who had escaped from Old World oppressions. He did not echo the voice of the religious abolitionist, such as William Lloyd Garrison; instead, he reiterated the ideas of Thomas Paine, who had written his essay "Common Sense" "in words that any literate person could understand," according to Howard Zinn. Thoreau did not gain his widest reading public until after his death, in the aftermath of the Civil

War, when his essay "Civil Disobedience" became a handbook for the rising worldwide rejection of colonialism and oppressive government. Tolstoy in czarist Russia, Ghandi in British India, and King in segregationist America made that essay their own polestars.

The Waning of Triumphalism

As the concept of morality as obedience has waned, triumphalism has lost its major justification, that it belongs to a divinely chosen people. Americans had begun to abandon the idea of a "chosen people" of God a long time ago, at least since the days when Ralph Waldo Emerson moved from the comfort of a mild Calvinist version of it to an undogmatic, open-minded Unitarianism. Many other active American thinkers and believers made the step along with Emerson. We are about to enter the new millennium on the crest of a wave of resurgent triumphalism. The triumphalist American might ask, "We won the cold war, didn't we? And we American Christians conquered the 'evil empire of godless communism,' didn't we? What could that be called except a triumph, indeed one which the whole world has to stand aside for and salute! So, how can triumphalism be said to be waning, fading away?" To sense the illusory permanence of power, we have only to reflect on such historical anomalies as the simultaneous presence in Victorian and Edwardian England of the icon of "Rule, Britannia, Britannia Rules the Waves," and the immensely popular works of Gilbert and Sullivan, such as *H.M.S. Pinafore,* in which the Royal Navy is lampooned in outrageous terms. Until the disaster of trench warfare in 1913-18, the irony did not come into full force: Britannia was an empty shell, a vacant castle. Not until after World War II did the sun fully set on the British Empire, and not until the liberation of the African colonies did the sins of the English and other European empire builders rise to the surface.

The European warlords had drawn lines on the maps of Europe and Africa that made human hash out of indigenous peoples in their homelands. At the end of the twentieth century, we still see what unutterable suffering has come to the former colonials whom the Europeans left with boundaries that locked some of them together in old ethnic hostilities and separated others from families and old friends.

Like our ancestors, we can be very much unaware of what is taking place in the world around us. We see what goes on, and we think we are reading the present correctly, but soon we notice circumstances that tell us we were mistaken. A previously unperceived reality has brought us to a world different from what anyone would have anticipated earlier. So, although triumphalism predominates historically, other things may be going on that are not yet apparent. We are no less prone to shortsightedness than previous generations. For a longer view of the morality at work in the world, we can look to South Africa, where a season of compassion and forgiveness is replacing a century of hatred and violence.

Many well-read church members will learn from this book and others that a whole "gospel" exists that does not rely on triumphalist grounds. Some may find in this gospel a welcome relief from the contradictions that have plagued them as they have sought to remain "true" to the apostolic tradition despite the distance they see between the Jesus that they have read about in the Gospels, and the kind of war god that their church has taught them to worship. But the increase in alternative scholarship and interpretation, together with the discovery of additional literature from the time of Jesus' life, is having an impact that shows no signs of lessening.

I have complex reasons for claiming that triumphalism is waning, and perhaps these include a little wishful thinking. Although I would be glad to live to see my claim borne out, neither my genes nor my girth will likely allow me the longevity that would be required for that. Perhaps my grandchildren will be the American generation to see the fruition of this long process of spiritual maturation that I identify as the waning of triumphalism.

Triumphalism for Individuals: "The Will of God for Me"

The personal level of what is called triumphalism encompasses many religious issues. A person who believes in triumphalism has a strong tendency to identify his desires for himself with the "Will of God for my life." This "will of God" concept grew out of the human tendency to anthropomorphize an external source of power, intelligence, or virtue. When we talk about "Mother Nature," or "Lady Luck," we refer to something that is not literally human as though it had some human form or characteristics. So, when we refer to the "will of God," we are portraying God with a set of human intentions. The notions of fate or destiny remain very strong in our ancestral memories. People have always known that we have little or no control over some events in life, and this engenders fear and even anger. The fear results from events or conditions that threaten us with harm or death but leave us with no way to prevent them. The anger results from events that not only have tragic consequences, but also thwart expectations, scattering to the winds well-laid plans before their fulfillment. Many religions accommodate these inevitable contingencies by placing such events under the control of nature or specific deities or powers that may or may not be within some range of human influence. This sets the stage for some human agents to be empowered to supplicate the deities or to accomplish a correction in situations that are believed to account for the unwanted events. For example, priests are persons who possess the secrets necessary to mollify the troubled powers or to perform rituals of submission and sacrifice to the appropriate deity.

A more graphic instance of anthropomorphism appears in the Japanese creation myth that involves two deities, Izanagi and Izanami.

> Izanagi asked his spouse, "How is your body formed?" She replied, "My body has one place which is formed insufficiently." Then Izanagi said, "My body has one place which is formed to excess. Therefore, I would like to take that place in my body which is formed to excess and insert it into that place in your body which is formed insufficiently, and thus give birth to the land. How would this be?" Then Izanami replied, saying, "That will be good." Then Izanagi said, "Then let us, you and me, walk in a circle around this heavenly pillar and meet and have conjugal intercourse."

It would be difficult to find a more specific portrayal of a divine force using human features and functions in a supernatural process such as creation. Some may consider this crude or even salacious imagery, unsuitable to a serious discussion of religion. However, in a naive but wholesome way it elevates the very human process of procreation to the level of a sublime relationship. Does this graphic depiction of the creation of the world bring God down to a tawdry level of human carnality, or does it elevate human passion and creativity to the lyrical level of cosmic significance? It may just as well be the latter, and as such it may make too much out of a good but very ordinary activity. But it seems a much preferable way to explain human sexuality than the original sin imagery of St. Augustine.

The idea of a supernatural, divine personal power that scrutinizes the comings and goings of each and every human individual has its merits. This idea seems to have developed in our culture out of the tradition of a "chosen people" that runs through both Jewish and Christian history. In this portrayal, God selects a family lineage to be a "chosen people." The original "chosen people" occupy a special place in human history, as do the descendants of Abraham, Isaac, and Jacob. The Apostles modified this portrayal into that of the new "chosen people," Christians who by the will of God are selected from out of humanity to be "saved" and elevated to eternal bliss in heaven. The Apostle Paul, St. Augustine, and later Luther, et al., further modified this concept so that the will of God applied to the particular path of each "called out" individual. In effect, this idea depicts God as the Great Scriptwriter who gives each Christian a role to play in the great drama of salvation. It is then up to each Christian to discern this role and to carry it to its conclusion just as God has designed it.

This general idea of divine direction of an individual's life developed in a historical progression. Socrates consulted his "daimon" to see if he were being warned not to do something; Shakespeare had Hamlet say, "There's a divinity that shapes our ends, rough hew them how we will"; and more recently, Fanny Crosby wrote a hymn, "All the Way My Savior Leads Me." These are variations on the idea of a divinely given, individualized pathway through the course of life. This seductive idea seems to have taken hold of the overheated religious imagination of recent partakers of the extreme individualism of post-Copernican Euro-Americans. Our American radical individualism that assumes that every single one of us acts as an independent agent with little if any essential reliance on other people fits well with this notion of divine calling to a prescribed path in life. We become actors in a cosmic drama, which we suppose includes other believers whose scripts are written by the same divine scriptwriter.

The idea of the will of God holds a unique fascination. A person who is serious about life, who thinks his own life may have some meaning, finds it a compelling idea that his own individual life has a place in the immense drama of eternity. The very thought that a particular plan of life has come from the eternal creator of everything is fascinating in itself.

Accepting the belief that even one's own lowly self may have a part to play in the larger scheme of things is a moving experience. For some, this realization holds the same qualities of excitement and fascination as the experience of a new romance. Even the most stolid person has probably felt the thrill of a new affection. Surprise, mystery, and excitement are stirred as though a new love has been revealed. Indeed, life becomes vibrant with a new and delightful rhythm. A romantic infatuation with another person and the thought of a divine plan for life share some interesting similarities. Both have "An irresistible power to transfix and hold spellbound." Indulgence in a fanciful infatuation and a serious belief in the divine plan are both out of rational bounds, not based on any credible evidence, and not consistent with any critical knowledge of what is involved. Each involves the investment of intense interest, the suspension of doubt, and the assumption of extravagant possibilities. Each gives the mind and heart the explosive power of affirmation. Romantic fascination in the abstract is always easier and more pleasant than actual acquaintance with the particular object of fascination. In fact, knowledge of the actual person may erode the fascination as quickly as it arose. Hence, on a practical level, it is just as dangerous to act on sheer fascination as it is to act on sheer belief in

God's will. Both may be fatal to better prospects that might not have been so compelling at first sight.

But, think of the possibility that the very stuff of daydreams might be the same as the content of the will of God. Pity the poor soul who has never indulged in honest daydreaming. What self-transcendence is provided in the thought of giving oneself to a purpose that is in keeping with the eternal values of nature, humanity, and God! What could open a grander expanse for imagining oneself doing wonderful things? When like-minded people confirm one's judgment, the self-enhancement is magnified. Any observers who raise doubts about the will of God are dismissed as simply playing the role of skeptical objectors. For the triumph of God's will requires that the faithful overcome obstacles—perhaps in the guise of parents, friends, or teachers—to keep the imagination working, dismissing the negative and affirming the positive. At the core of doing God's will for one's life lies a moral qualification: submission to the ultimate authority, which then sanctifies all that is done in carrying out that submission. No wonder people will follow the most improbable of human leaders, like Jim Jones. If following that leader is the same for them as submitting to the will of God, the intensity of their devotion becomes more credible to outsiders.

As a battle-scarred veteran of many inner struggles over the will of God, I am prepared to accept the irrationality of following charismatic religious leaders. At the same time I understand that such followers are not necessarily weak or stupid people. I know how compelling religious fascination can be, and how powerfully influential the idea of the will of God can be. I have yielded much of my life and devotion to both fascination and to the idea of the will of God, and I have lived to regret much of the results of both. If I had been more concerned about knowing myself and what I was getting into, and less impressed with the megalomaniacal aspect of what I had imagined to lie ahead of me, I would have acted differently and would have less to regret.

This does not constitute an attack on the integrity of those who make an earnest effort to do the will of God in their lives. I consider them and myself the victims of bad teaching. I am now not trying to trivialize them, but rather to open a discussion that is long overdue among traditional Christians. Am I right in suspecting that a person's intense involvement with doing the will of God is likely to coincide with that person's youthful or early exposure to enthusiastic religion? Do more mature individuals or older people with less invested in enthusiastic religion show less willingness to sharply change the direction of their lives on the basis of a new "revelation" of God's will? Worldly experience dampens the credibility a person is likely to grant to eccentric leaders and exhorters of God's will.

A strong correlation seems to exist between hearing God's call to a specific and peculiar change in life's direction and many of the critical periods of life, such as puberty, adolescence, midlife crises, and interruptions of life caused by loss or separation. Many people seem to be susceptible to such "leadings" at critical phases, and their spiritual advisors encourage enthusiastic leaps into exotic but unwise commitments. An older pastor, priest, or teacher may look at the "just about to take a plunge" individual and feel some nostalgia for the excitement of that stage of life. Their temptation is to urge a full-speed commitment to radical change, when a cooler look at the whole situation would be more helpful. Who wants to play the skeptic's role when a reinforcement of certainty seems so much desired? And so, a seeker after a new way to face the future becomes escorted onto the slippery and shifting path of complete faith in a fascinating but untested possibility.

A young woman student once asked me if I knew a certain friend of hers, a young man named Tommy. I replied that I did know him and his parents, and that I considered him a fine fellow. I suspected that she had more in mind than mere curiosity about my acquaintance with him, and she surely had! She said that after graduation he had moved to Chicago and obtained a job and an apartment of his own. He had invited her to come to Chicago and spend a weekend with him. As she talked, her eyes glowed with fascination at the prospect of seeing the city in the company of a handsome and experienced young man. When she told of that plan, it gave me the sort of feeling that I had when a friend's daughter informed me that she was thinking of hitchhiking to California instead of returning to college.

What do you say? She wanted to go so badly that she was already savoring the prospect, and she knew that I would not tell her not to go, because of our discussions in ethics class about the process of moral choice. I told her that I had not realized that she and Tommy were so well acquainted or so far along in their relationship. Her eyes lost some luster as she revealed that they had only dated a few times during the previous year, while they worked at the same place. From her tone and demeanor I sensed that she was beginning to see my point. I said that I thought she would have a wonderful time, and that Tommy would be a very lucky young man, but that he would probably expect more of her than she might be ready to give. I suggested that she should do what was consistent with her own values about herself, and what would be consistent with her future, especially in regard to Tommy. She walked away with the slightest shrug and grin. Later, she told me that she had invited Tommy to the local homecoming game and dance. Afterward, Tommy's father told me that his son had spent the weekend in question visiting his grandmother at her home in Evanston. Thus does the pull of fascination and imagination succumb to the effects of serious thought and real life.

A parable of unknown origin imparts the best example of proclaiming the will of God for individual persons. A minister ended a sermon by telling his congregation that he was going to reveal to them God's will for all of their lives. He went to the right side of the room and said to those on that side, "Love your neighbors." He then went to the left side and said to those on that side, "Love one another." Then he went to the center and said to all, "Walk humbly before God."

People who admonish others to seek and to submit to the will of God typically make their assertions based on certain claims to knowledge. I claim that no one can dependably apprehend such an abstraction as the will of God for a particular person. Sheer partisan power plays are the rule rather than the exception. Some organizations or their leaders claim that they are simply doing the will of God, but then we see those leaders treat each other as though they are out destroy their rivals. Real issues get trampled underfoot, and human spirits are more likely to be grounded than to soar. On more than one occasion I have seen an earnest believer happen upon a scene of rancorous squabbling among church officials, and then turn away in disgust, regretting that he or she had gotten too close to the top rungs of the ladder of authority.

Dedication is the one great and overriding reward that will come to the believer who earnestly sets out to follow the will of God. This undertaking, as few other things in life can do, demands great dedication that focuses a person's life upon a goal. It provides a transcendence of the ordinary things of the world and renders trivial everything that would stand in the way. Dedicating one's life to a cause that is believed to be of ultimate worth offers a great reward. Commitment is empowering. Religious dwarfs have become like giants under the spell of an overpowering purpose. People have told me that they hold onto the traditional doctrines of Christianity primarily because they fear that if doubt takes root in their minds, they will lose their sense of purpose in life. They say, in effect, "If I stop believing in God as I always have, won't I throw away my whole reason for living?" My response is that there remains enough to be improved in the conditions of ordinary human life to provide ample purpose for all of us.

Pursuing the will of God has one risk that outweighs the value of centering one's life on one grand purpose. That is the danger that one will abandon all inquiry into what the will of God is, if there is indeed a true will of God for the individual life. If one uncritically accepts the value of dedication to an overwhelming purpose, one faces the danger that single-minded devotion to this idea will drive out all the healthy caution and questioning that everyone needs to gain mature wisdom. The tradition tells us that the will-of-God notion displaces all questions and subsumes all inquiry to intention. We are told to be most certain that there is a will of God for each individual, and that each individual can know this plan in detail; it is necessary only to believe! If we really want to know God's plan, it will be revealed to us. We are further told that if we do not know these things, it is because we lack sincerity or innocence or both. This notion goes back to St. Augustine, who said, "If I submit to the will of God, then I will know." He claimed that he did not need to look at the ordinary affairs of life, or inquire into the wisdom of people generally, but would only have to give unreserved assent to the traditional teachings of the ecclesiastical authorities, and he would come to understand all that was necessary.

Knowledge is a deceptively difficult topic, especially when it concerns God. But what are we to think when we find that a major biblical figure has undergone a major change in his concept of God? This happened to the Apostle Paul in his conversion experience, his famous Damascus Road enlightenment. Before that experience, Jewish beliefs in God, which he shared with other religious Jews of his time, shaped his concept of God. Paul says that he belonged to the Pharisees. That sect believed Jesus to be a renegade Jewish rebel who had forsaken his roots, become an outlaw, and been executed by the Romans. After his conversion, Paul came to believe that God had sent Jesus to redeem not only Israel, but all of humanity. Did God change from a Jewish deity to a universal redeemer of humanity, or did Paul change his mind about God? Paul gives us a clue about what might have happened when he explains such a change of mind in one of his letters:

> When I was a child, I spoke like a child, I thought like a child, I reasoned like a child; when I became a man, I gave up childish ways. For now we see in a mirror dimly, but then face to face. Now I know in part; then I shall understand fully, even as I have been fully understood. (1 Cor. 13:11-12)

Paul tells us that it is normal and natural for knowledge to progress from the partial to the complete and from the immature to the mature. He regards his knowledge of God before his ecstatic experiences as being different from his knowledge of God afterwards. God had not changed, but Paul's knowledge of God had. Paul here endorsed the idea that a godly person can have a change of mind about God. Thus, Paul seems to be saying that it would be imprudent to consider any particular idea about God as permanent and unchangeable, even an idea of the will of God. This suggests humility when stating what the will of God may be.

Does this not give us reason for modesty in our assertions about our concept of God? Do we not need to maintain a decent proportionality between the degree of certainty we can claim and the seriousness of the matters about which we speak? When we are talking about the "will of God" for someone's life, we should be careful that our present version of God's will is in keeping with the limitations of our present knowledge.

Past and Future: Triumphalism or Reconciliation?

The triumphal attitude assumes that Christians have an ordained mission to conquer the world in the name of Christ. This idea is the ally and blood brother of the concept of "whiteness," the assumption that a special status of advantage and worth attaches to having what passes as "white" skin. Which came first? Historically, triumphalism appeared in the ancient world at a time when I assume the concept of "whiteness" did not exist in its present Euro-American form. But in the history of Euro-American colonization and migration around the world, the adulation of "whiteness" has played a special role; in the United States, it has surfaced in the unfolding racism that has kept African-Americans and native Americans in truly degraded conditions. In one of the major sources of shame to "white" American Christians, their religion has not yet required them to come to grips with this national tragedy in any institutional way.

The moral stature of America is at present, as it always has been, an unfinished story. Although the country has existed for only a few hundred years, we have seen enormous shifts in the nation's direction and pace. Our history has compressed into a few centuries a sweep of events and developments that has hardly been equaled by any other nation, even in thousands of years. For example, the Louisiana Purchase practically doubled the land mass of the United States overnight, and without a shot being fired. Jefferson bragged that he had in one stroke showed Europe how to expand a country without war or bloodshed, despite the questionable constitutional legality of the accession. Jefferson's enemies saw it as a grandiose boondoggle that wasted good federal money on a worthless expanse of wilderness that was valuable only to the "savages" who roamed aimlessly over it. We might now question whether the Louisiana Purchase was immoral: it transferred ownership of property that did not belong to the sellers and ignored the homestead rights of millions of people who had lived peacefully on the land for millennia. Frenchmen and Americans treated the American Indians as if European-style land ownership customs superseded native American birthrights. This is analogous to Russia selling the Ohio Valley to Italy. Such a thing would have caused a riot in Congress, and Jefferson would have spearheaded it. The analogy is not strictly accurate in detail, but it is near enough to convey the thought. Nevertheless, Jefferson had to scurry to make the purchase into a credit to his tenure as the president of the United States. To his discredit Jefferson, as a fellow human being of the American Indians, extended Euro-American civilization to where it had never been before, and to where it could only destroy an ancient and unthreatening native civilization.

Sweeping changes have taken place in unexpected ways and by unprecedented means. In 1850 Congress passed the Fugitive Slave Law and the president signed it into law. This was the high-water mark of legal slavery in the United States. The powerful slave states could make every citizen in the country into a virtual slave-catcher. This infamous law defined every person of the slightest shade of color as a suspected runaway slave. It required that any white citizen who saw a person of color cooperate in the apprehension of that person as a possible escaped slave. The person of color had to prove on the spot that he or she was not in fact a slave who had escaped from a slaveholder. Otherwise, the person of color was subject to arrest and return to whatever slaveholder might make the first claim. Courts and governors of the free states witnessed the spectacle of having a citizen—perhaps a resident and neighbor in that state for many years—being brought into the dock to be subjected to the legal system of the slave states. This law and its consequences provided one of the decisive pieces of evidence that brought the North to recognize that they also were allies of slaveholders, no matter what freedom they claimed for themselves. Fewer than twenty years after the passage of this crown jewel of the infamous slave legal system, the system had disappeared from the United States.

Serious changes in our national history have taken unusual courses. Whereas Europe endured the Thirty Years' War after the Reformation, and Ireland still fights its own religious war, John F. Kennedy went to Houston in 1960 and dehorned the Texas Baptists, settling the question of whether or not a Roman Catholic could be elected president and interrupting the unbroken stream of Protestants and other non-Catholics, such as Jefferson, who had previously held the office. What seems like permanence is always temporary: after a short time, more change occurs.

Triumphalism, like the supremacy of whiteness, needs to wither, shrivel, and dry up at the roots for the good of our American public and for the good of individual believers in Christianity. The churches need to bring people together to promote community and to offer reconciliation to antagonistic groups of neighbors.

Triumphalism feeds on people's tendency to separate when they might otherwise feel like neighbors, and it fuels the group and individual pride and arrogance that make enemies of people who would otherwise only be considered different sorts of healthy and slightly off-center Americans. The ideal of "We the people" cannot thrive where triumphalism is rampant. American triumphalism has led to the spirit of "Manifest Destiny," the belief that the United States is the divinely ordained model for all successful future human societies. But, can this spirit be our motivation for dominating the rest of the world without that same spirit being a divisive malignancy that corrodes our internal social life? The triumphalist spirit has contributed to the demise of past nations and empires that have devoted themselves to it. In the same way, the supremacy of whiteness has retarded America's progress toward civic and social stability. When we look at the Old South, we can see that slavery isolated those states from the mainstream of American progress, leaving any advancements made after the Revolution to the Northern and Midwestern states, where immigration and innovation were forging an industrial and agricultural powerhouse. After the Second World War, the GI Bill of Rights, and the repeal of Jim Crow laws, the remnants of the Confederacy have blossomed. How much of the nation's progress might have taken place in the Sun Belt, had the dead hand of slavery not throttled it?

A further question must be raised: Can religious people live a good life if triumphalism is not an integral part of their religious tradition? Can we hope to find the peace of mind and the satisfaction of our deep spiritual needs if we do not have the old assurances of God and heaven, even if we no longer find those assurances credible? Will the waning of triumphalism and the rising of an inclusive and humane attitude toward a wide variety of religious beliefs be compatible with healthy spiritual life for individuals and institutions? I believe that the future possibility of healthy spiritual life for Americans rests on the emergence of primary Christian and other religious beliefs that discard triumphalism, eventually making it as much a relic as divine-right monarchy. Triumphalism requires a mind-set that refuses to see the reality of our common human identity. It replaces the unity of humanity with a self-anointing as God's chosen people. The motives of ordinary human greed and arrogance for domination hide behind a mask of self-serving claims that we are only following God's will in imposing and extending domination.

As the future becomes more and more globally oriented, our national horizons become clouded with deep and vital questions about our entire American public, and whose color and ethnicity is the "correct" one. On the other hand, could the "American Dream" become an inspiration for the reconciliation of diverse people? Are we going to see ourselves as a member of the inclusive global community, in which there is a spirit of universal public rights and responsibilities? Or, will we see ourselves as a vast collection of pseudo-independent selves, each of whom thinks that alone it is possible and desirable to find an island of prosperity in a sea of irrelevant poverty? Which of these perspectives will our religious values support?

All of these levels of triumphalism—national, social, and personal—comprise our American and Christian culture. It is not my claim that triumphalism alone caused certain things to happen. I do not think, for instance, that the Civil War was fought solely because the two sides, the Confederacy and the Union, each had convictions of being under divine command and support in its efforts to defeat the other, and thus to preserve human slavery or to wipe it out. Many different issues of historical precedent, economic advantage, and personal benefits contributed to the war. At any level of life, only rarely can events be said to have just one cause. I do not know how important the tradition of national triumphalism or religious triumphalism or personal triumphalism was as a cause of the Civil War. Historians have argued those claims before and will argue them again. But I do claim that in the Civil War, as in other similar affairs, triumphalism contributed to the sentiment that war was the only recourse, and that God was on the side of all combatants, as long as they still fought. Triumphalism has strongly biased the nation, our society, and many of us personally to believe that our mission has divine direction and support, and this belief often overrides our consideration of more comprehensive and productive national purposes.

The Civil War attempted to resolve the many issues remaining after the founding of the nation in regard to the place of slavery under the new constitution. Were property rights in human beings equal to property rights in land, cattle, and so on? Did the federal government have an interest in the human rights of all native-born inhabitants including slaves, or only those who were born free? Did the framers of the Constitution expect slavery to wither away peacefully, because the importation of slaves became illegal after 1808? Do states have a right to withdraw from the Union, if they had originally volunteered to join it? How did the growing economic and ethnic differences among the states affect relations between the North and the South? Most growth in the free population occurred in the North, through immigration, while the South grew at a much slower rate through natural breeding. The nation's industrialization burgeoned overwhelmingly in the North, in cities that swelled with large, skilled work forces of free citizens. So what caused the Civil War? A better question would be, Why was the solution to the existence of slavery, and all the other problems that faced a diverse and growing nation, assumed to be a war between brothers and cousins? Why were citizens on both sides convinced that their personal and familial values depended on winning such a war?

The issues underlying the Civil War did not require a divinely ordained war for their resolution; in fact, the war did not even remotely settle the issues that were then at work in the nation, North and South. Triumphalism supported the drift toward war and supported the continuation of the war—with its terrible toll of 600,000 Americans dead—even after it was clear that no resolution to racial, legal, or economic issues could be won. Without triumphalism molding our cultural expectations, there might have been a gradual, rational, planned emancipation, as there had been in other countries, possibly with better results for the progress of newly freed African-American citizens. Without such triumphalism, our nation would have had a better chance to bring about the betterment of life for all its citizens, through freedom from slave-bondage as well as through full participation for all citizens in building a thriving nation. But with triumphalism as a deeply ingrained element of our culture, and embedded in our public religion, solutions to all vital issues such as those of slavery and union will always be harder to find. Progress in contemporary issues, such as full opportunity for all Americans to participate in a thriving nation, is sure to be more costly in effort and poorer in results if triumphalism continues to plague our sense of values.

The presence of triumphalism in American culture promotes unjustifiable glorification of our national place in the whole human scheme of things. We hold fast to the notion that we are the new "chosen people," destined by God's design to outshine all other nations in our righteousness and our good works. Our "superpower" position in the world supposedly attests to this claim. We have outdone all our old foes. The world now looks to us as its model of the rich, successful, privileged nation of the future. We tell ourselves that it is all because we have made this continent into the most productive and thriving land on earth. We claim that only by our wisdom and hard work have we conquered all our enemies in military, commercial, and cultural contests. As the only remaining "superpower," we will guide all others into becoming imitations of ourselves.

The stark reality of cold print makes the hollowness of triumphalist sentiments even more apparent than when we hear them shouted to the crowd in a political rally. Such political speech provides another case of bad theater chasing out good thinking. In our cooler moments, many of us have realized that we have been incredibly favored, not by an arbitrary deity, but by a wonderful natural system by which life grows and thrives according to the same laws in all nations.

I recently encountered a highly placed electronic engineer who confronted a common but resistant problem with his counterparts from other companies. What was his almost heretical recommendation to his fellow workers? "When all else fails, cooperate!" We all experience the values of cooperation and the limits of competition in the daily flow of life. We share the family of our basic humanity with all those not like ourselves in color, class, and religion, as well as those who are our brothers and sisters in reality. We feel the warm kinship of those people of good will who visit us from far away, and those whom we meet in personal encounters. When we share a slice of real life with someone different from ourselves, it is much easier to think, "neighbor," than "enemy." All for good reason: we are all part of the organism that constitutes humanity, past and present, near and far, same and different.

4

Many Things Are Known, But All Incompletely
The Origin of Knowledge

THE BRAIN and its extended neural system constitute the organ of consciousness, sensation, and thought, functions central to human life. The brain is also the seat of personhood, as long as an individual has life. The physiology of the brain has developed over eons, so the neural system we share with other creatures like ourselves has remarkable similarities. Creationists believe that the brain is so wondrous that an intelligent creator must have designed it as it now is. This special-creation argument can easily be dismissed since human and nonhuman brains are alike cases of natural development. The more important questions for us are what it means to have this marvelous facility, and how can it be used for maximum benefit.

Blaise Pascal, the seventeenth-century mathematician and theological adventurer, used his mental facilities to a superlative degree. He created a primitive computer and consorted with the premier scientists of his time. But he also perceived his world as would an authentic Christian mystic. In his book *Pensees,* Pascal explored the mysteries of life, death, and God.

> Man is only a reed, the weakest in nature, but he is a thinking reed. There is no need for the whole universe to take up arms to crush him; a vapor, a drop of water is enough to kill him. But even if the universe were to crush him, man would still be nobler than his slayer, because he knows that he is dying and the advantage the universe has over him. The universe knows none of this.

The human individual has this cognitive function with an exquisite capacity that can be experienced as thought and expressed as knowledge of itself and much of what is going on in the universe. A human child between the ages of one and three years normally develops more specific awareness of its surroundings than the rest of the nonhuman universe combined. The processes of thought and language seem to develop reciprocally, so that each depends on the other for its growth.

A story about a little Bronx schoolgirl named Sylvia poses an interesting analogy to the tenacious belief in God's will and illustrates an interesting aspect of human development. Sylvia had classmates named Rosita, Maria, and Heidi. When Sylvia visited the homes of her friends, she became impressed with the different languages spoken by her friends' parents. In each home, Sylvia noticed with some amazement, her friend and her friend's parents spoke the very same language. She found it amazing that Rosita spoke Spanish to her parents, Maria spoke Italian to hers, and Heidi spoke German to hers. Sylvia wondered, what if Rosita had been born to speak German to her parents as Heidi did? Or if Maria spoke Yiddish to her parents as she herself did, instead of the Italian that Maria's parents understood? How marvelous that all children had been born to speak the same language that their parents understood! How fortunate they all were! Was she seeing a miracle before her eyes? Sylvia believed this impressive process seemed to call for a supernatural explanation. When she grew older and recognized that people all over the world developed language skills this way, she realized that she had witnessed a simply natural process, with no magic or miracle involved.

The language learning in "Sylvia's story" illustrates the primary functions of imitation and assimilation. Not only can a human child think and speak in interaction with parents and others, but that child also self-corrects in the process. As the child acquires more and more precise command over thought and language, the accuracy of its intended communicative message grows. Quality of expression bears as much importance to the social fabric of a family as quantity of communication. The speaking and listening person becomes aware that some thoughts and words receive approval, and others are met with disdain. We assume that certain things we say must be true because listeners seem to understand and approve them. Other ideas that we suppose are false are either not understood or are not approved. In time we learn to use other, more complicated means and tests to distinguish the true from the false. Comprehending the difference between true and false turns out to be far more complicated than any of us could have imagined as children. One of my daughters went through a developmental period in which she grew extremely sensitive to the concepts of true and false. She would frequently stop me in the midst of a fanciful story and ask, "But is that true, or are you just making it up?"

My daughter had prematurely taken her first steps on the journey from uncritical to critical knowledge. At first, we take any item quite literally, as a true fact.

Later, we are shocked to learn that not everything can be taken as true without qualification. But an even greater shock awaits us when we learn that nothing at all can be relied upon as true without qualification. It is often dismaying to find that our knowledge is all subject to question, and that some of what we have taken for granted and held familiarly and confidently is really not to be taken literally. When we feel connected and satisfied with some one or some thing, it is a dark moment indeed when we realize that we have invested our emotion in an illusion. This bitter realization must be accepted. Presuming knowledge to be true against all evidence to the contrary incurs the risk of great loss.

Our knowledge is more a work of art than a chart or graph, which simply gives neutral facts untinted by pleasure and pain. The technical name of this personalized understanding is "cognitive relativism," which means that any knowledge is related to and dependent on the person who knows it. It also means that no knowledge is beyond question. However, this does not imply that any knowledge that I want to be true is true either because I believe that it is true or because I want it to be true. I cannot make something true just by deciding that it is true for myself. Cognitive relativism does not mean that the world outside my skin is not the same world that is outside your skin. What it does mean is that what I may know about our shared world is not identical to what you may know about it. My knowledge of it may be more nearly true than yours. The parent-child relationship usually typifies this instance. My knowledge of the thunderstorm with all its fright and fury may well be different from and more true than my young daughter's knowledge of the storm. One of us may be more frightened than the other, due to what we each know about lightning and thunder. I may fear the lightning more, while she may be more terrified of the thunder.

Cognitive relativism means that knowledge is contextual to the circumstances under which it has arisen. Knowledge is always known by some knowing mind and has some human source.

Some religious devotees want to communicate their spiritual experience, which they attribute to a divine visitation, but they cannot find words with which to express themselves, because the effect on the faithful has been so shattering. However, this divine visitation becomes the springboard from which the person divinely visited, or a surrogate, offers detailed information about God, nature, and humanity. All of these truths merit acceptance because of the special authority ordained by the experience of divine visitation. If what appears to be an experience of dizziness or trance or ecstasy is instead taken for spiritual possession, then some people would find this sort of authority credible. Those who take such things for granted might believe the truth of the information conveyed following such an experience, but others might be less impressed.

Much of what the ancient world took as religious revelation arose from such personal experiences. Many sacred scriptures record such events and their aftermath. Religious believers often give these accounts the status of absolute truth. Adherents assign such qualities as "inerrant," "infallible," and "inspired" to their own scriptures, but not to that of any other group. This revelatory literature comes mostly from the ancient world, but in the nineteenth century, the Mormons and the Christian Scientists have adopted their own version of the authoritative "sacred book" as the basis of faith and practice.

This discussion of the relativism of knowledge of God does not attack the claim that God exists, but it does challenge the claims of any one and only "true," fixed, and final *concept* of God and all that is involved in belief in God. The sincerity or integrity of various believers in God is not at issue, but the question arises whether anyone can claim final knowledge of God simply on the basis of that person's sincerity and strength of conviction. Some claims are made that a person's beliefs could only have come by supernatural means. For instance, the Apostle Paul seems certain that "his gospel" was God's truth based on the revelation that he believed he had of "The Risen Christ." In a vision, an epiphany, an appearance of the post-resurrection Jesus, Paul believed that Jesus had communicated the details of "his gospel" to him. Paul resorted to this certification when he had disputed with his fellow apostles or other Christian advocates. It must have been a miracle, as Paul and his followers saw it.

But, suppose that someone else makes the same claims to divine revelation as Paul makes, and this same individual shows evidence of a spectacular transformation in his life? Does this mean that his visions and beliefs are to be given the same weight as those of Paul? Or, are they both to be accounted for by natural social and psychological processes? We know very little of Paul the man, and most of what we know comes from the personal records that bear his name. Only the record of the writer of the Acts of the Apostles in the New Testament gives any secondhand view of Paul, and this record seems to have been written with the same focus as the writing of Paul.

When in our own time we encounter amazing conversions—such as that of Malcolm Little, who became Malcolm X—we learn only part of what went on in the converted person's life. Different versions of Malcolm's story exist: in some he is a hero and to others a villain. But we can hardly question that he experienced a profound religious conversion. Much of our understanding of the man rests on how we see him in the context of his early life, in his growth away from the civil rights principles of his youth, in his final emergence as a person motivated by strong, but very different, principles while in prison. Also his life presents some continuity there, as well as vast differences. At the very end of his life, however, Malcolm's life takes an even more ambiguous direction. Even though we lived in the same world as he did, and he, his friends, and his enemies have related their versions of his story, who can believe that we have the final and fixed truth about the man? How much less can we have the final story of that striking man Paul, godfather to the infant church?

As I noted in a previous chapter, two highly relevant passages from the New Testament, one from Paul and one from Jesus, throw some light on the relativism of knowledge, including religious knowledge. In the "Hymn to Love" in the thirteenth chapter of First Corinthians, the Apostle Paul refers to the difference between his childhood understanding and his adult understanding, and also to his partial knowledge "now" and his expectation of full knowledge in some future "then." Paul clearly sees how the limited context of his childhood experiences contrasts with his experiential knowledge of his world as an adult. He does not claim that his childish knowledge was false, but that it was surely very different from his adult knowledge. The old way of seeing things made sense to the child, but would hardly be adequate for a person of mature years and full adult responsibilities. The references to the "now," in which his knowledge was first partial, and "then," in which it will subsequently be full and complete, show a development in comprehension about the context of knowledge from the present to a future time. The Apostle no doubt looks forward to a future when he expects a grand and glorious climax to human history, when "Every knee will bow and every tongue confess that Jesus is Lord," or perhaps when he will die and be resurrected. Whatever Paul's expectation and whatever its fulfillment, it is clear that he does not claim full understanding in the "now" time.

The difference between Paul's statements of recognition of the relativism of his knowledge, and his claims of certainty about the finer details of God's plans and dealings with the church and humanity makes us wonder. Pauline scholars regard him as more of an enthusiast than a profound thinker. In his book *The Genius of Paul*, Samuel Sandmel writes:

> We need to recognize, as is now uniformly the scholarly conclusion, that Paul was not primarily a systematic thinker, not a definer of terms, and

not a classifier of views, opinions and expressions of either contemporaries or predecessors.

Whenever one reads a systematic study of Paul's doctrine, the system is that of the interpreter; it is never Paul's own. Paul had no metaphysical system.

Paul's writings appear scattered in substance because they were like tracts dashed off in the midst of travels, or answers to specific but missing messages sent to him from his churches and friends. Intermediaries sometimes delivered these messages by word of mouth, and they were often so urgent that Paul dared not wait for clarifications. Some told of disputes among believers, and some reported challenges to his authority, to which he replied sternly. At one point, he was moved to imprecation: "But even if we, or an angel from heaven should preach to you a gospel contrary to that which we preached to you, let him be accursed" (Gal. 1:6). Paul's memory of his childish thoughts and his recognition of his partial understanding, as related in his "Hymn to Love," apparently did not temper his apostolic dogmatism. His disputatious writings over points of doctrine sometimes lose their credibility at the distance from which we see them. Paul uses a forensic style, as though he is presenting a case in court and weighing every point in favor of his current client, mindless of the fact that in the next case he will plead the same point in favor of a different and perhaps conflicting conclusion. Subsequent theologians have used his scattered arguments in a way that only compounds the problem of clearly understanding "his gospel." If Paul had availed himself of the humility and tentativeness that he had expressed so clearly in his "Hymn to Love," how different might the results of his gospel have been for future believers!

Just how serious is the discrepancy between Paul's "gospel" and his recognition of the supremacy of love and tentativeness of knowledge? Paul bases his "gospel" upon a scheme of absolute dependence upon another, a God-man, as a substitute sin offering for himself, Paul. He believes that this satisfies God's demand for Paul's righteousness and nullifies any punishment that Paul has incurred through sin against God. Paul maintains that his submission to the terms of this "gospel" further supersedes all earthly commitments, even those duties of moral and social concern to which his Jewish heritage binds him. Strangely, it removes him from any significant interest in the life example and teachings of Jesus. Paul's view reduces the whole spiritual element of life to a verbal formula, as if the fulfillment of human spiritual capacity were as simple as the satisfaction of an invoice for goods or a legal contract. Paul further holds that his belief in his "gospel" not only applies to him and his immortal destiny, but also to that of all of humanity, past, present, and future. He claims that the visionary revelation that he has received from "Jesus Christ" independently of any human agency including his own, renders null and void any beliefs that depart from his own "gospel." For better or worse, Paul's claim is that his "gospel," based on his experiences of the "Risen Christ," gives the unchanging truth. This definition has shaped and propelled the growth of Christendom.

We have to wonder if the writer of the Epistle to the Galatians, who called down curses on anyone who deviated from his "gospel," is also the writer of the "Love Hymn." Professor Wayne A. Meeks, one recognized expert, says in a footnote:

> Chapter thirteen is a self-contained unit, composed in the style of an encomium on a virtue so familiar in Greek literature (the praises of Eros in Plato's Symposium are the most famous)....the depreciation of gnosis (knowledge) is quite consonant with Paul's earlier admonitions....It is quite possible, therefore, that Paul himself inserted the previously composed rhetorical unit here.

Professor Meeks refers to other instances in which Paul argues that love is superior to knowledge, where Paul states that "If I understand all mysteries and all knowledge...and have not love, I am nothing." It is not clear whether Paul refers here to the "mysteries" prevalent in the popular religions of his time or to some leftover questions from Jewish lore. When he does refer specifically to knowledge, as quoted earlier, he does not deny it, but rather qualifies it. Paul expects to "understand fully, as he is fully understood" as part of the glorious future—most fervently to be desired—that he believes will be his reward.

In contrast to his recognition of the tentative quality of his knowledge, Paul underlines his dogmatism with curses upon any who deviate from his version of the gospel. His followers in preaching Christ believe Paul's imprecation upon dissidents refers to the whole scope of Christian doctrine, so Paul's writings become the criterion for revelation from God. However, when questions arose, parties discussing his writings would quote the Apostle Paul to support both sides of the issue, and each side would anathematize the other in Paul's style. A bloody trail through Christendom marks the ecclesiastical disputes in which one group of Christians killed members of another group in observance of the triumph of true knowledge. These Christians were carrying out the spirit of Paul's doctrinal imperialism and the letter of his curses.

Triumphalism rises like a whirlwind from Paul and his fellow champions of absolute revealed knowledge. The contradictions between one version of absolute knowledge and another version of absolute knowledge have scandalized earnest believers down through the centuries. The dogmatism and self-serving authoritarianism that so marked the writings of the Apostle Paul helped poison the search for knowledge in Christendom. For many Christians, Paul's overflowing spirit of love toward God and humanity, which he verbally magnifies, usually overshadows and justifies this venomous attitude. No doubt people of Paul's triumphant spirit love their followers and God. Even such difficult Christians as Jim Jones and David Koresh loved their uncritical followers, as long as they were submissive. However, we note that this kind of love shows little respect for those who are loved, especially when a loved one asks an unwelcome question.

Paul and Jesus each faced challenges with a totally different spirit. Humility, caution, and compassion characterized Jesus' attitude toward his followers. When confronted by the Jewish authorities who were about to stone a woman whom they accused of adultery, Jesus did not comment on the lawfulness of their action. He did not overrule the ancient injunction against adultery. But he did humiliate the accusers when he said, "Let him who is without sin among you be the first to throw a stone at her." His words so shamed the zealots that they left the woman unscathed. Jesus found a creative way to elicit a serious, respectful response from a hostile crowd. In doing so, he showed respect for the accused woman and also secured a respectful response from her. The accusers had expected to provoke Jesus; instead, he prevailed and gave all parties some opportunity to emerge from the confrontation with a better sense of the complexities of human life and the dignity of each person in a respected community.

Jesus felt momentary indignation at hypocrisy and exploitation, but his respect for the "poor in spirit" and those who had been excluded from polite society shines through in the murkiest situations. Triumphalism cannot compare with the humility, caution, and compassion that characterized Jesus.

Jesus' "Sermon on the Mount" helps us focus on the incompleteness of knowledge. In one extended passage in the fifth chapter of Matthew's Gospel, Jesus says to his hearers:

> You have heard that it was said to the men of old, you shall not kill; and whoever kills will be liable to judgment. But I say unto you that everyone who is angry with his brother shall be liable to judgment. (Mt. 5:21–22)

He repeats this pattern, "You have heard that it was said...but I say unto you...," in each case quoting an item from the ancient laws of Moses. But he gives a new meaning to the Mosaic code, uniformly distinguishing between a rule to be obeyed and an attitude and motive to be cultivated for enriching the relationships of people in commonplace experience. He does not attack the ancient law but does restate its meaning and purpose. Moral value is elevated from the level of obedience to a specific command to the level of inward intent for reconciliation, specifically, the reconciliation of those broken relationships between people that mar their lives. The triumphalist will claim that the ancient lawgivers gave a fixed and final statement of God's will for moral behavior. Jesus advanced the meaning of moral behavior by imparting a more comprehensive basis for conducting a morally responsible life. Would an even more comprehensive statement appear at some time in the future? Another day in another time and world will make such a question relevant, and I insist that we have witnessed such developments.

There is a marked contrast in the ways that Jesus and Paul made allowance for growth in knowledge. Jesus restated the old laws in more humane ways, engaging in overt disagreements with authorities who sought to trap him. At best, Paul made only scant mention of the issue in a vague poetic setting. Both Jesus and Paul dealt with issues of knowledge that would have the most profound importance for future generations. We now know that our most basic and intimate problems and desires are shaped and resolved in the framework of Jesus' and Paul's teachings. Interpretations of those teachings have largely defined moral issues in Western civilization. All too often, however, these teachings have been transformed into doctrines that are represented as fixed and final knowledge of God's will. Too many times, the leaders of Christendom have abandoned the pole stars of humility, caution, and compassion for arrogant and punitive purposes of exploitation.

Augustine of Hippo: "Believing" and Knowing

The Crown Prince of Christendom, Augustine, Bishop of Hippo (354–430 C.E.), synthesized the major doctrines of the early church. The outlines of Augustine's life are familiar by now. Born in a rural area of the Roman province of North Africa to a minor Roman official and a native Christian mother, Augustine received the best education his father could provide. As a scholar, Augustine moved to Rome and then to Milan, in pursuit of the profession of rhetorician, one who produced elegant oratory and taught the skill of persuasion by effusive speech. The role of rhetorician roughly equals the function of a modern lawyer who would coach his clients to present and win their cases, whether in serious matters or simply in the give-and-take of polite society. The young Augustine might have been an ancient counterpart of the highly successful Dale Carnegie, who inspired thousands of Americans with his book *How to Win Friends and Influence People.* Eventually, Augustine went to study with Ambrose, the Bishop of Milan, who was unrivaled as a rhetorician. With Ambrose as his mentor, Augustine became a Christian after undergoing a profound psychological experience.

The life of the venerated bishop of Hippo spanned the last days of pagan Rome and the beginning of Christian Rome. The time and the man were made for each other. Augustine needed a giant stage upon which to play his heroic role, and the era needed a giant mind to write its story and to lay the foundations of a future civilization. The stature that Western civilization accords Augustine reflects the magnificence of his life and work. He is regarded as an exemplary writer of high classical Latin and is appreciated by scholars of both secular and religious literature. Within his own Christian tradition, he must be considered second only to the Apostle Paul as a definitive voice in the shaping of the church. When Martin Luther sought to return the church to its original basis, he followed the pattern set out by Augustine, whose name Luther's ecclesiastical order carried.

In his early twenties, Augustine became a follower of Manichaeism, a blending of Gnostic and Zoroastrian elements. Mani (216-276 C.E.), a Jewish-Christian of Persian birth and one of many later self-proclaimed apostles, syncretized elements of ancient Zoroastrianism and Christianity with elements of the cosmological mythologies of the Near East. Manichaeism was modified as it spread from India to Rome, and it eventually rivaled Pauline Christianity in the third century. Some of its more extreme doctrines and practices were considered bizarre even for the time in which it flourished. For instance, they proclaimed a "new gospel" in which it was revealed that all physical things, including human bodies, are the evil prisons of pure particles of light. The clouds of triumph of apostolic Christianity obscured scholarly understanding of this religion, but the church absorbed many Manichaean ideas. Manichaeism survived until the Middle Ages as a competitor with the church under official ecclesiastical condemnation.

Many pagans and Christians of Augustine's time identified themselves with this sect, which vied in a struggle for the soul of Christianity. Because orthodox Christians wrote the history of the times, the Manichaeans have been relegated to the dust of defeat in official accounts. It serves the present ecclesiastical purpose to exaggerate the early church's distance from this and other heresies. Thus, many scholars have systematically minimized the relationship of Augustine to the Manichaeans. Scholars who thought Augustine worth serious study devoted themselves to increasing his distance from the Manichaeans. Those researchers who might have been more open to Augustine's involvement with the Manichaeans have not seen the value in doing the necessary work. However, a new wave of women scholars, such as Uta Ranke-Heinemann in her book, *Eunuchs for the Kingdom of Heaven,* has shown interest in exploring the relationship between Augustine and the Manichaeans.

All of Augustine's biographers see the dividing point in his life as his conversion, which took place in his thirtieth year. Augustine himself also saw and described his life this way. However, little about Augustine's life changed with his conversion. Although conversions traditionally appear to the convert to herald a movement from dark to light, from death to life, William James came closer to the truth. As a critical psychologist and philosopher, James claims that conversion indicates an integration of elements that were already present but in conflict. James describes conversion as the coming to integration of "the divided self" through an explosive emotional climax in which a feeling of transcendence replaces the frustrations of the past. This involves the integration of conflicting elements of inner consciousness into an orderly arrangement under the control of a new, dominant vision, so that differing elements are redefined by that new and overarching element. One result may be some resolution of old internal psychological conflicts. But the same elements are still there, and the degree of successful integration depends on long and arduous work, if it happens at all. James points out that he does not regard Augustine's conversion as an adoption of the version of Christian confession commonly held at that time, but rather as a philosophical insight into the Neoplatonic version of spiritualized reality. Augustine's embrace of a more complete Christianity such as the apostles had taught, and his mother had exemplified, would come only some years later.

In Augustine's early life, his mother Monica served as the ever-present, visible example of the pagan/Christian religious stew that permeated the late Roman empire, especially in what we now call North Africa. At the time of Augustine's birth in 364, the victory of Constantine over Roman Italy in 312 and his first patronage of Christianity still lay within living memory. At the time of Constantine's conversion, no simple majority culture existed under the rule of the Church, as Augustine would later envision its future. Roman religion was dying, but dying hard.

Patricus, Augustine's father, was a solid Roman citizen, pagan to the core. Along with a naive version of Christianity, Monica embraced much of the superstitions that are familiar to naive people of all backwater origins. Monica could scarcely have reflected anything like a mature version of the future Christian faith, due to the unsettled state of the Christian churches in her childhood, and what Augustine describes as the backwardness of her home life. Even in older Christian centers, theological and practical issues were far from being resolved. What Augustine learned from his mother was not Christianity but some Christian vocabulary, along with simple and unquestioning piety toward fate and the supernatural. It is no more a wonder that Augustine should some day "come home" to the faith that kindled the fires in his mother's bosom than that he should learn to speak in her native tongue. The wonder is that the journey took him so long a time, and that he traveled so short a distance.

Augustine's two major written works are his *Confessions*, and his *City of God*. Classical in language and themes, these writings helped shape the culture of Europe as much as the later King James Bible and the plays of Shakespeare. John O'Meara entitles his book on *The City of God*, *The Charter of Christendom*. *The City of God* served as the basic text of the orthodox (catholic) religion of Christianity. The concepts in this text dominated Roman Catholic thinking until the Middle Ages, when Thomas Aquinas sought to synthesize Augustine's mysticism with Aristotelian logic. In the sixteenth century, when Luther and Calvin sought to reform the medieval church, they returned to Augustine as their ideal. Martin Luther started his church career as an Augustinian monk and never departed from that Augustinian model in his concepts of faith and destiny.

When Augustine defines God as a supreme sovereign, and the members of the Church as his governors and agents on earth, we all become part of this struggle between the City of God and the City of Man. Augustine defines the ultimate nature of humanity as a dualism of spiritual soul and fleshly body. He further categorizes the soul as the worthy part and the flesh as the unworthy part. This leaves us with a complex and unwieldy version of sexuality and its pains and pleasures, and with the disproportion of minor transgressions and eternal punishments. Our civilization becomes weighted down with the belief in and practice of domination of the godly over the ungodly, and the division of humanity forever between the dominant, totally favored by God, and the nondominant, totally disfavored by God. The complexities of Augustine's system of beliefs are too many and too abstract to allow more than a mere mention here. However, Augustine and his followers maintain with iron-bound determination that every belief is known with equal certainty as all others. Thus, a practical issue such as mandatory male priesthood lies beyond discussion, as does the dogma of the Holy Trinity. These and some other derivative ideas and beliefs represent the core problem of our world, both for believers in the system and those who live in the world with those believers. For instance, I heard a discussion of why creationism should be taught in public schools. If there were no creation, then there would be no fall from innocence in the Garden of Eden, and hence no human sin to require the death of a savior. So, the creation or evolution issue also encompasses the meaning of human mistakes or sins, and the remission of those sins by God. The followers of Augustine are as certain of one part of the system as of all the rest due to their reliance upon the self-validating traditional authorities.

Augustine claimed that a person could only know the Truth—a true conception of nature, man, and God—through submission to the will of God. In his *Commentary on the Gospel of John,* Augustine quotes Jesus at John 7:17: "If any man's will is to do his will, he shall know whether the teaching is from God or whether I am speaking on my own authority."

Augustine then gives his interpretation:

> Therefore do not seek to understand in order to believe, but believe that thou mayest understand....Therefore I would counsel the obedience of believing toward the possibility of understanding.

The pivotal part of Augustine's explanation of the source of Christian knowledge is the connection he makes between "believing" and "obedience" on one hand, and then the connection between "believing" and "understanding" on the other. He effectively empties "believing" of its meaning of "confirming a claim" and instead invests it with the action of "willing submission." This substitution replaces an intellectual comprehension with a will to comply. For example, a teacher might grade a student not on the student's performance on a test, but on the student's willingness to take the teacher's opinions uncritically. In the second connection, Augustine implies that the result of this "willing submission" is the intellectual grasp of a truth. In this case, the analogy can be made with the teacher who, in giving a student a passing grade, simply disregards the student's failure to learn anything from the course and rewards him for accepting without question all that the teacher has said.

On inspection, the inner logic of Augustine's claim of a basis for understanding is glaringly problematic. He insists that my understanding, that is, coming to know how to give an account of what is being claimed, depends on my prior agreement with it. This would seem to require that I simply agree to accept whatever is claimed before I have even heard it. Augustine would have us say to him, in effect: "Don't bother to explain what you have to say, because I already accept it since you say it. My mind has no evaluative function in hearing a claim made and then giving assent to it. On such a basis, when I trust my money to a bank, I would never thereafter review a statement that tells me how much money I have on balance, and I would never wonder if I were getting a fair accounting."

In all these instances, I should have no concern about the credibility of what I am being told, because I trust whoever told me the information. The same person who tells me to trust him is the one who tells me that whatever he says is so. This circular reasoning typifies the pious attitude, ancient and modern. It fits quite well into the self-anointing tradition of pietistic religion. The scriptures declare that they, the scriptures, are inspired; the apostles are authoritative because the scriptures say that they are; and the apostles in turn reaffirm the inspiration of the scriptures that anoint them.

Some scholars have defended this version of knowledge as "intuitive." The model here is the mathematical or logical statement that is known to be true on mere inspection, such as the sum is greater than any of its parts, or, anything that happens is possible. Expanded, this model includes such insights that seem to be totally given without mediating reasoning: I knew that I must believe her instead of him. Intuition is further romanticized as "love at first sight." There is no arguing with such beliefs, because no arguable claim is made. But neither must its truth be taken for granted just because there is an overwhelming feeling of certainty.

The pious believer is in step with Christendom when he rests in the intuition of God and all that pertains to religious feeling. Nothing else, not reason or intellectual rigor, is needed or would be of any benefit over and above the feeling of satisfaction that is his by faith. But, when that pious believer advocates a truth that he expects other people to honor, he is like the star-struck lover who trusts that everyone else will see his beloved's beauty as he does. At the opening of the *Confessions,* Augustine speaks—and speaks well—of his heart's longing for God: "You have made us for yourself, and our heart is restless until it rests in you." In this passage Augustine reaches a height of religious intuition that reason cannot affect. However, when he or another pious believer derives from that intuition an implication of universal truth about the world and humanity, then he enters the arena of ideas, where we all have to find our own grounds for decisions. To suppose that we have grounds for truth-claims about nature, man, and God just because we are talking about God, or because we believe something about God and are warmed by the feeling of God's presence, requires that we offer the same credibility to all other believers, no matter what they believe. Augustine and his followers, down through the centuries until today, are ever-ready to rule as "false" any statement about God that disagrees with their own beliefs, even if their adversaries are themselves ardent believers in Augustine's God.

How Augustine Got That Way

I now lack the overwhelming inclination to accept traditional authorities that Augustine had, an inclination that I once shared with him but to a lesser extent. The beginning of my change of direction regarding acceptance of traditional textual authority came when I was fortunate to be a doctoral student in the Department of Philosophy of Boston University in the years 1958-61. In my very first year, I had the seminar in History of Philosophy with one of my secular patron saints, Professor Peter A. Bertocci. The text we used for the beginning portion of that seminar was *The Presocratic Philosophers,* by G. S. Kirk and J. E. Raven. In their early pages, they make an unpretentious comment on their use of Aristotle's treatment of his philosophical predecessors:

> Aristotle gave more serious attention to his philosophic predecessors than Plato had done...however, his judgments are often distorted by his view of earlier philosophy as a stumbling progress towards the truth that Aristotle himself revealed in his physical doctrines, especially those concerning causation. There are also, of course, many acute and valuable criticisms, and of factual information.

The Kirk and Raven book provides a marvelous example of the superior scholar's way of dealing with texts. Although they never call Aristotle a liar and a cheat, they demonstrate that the figure who towers over classical and medieval philosophy had his own agenda in his treatment of his sources. They do not attack Aristotle, but display in successive pages the Greek text from authentic fragments of the Presocratic Philosophers, along with their competent translation, and then the appropriate textual comments of Aristotle and other ancient writers. Aristotle shapes his comments to bolster the impression that those previous thinkers endorsed his position in anticipation. It is clear even to an apprentice student that many scholars of early Greek thought have given us a distorted view of that period as they saw it through the eyes of Aristotle. Accordingly, the scholars who wrote the texts that I had encountered as an undergraduate student of philosophy did not portray the presocratics as the robust, imaginative giants that Kirk and Raven gave us. At any rate, after I left Bob Jones College, I came to have a critical approach to all scholarly texts, and I wonder now that I ever had any other attitude toward Augustine or anyone else.

The man Augustine did not invent piety, but in his own life he gave the model for it to Christendom. I suspect that he got his version of piety from his mother, Monica. If Monica ever had any question about her right and duty to mold her son in her own rigid and self-righteous image, Augustine does not reflect it in his extended account of her. He rebelled against her moralistic demands as an adolescent and sought to escape from her influence when a man, but he never stepped back to see her as anything but an absolute fixture of rectitude. He preserved his belief in her moral superiority behind a facade of sentiment. No picture of her as a person of flesh and blood comes through in his writings. He did not see her, but only the halo that she assumed and he accepted as authentic.

Philosophical culture in Augustine's time had begun its downslide from its classical heights. The works of Plato and Aristotle were centuries old and were read more in digest form than in serious criticism. Because everyone assumed that they already knew what the ancient philosophers had to say, few bothered to read their texts as primary sources. The Greek-style philosopher of Augustine's day was Plotinus, a third-century Egyptian who came to Rome and was seen as one who might synthesize the pagan polytheism of the Roman past and the emerging Judeo-Christian monotheism. Plotinus' philosophy is called Neo-Platonism, its association with Plato being overstated. The only philosophical attribute that they share is an undaunting confidence that a coherent conceptual account can be given for the One and the Many, and that this account will have as its basis the concept of the highest reality as the abstract nature of the invisible and unitary Whole, or God.

Dualism of the One, conceived of as a spiritual unity, and the Many, conceived of as the material world, the multitude of physical things, preoccupied the Hellenic mind. Plato accepted this dualism, which he explained as a dualism of the "realm of the perfect ideas" and the "realm of things," a shadow land that makes no sense except by reference to the perfect ideas. With Plato, to be real meant to be self-explanatory. Therefore, because the world of things cannot be understood except by reference to the immaterial concepts in the non-physical soul, then material things must lack full reality. The Real One is in a conceptual dualism with the Illusory Many.

The moral and political experiences of life showed Plato that this scheme has a fatal flaw: it presumes that the abstract realm of ideas really serves the needs of the material world, the world of men and cities and dialogues. The Real exists for the benefit of the lesser reality. The resolution of this dilemma is the understanding that it really is the knowledge of the real that serves the lesser reality, and it is this lesser reality that men, the thinkers, inhabit. No matter what the theoretical priority of the realm of ideas, Plato does not assert that there is something in the universe of higher moral value than the society of thinking souls. This keeps him from taking the step that Plotinus took, and that Augustine would later follow; that is, the movement from a conceptual higher realm to explain the lower realm, to the assertion that the lower realm itself is of no lasting value. Plotinus and Augustine also accept this as grounds for the movement from the imperfection of the lower realm, to the assumption that the lower realm must be destined to serve the glorification of the higher. For Plato, the fact that the soul can conceive of the ideas does not mean that those ideas are our masters, but rather that our minds have the capacity to merit immortality.

Plotinus and Augustine believed that the One is the source of knowledge, and that it is the One that determines what is known and that only the One deserves to be served. Plotinus said that the One is the unchanging, uncreated, immaterial absolute, and that there is nothing that does not emanate from the One. Because material things are dependent on the One for their being, and their being known, those material things must be less than fully real. Only the One, that which is fully rational, meaning that which can be conceived without reference or dependence on anything outside itself, is fully real. And if only that which is fully real can be perfect, then this is the truth about the universe: all material things exist only provisionally, and not independently. Men, cities, and all their furnishings are only fragments that are meaningless in themselves and must be understood as of lesser value than the perfection of the One.

This Neo-Platonic conception had the religious value of expressing mystery in available imagery. It also deflected the religious need for the involvement of a living God in commonplace life. For our purposes, we can say that the Neo-Platonist, with his concept of God as the Perfect Unity, gains abstract coherence at the expense of empirical coherence. The rational unity of the immaterial One is gained as the reality of the commonplace world is denied.

Augustine's ultimate intellectual goal is strongly presented in the seventh book of the *Confessions*. This goal is the vision of Perfect Being, which he found in Plotinus. From the time of his indoctrination into the Neo-Platonic philosophy onward, he had ultimate confidence in his ability to defend the most esoteric doctrines with this mighty tool. The difficulty that has dogged his followers in orthodox Christendom is the gulf between the concept of Perfect Being and the God of Jesus, the same Jesus who walked the earth as a son of man. The abstract coherence that Plotinus gained is an explanation for the dilemma of the Perfect Being and an imperfect world, which accepts the denial of the reality of the commonplace world. The Neo-Platonic mind can thus spin the web to connect all the conceptual points of immaterial Being. But Augustine and his followers have answered the call of the Teacher who gave them a message for the people of the world, that a Father in Heaven loves them. This message dealt with suffering and loss, reconciliation, and redemption. In present philosophical language, we would admonish Augustine to seek after empirical coherence, that is, to seek a way of seeing things together that takes the world seriously and deals with its inconsistencies without giving up on the more troublesome aspects of a person's life, such as having a body with feelings and passions and a conscience for moral values.

Augustine As a Sophist

I will attempt to deal with the issue of emotion and reason as it occurs in Augustine's system. In so doing, I will not depend on the differences between the fourth and the twentieth century, as though the problem is that Augustine was just not lucky enough to live in our century and know as much as we do. The work of Descartes, Locke, Kant, and others has given us some advantage, but I prefer to deal with Augustine on his own terms, as best I can do so. Augustine did not follow the great Athenian Plato, as he perhaps thought he did, because Augustine had little access to Plato's work. Not only did Augustine not follow Plato, but he also departed from the Socratic/Platonic model and method in the same ways as other opponents of Plato did. The bishop shows himself to be closer to Plato's opponents, the Sophists. This shortcoming in Augustine's thinking makes him an unreliable guide in religious thought. The Sophists did not produce any lasting contribution to critical knowledge. Their best effort lay in their articulation of the centrality of humanity in any scheme of reality. In their favor, the Sophists and Socrates/Plato agreed on that one generalization, the primacy of humanity, but the Sophists made this reference to the human individual, and Socrates/Plato always insisted on the primacy of the human public, the human community.

The best-known Sophist was Protagoras (485–410 B.C.E.), who is commonly credited with the formula for classical humanism, Man is the measure of all things: of those that are that they are; of those that are not, that they are not. This belief so closely reiterated what Socrates believed that Socrates himself was sometimes mistaken for a Sophist. Indeed, one of the charges for which Socrates was condemned to death was that he had corrupted the youth of Athens—an aspersion often cast upon the Sophists by their uncritical detractors. Socrates chose not to distance himself from that idea in his defense against the charges. The subtle difference eluded the jury of common folk Athenians. Socrates saw "man" as the measure in the collective sense, whereas Protagoras saw "man" in the individual sense. Socrates believed that truth arises out of the interaction of candid and earnest seekers who talk and listen in their search for truth. They can find concepts that they can all understand, and by which they can reach a common agreement as to the better way of thinking about a life worth living, which Socrates called the "examined life." Protagoras, on the other hand, seems to have believed that each individual "man" is so contained in his own mind that no serious exchange of concepts is possible: only a final skepticism of all concepts remains because no one has access to the concepts in the mind of any another.

How much had the post-conversion Augustine changed his way of handling arguments? His thinking had shifted away from the ideas propounded by the intellectual skeptics of his time to the Christian tradition as embodied in the Bible and the teachings of the Church Fathers. But how much did Augustine move away from the sophistic style of exaggeration and shift his intellectual context—which he freely admits to as a Manichaean—to a more conscious examination of the inconsistencies involved in his own ecclesiastical positions? His new bases of evidence were miracles and prophecy, which were the currency of the oriental religions that had flooded the Hellenistic world. Although we do not fault him for accepting this mysticism, we must expect him to become more responsible when he later uses inconsistent, contradictory arguments as he formulates claims against his opponents.

This lapse in responsibility for examining his own assumptions shows up most glaringly in Augustine's reliance on tradition and authority, and in his confusion of submitting and learning. This is the same conflict as noted earlier over will, or emotion, and reason, or dialectical thinking. This dispute, alive in Plato's time, still had currency between the Stoic philosophers and Sophists of Augustine's time.

Augustine's teaching here attempts to make the believer think that his understanding of the Church's doctrine depends upon his submission to the commands that he receives from the Church. If the believer fails to understand, his "willing" is defective, and he does not need to study further, but to repent and make contrition. Any lack of understanding is the believer's fault, not the irrationality of the doctrine or the method of the Church. As a consequence, the Church has practical control over the believer and the Church's teaching gives up intellectual credence.

The authority can impose whatever conditions of compliance it chooses, and the believer has no alternative but to comply, because he does not know, and cannot expect to know, what the authority knows. There are no proper questions to ask, because the problem is not intellectual but volitional. It is the motives, the intentions, of the believer that must change. No matter what the believer thinks, his motives must be defective if he still does not understand.

The believer's only recourse is either to forego questions or to get out of the system altogether. Ecclesiastical dogma is not open to questions; only intentions can be open to question. Many do get out of the system, but many, of course, do not. Most who do not leave the Church simply do not think through the assumptions given them and then ask if alternative assumptions can be made.

The Legacy of Triumphalism

Rigid, narrow conformity had already characterized ecclesiastical thought by the time that Augustine came onto the scene. When the Roman Emperor Constantine first legally recognized the Church, he expected that this new and vigorous sect would provide a unifying influence for his sagging imperial authority. If he could promote a single religion as the centerpiece of the diverse ethnic and language groups, then he might be spared some of the inter-empire bickering and fighting that weakened his position against the threatening outsiders to the north. But a troublesome controversy roiled among the Christians about the status of Jesus relative to God the Father. The doctrine of the Trinity as a resolution eventually emerged at a general meeting of the heads of the church in Nicea in 325 C.E. Constantine told those assembled to settle the matter and write a formula that might be the basis for Christian belief all over the Empire. They produced the Nicean Creed. In its final form, this creed supports the idea that Jesus is not subordinate to the Father, but is "of one substance with the Father." The creed also curses anyone who uses language that suggests that Jesus was created or was alterable or changeable. Instead of settling the matter, the creed inflamed the controversy. Some churches stubbornly continued to use liturgical language positing that "the Son has a beginning, but God is without beginning."

The struggle sought to find possible ways of stating the impossible: the fairly obvious contradiction between the doctrines of the divinity of Jesus and the humanity of Jesus, especially when "full divinity" juxtaposed against "full humanity." The ideal of "making everything about God an absolute" required full divinity for Jesus so that he could merit worship as divine; Jesus also needed full humanity, so that he could be the perfect sacrifice for the sins of mankind. The impossibility of joining two absolutes into one hyper-absolute never seems to have occurred to the pious theologians, ancient or modern.

The historical evidence of what went on in these disputes remains obscure. The authorized versions of the proceedings have been sanitized to suppress the egos and ambitions of the ecclesiastical disputants. Whatever the historical evidence on these matters, the net results for the Church and for Western civilization seems apparent: the doctrines of Christendom were going to be fought over in the same ways as political, economic, and social policies are. Raw power would determine outcomes that are masked as divinely ordained statements and communicated in formulae that are imposed upon all. The combination of ecclesiastical and secular authority, working together to enforce obedience to both princes and priests, would secure the submission of the faithful.

Triumphalism, the claim that one religion alone has a legitimate right to approve or to veto all matters of moral belief and behavior, became translated into the claim that one institution, the visible Church, must set the criteria for judging civil law and culture. In this light, the specific contents of the creeds have less importance in the larger sweep of issues than the fact that imperial needs allowed a single statement of belief to become the norm for Christian faith and practice. This was a slippery slope indeed. To assume that only one formula could define Christian beliefs set believer against believer, turning the "loving community" into a boisterous, wrangling mob. To assume that secular rulers had power to settle disputes that arose from these wrangles, using punitive measures that ranged from deprivation of civil rights to torture and death, both scandalized and terrorized Christians down to our time.

Hosius, Bishop of Cordova (296-357) raised his voice against the mingling of secular and ecclesiastical power. The bishop wrote to the Emperor Constantius, successor to Constantine:

> Do not interfere in matters ecclesiastical, nor give us orders on such questions, but learn about them from us. For into your hands God has put the kingdom; the affairs of his Church he has committed to us.... "render unto Caesar's the things that are Caesar's and unto God the things that are God's." We are not permitted to exercise an earthly rule; and you, Sire, are not authorized to burn incense.

The seekers of high office in the Church drowned out the sanity of Hosius's plea. Elias J. Bickerman, Professor of History at Columbia University, says, "Bishops accordingly lived in great style, and episcopal elections were often violently contested: one in Rome left 137 dead in a day's fighting."

Reducing religious teaching to a formula for rote learning had devastating effects on the diversity of the multiple communities of believers. The usually creative process that translates feelings into words leaves out the richness and uniqueness of the felt experience of God. To try to cramp such feeling into an inflexible set of words is to rob individual expression of the validity of its feelings. Not only does the individual lose the infinite shades of meaning that might be remembered as he or she reflects on the experience of God, but the community surrounding that individual will lose the prophetic insights the individual might have been able to express had the words been freely expressed. The old covenant language that played so prominent a role in the Hebrew identity became assimilated in the Christian ecclesiastical terminology. The church was the "New Israel," God's newly chosen people. Paul seems to have taught, at some points, that God had foreordained that the people of the old Israel would fulfill the ancient covenant promise by becoming Christians. He and others considered themselves as Christians to be God's chosen people. So, God decrees the separation of humanity into two groups, the saved and the unsaved in primary terms, and then the saved further separated themselves into the carnal-worldly, and the spiritual-holy. The "us-them" kind of tribalism that anthropologists tell us characterizes most societies is sanitized and legitimized. In Christendom, we are told that God ordains the demarcation of "us" as good people and "them" as bad people, with "us" being the Christians and "them" being anyone else, sometimes people of another skin color or language or culture. This is another slippery-slope argument that once crested in the early Church but has plunged headlong into the fragmentation of humanity into desirable and undesirable pieces. The reconciling of person to person and the universal family as the Kingdom of Heaven, about which Jesus spoke, are left for another mission, outside the realm of the ecclesiastical concerns.

The early Church ventured onto the idea that God requires blood sacrifice for the remission of sins. This idea goes back into the dark reaches of Hebrew history; at its worst it surfaces in the story of Abraham preparing to kill his son Isaac as a sacrificial offering. Indeed, the story tells us that God stopped Abraham before he completed the sacrifice, which Abraham believed he was divinely commanded to do. The idea that God would require the shedding of human blood seems not to have been repugnant to Abraham. In the Christian version of blood sacrifice, Jesus is killed on a Roman cross as a sacrifice for the sins of those who will be saved. The doctrine says that it is this mysterious blood of Jesus—not that blood which had flowed in the veins of the living person, but the blood that poured from Jesus' wounds and dripped down the cross to the ground—that makes it possible for God to remit the sins of those who obey God, as Christians. This makes God the sponsor of deadly violence.

As a person who grew up in a non-Catholic environment, I have been shocked when I have seen the image of a miniature dead human body on a small cross hanging on the wall of a room in a Catholic hospital or school. This is the most common and universal symbol of Roman Catholic Christianity, as the empty cross is symbolic of Protestant Christianity. The worst result of our culture retaining the idea of God's sponsoring violent death is not the archaic representation of the crucified Jesus, but the ease with which we give social approval to killing people, whether it be by state-ordered execution or by the random killing of soldiers and civilians in massive warfare. Other cultures expect socially approved killing to occur, and the Christian doctrine by itself does not cause our executions and war killing. But our Christianity seems to do little to restrain our socially approved killing. We pattern our social killing after Old Testament models of conquest and slaughter of enemy families and lynching of off-caste people. Our young men have been taught to kill other people as enemies, in places as various as My Lai and Hiroshima, and then have been welcomed home as heroes, giants in the land.

Those young men are merely abused victims of a society that has so long and so often rewarded people for killing others who were unknown to them. Christendom made us a bloodthirsty culture, and then to think it quite natural to be so. Therein lies the greatest tragedy: we embrace our violent society without a hint of remorse. No matter what Jesus said or meant, the culture has distorted his life and message and rendered them almost meaningless. Christendom will bear this triumphalist millstone throughout history.

5

Religion and Community

SAINT AUGUSTINE BELIEVED that a person's readiness to do God's will enables that person to know God, salvation, and the good life. The concept of knowledge that Augustine developed assumes that final and fixed knowledge is possible through divine revelation. Common sense denies the validity of such a concept; yet it nevertheless is necessary for the triumphalist attitude. Indeed, Augustine might be considered the architect of thoroughgoing triumphalism in Christendom. He broadened the Apostle Paul's spiritual triumphalism to include the vision of a secular order presided over by a monarch who promotes and protects the Church. This idea, later known as the "Divine Right of Kings," became a building block of Christendom.

This doctrine of divine right of kings is not simply a convenient political designation for a monarch, a single ruler in an established jurisdiction. The "divine" or superhuman designation adds a dimension of religious endorsement to the status of that royal individual, which sets that special person above and apart from all other human individuals. Such a designation elevates the mortal institution of monarchy, but it also reflects the arbitrary majesty of the divinity who has decreed that this should be the case. No one imagines that some highly self-assured individual human being made overtures to the deity and won a divine decree that kings should rule by divine right. We are supposed to believe that the doctrine originated because God saw fit to reveal his divine will that it be so. In fact, the idea was latent in ancient Roman emperor worship and waxed and waned with various waves of power and personality. One of the foremost secular theorists, Thomas Hobbes (1588–1679), used the phrase "the mortal god" to refer to a sovereign's effort to make himself an uncontestable and invincible ruler, with power on earth to match the divine power in the other world.

The Sun King of France, Louis the Fourteenth, epitomized the modern absolute monarch. He dazzled kings and commoners with his wealth and style and was canonized by the Roman Church. We see in Louis as monarch of France, and the Pope as monarch of the Church, the exemplars of God as the monarch of the universe. If St. Augustine could have fancied himself as a bishop in Louis's domain, he would have found himself right at home.

However, not much would be more contrary to a human community than a divine-right-monarchy doctrine. On a personal level, it subverts moral responsibility by making obedience to the king, however good or evil, the highest moral obligation. This abrogates the possibility of personal responsibility for intending and carrying out decisions that benefit other people. Individual commitments to other persons are always compromised as long as the king always commands first priority. At the social level, custom decrees that any disobedience to the king equals disobedience to God and will be punished accordingly, with divine wrath. The idea of citizenship with its rights and responsibilities is nullified at the start. No one person in recorded history has ever displayed in his office so many of the attributes of what I have called triumphalism as Louis XIV. When George Washington refused a crown and insisted on being called "Mister President," he took a decisive step toward American democracy, away from Louis's example.

I previously stated that this triumphalism has its most devastating effect on individuals when it infects morality by devaluing the relationships of persons to persons, societies to societies. In theory, the autonomy of individuals is an intrinsic personal value; however, in practical matters, a degree of independence of persons from each other must be recognized. The manner in which this separation is perceived affects the achievement of moral value. While triumphalism emphasizes our divisions, it separates us not only in practical decision-making experience, but it also amplifies the antagonism, hostility, and hardening between those who rule and those who are ruled. Thus, the spiritual nurture of individuals is hindered at the very point at which it should be promoted. Contrary to the divisiveness of triumphalism, Jesus gave priority to the reconciliation of the breaks in relationships and to the restoration of nurturing functions between persons.

Our ancient ancestors used the concept of "soul" to distinguish us and our humanity in its most essential character from other sorts of animals. Whether seen as rational or as spiritual, the soul was thought to be the unique substance of humanity. Today, we are more likely to think of the functions of humans and other animals as their distinctive characteristics. Functions can give us better describable and quantifiable evidence than substances. This type of evidence is a prerequisite for scientific inquiry. So, the functions of language-making and usage, symbolic representation, and creativity are usually cited as distinguishing human activities. But we still have a concept of universal humanity, whether we discuss it as souls or as functions. No doubt we would think more productively about the unity of humanity if we did not give so much attention to the false hostilities that cause us to divide it.

Triumphalists need enemies, aliens, "others" over whom they can believe themselves to be superior. The interlocking communities of our society have become fragmented as a result of triumphalist attitudes, especially religious triumphalism.

Authoritarianism grows out of triumphalist Christianity when it conceives of God as the ultimate arbitrary authority, who needs no justification for whatever he does or does not do. We are supposed to believe that God is above any moral judgments: "Whatever God does is right." Any questioning of God's authority is treason and calls for banishment from Christian society. Rulers of the secular and the ecclesiastical orders have assumed this model of hierarchical governance. Over time, the male, the white, and the wealthy have become surrogates for divine authority. What effect does this worldly situation have on humanity? There is no reason to ask such a question within the assumptions of triumphalism, but it is precisely those assumptions that we must examine and replace.

Authoritarianism breeds both fear and imitation. The fear comes from the awareness that the authority has the capacity to punish those under it. Imitation stems from the recognition that methods of intimidation are usually very effective. One who wants to get along in an authoritarian system will become accustomed to intimidating whoever will stand for it. Those who cannot intimidate others will suffer from increased intimidation from those who can. I was once told that if I wanted to succeed in academic administration, I would need to learn to enjoy seeing my colleagues squirm. I did not agree with that opinion, so I did not rise above the basement floor of academic administration. Some very effective but unintimidating academic elder statesmen helped me learn better ways of moving through the administrative mazes.

Authority by itself does not nurture. Its own loose-cannon ways might win some battles, and sometimes it will level a weak barrier and seem to conquer. But power alone does not know either the limitations of its own strength or how to use that strength. Power alone does not know how to plant and nourish its own replacements, nor does it really care about that. Authority can only follow its own narrow path and flourish as long as others are sufficiently intimidated. Its apparent allies are really its worst enemies, who will become openly rebellious when the intimidation grows hollow. But even with temporary success, the authoritarian may be like a king of thieves, glad to be king of something, even something unworthy.

The authoritarian cannot nurture anyone else. To nurture, an element of trust must exist between the nurturer and the nurtured. The one who nurtures must listen and respond with respect. In an authoritarian situation, one can never expect the person in power to listen with respect. The authoritarian will hear, but only with suspicion, with the intent to misuse what is heard to strengthen his position. The unwary speaker will find the authoritarian listener to be his adversary and a link in the chain of authority that will bind him. So, authority poisons confidence and thwarts nurture. In a situation built on authority, where does one find the respect and trust that can promote understanding and growth?

I attended Bob Jones College, later known as Bob Jones University, an institution built on crude authoritarianism. If I had asked if the college had been built on authority, I would have been told, "Yes, the authority of the Bible and the Apostles' Creed, and the Fundamentalist program." I would have agreed wholeheartedly with that position, because that was the reason I had chosen that college. The institution continues in that direction to this day, without a waver or stutter. In some cases, I think some of the individuals involved were misguided. The staff expended great efforts to instill in us a sense of our own vulnerability to various temptations. We were constantly made aware that we were being watched and heard, and that any deviation from accepted behavior would be punished swiftly and with the utmost humiliation.

I lacked the inclination to commit grosser violations of the rules, such as touching a girl, or skipping chapel, or smoking a cigarette. However, I made the mistake of expressing an opinion contrary to a teacher's statement in class. I compounded that mistake by referring to the incident in a dormitory "prayer group." To my surprise I learned that the administrators required the "captain" of the "prayer group" to report any deviation within the group. I simply had not appreciated the thoroughness of the authoritarian system. No one ever discussed whatever I said or meant and whatever prompted me to speak out. I was simply not wanted at the college anymore. I left voluntarily, just before I would have been expelled. My mental denseness did not allow me to comprehend the corrosive effects of the system. Unfortunately, I lacked the good sense and advice from anyone else not to think it my destiny to return and prove that I could finish what I had started to do. With great self-satisfaction, I demonstrated that I could fit myself into a malignant situation and finish my work, but it would take me many years to recover from that corrosive experience. I believed that I had a direct assignment from God to go to that school and accomplish what I was supposed to do there. It never occurred to me that getting an education ranked as my most important priority at that time of my life. The misguided notion that I was "called" to attend that college sidetracked my academic purpose. Several years of harsh and at times embarrassing exposure of my lack of education led me to acknowledge this.

As a corollary to that sordid tale, I had the happy fortune to attend Harvard Divinity School. As a special student there, I found a combination of opportunities for work and study and began to grasp the educational deficit that resulted from my "God's will" experience at Bob Jones College.

Not only did I experience a genuinely superior educational opportunity at Harvard Divinity School, but I also met one of the heroes of my life, Professor Henry Joel Cadbury. This man could listen respectfully to an unwashed and untutored fundamentalist preacher from an impoverished academic background and help him aspire to real intelligence. Near retirement, Professor Cadbury had already been recognized by the scholarly world as a superior translator of Scripture. He had accepted the Nobel Peace Prize from the king of Norway on behalf of the American Friends Service Committee. Quaker Henry Cadbury had to borrow a tuxedo for the formal occasion; despite his worldwide academic and Quaker leadership he had not needed formal dress prior to that.

Professor Cadbury was one of my teacher models, but he was foremost my bridge from the educational backwoods into the academic metropolis. When I completed my academic degrees and became a qualified teacher, he wrote me a congratulatory note and provided helpful recommendations. Although he was not a philosopher of religion, his interests spanned the world of religious experience and knowledge. He gave me unusual access to his Quaker background and helped me understand some of the divisions within American Quakerism, and what I would need to know in that environment. He intimated that I might be more useful in the classroom than in a series of pulpits, and I soon agreed with him. Cadbury displayed the ideal of nurturing authority, that rare service by which a person of superior qualifications gives the gift of respect and dialogue to one who lacks the discernment to appreciate these gifts. Patience and humility characterize this intrinsic authority. What a difference from the arrogant authority that has taken on the guise of Christianity among the triumphalists!

Triumphalism Against Community

Many advanced ancient religions contributed to the notion of social dualism by tending to divide humanity into two parts and separate it along lines such as believers and nonbelievers, elect and nonelect, or chosen and nonchosen. Similarly, political and kinship terms like clans, tribes, and nations demarcated one group from another, naming and experiencing some as native, others as alien. This is reflected in the myths and legends of the ancient past and in the records of alliances and hostilities between historical groups that have distinctive names. Every individual is born into one named group and not any other, and every group has its own specific story, in which it invests significant emotional and practical commitment to validate its identity.

As we have become more aware of ourselves and others as part of a larger human breed, with more in common than our ancestors could have imagined, we have become accustomed to thinking of a universal "human nature" that we share with each other and with our ancestors and our descendants as well. We have come to distinguish this "human nature" from "animal nature," and we understand we humans differ from animals in a qualitatively different way from the way we differ from other groups of human beings: in our functions of language and reflection. Ideally, the universal human community would consist of all who share this "nature." However, triumphalist Christianity mandates the total division of this community, both practically with terms such as individuals, families, and tribes, and also ultimately into godly and ungodly, "saved and lost" groups.

Our notion of community has always included a notion of division between the approved "inside" group and the alien "outside" group. Sometimes, the "insiders" even consider themselves superior to the others in some esoteric way, and the division blots out their shared identity. Many Americans have believed that the designations of "white" or "black" take precedence over designations such as American, or even human. That is how we have come to be what Andrew Hacker calls *Two Nations, Separate and Unequal,* in his book of that title.

The two nations are the predominant white one and the subordinate black one. The problems arising from the separateness of the "two nations" originated in the mutual disrespect that was born of, bred into, and institutionalized in slavery. This mutual disrespect affects our American culture, both in formal laws and practices and in informal popular attitudes and tastes. As late as 1965, two students of mine had a problem finding a location for their wedding. The bride was a native of Kansas City, Missouri. The groom was from Denver, a third-generation Presbyterian, and the son of Korean immigrants. The couple belatedly found that they could not get a marriage license in Missouri because of an old law that prohibited the marriage of a Caucasian and a person of Asian ancestry. They traveled across the river to Kansas for a legal civil marriage in the morning and came back to the church in Missouri for an afternoon wedding. Triumphalist morality failed to thwart a resourceful young Presbyterian couple.

Because the white slaveholders began and sustained slavery and stole the Africans from their homelands, it is not difficult for me to see the moral problem of slavery as a white person's problem. Black people have to face the practical problems that persist in our nation as a result of the deep evils of slavery. The moral problems remain deeply embedded in the religious beliefs of the white society that enacted the slavery, with the resulting rift in our national society. What I will call "whiteness" in a later chapter is at the heart of this moral and religious problem.

In the Southland of my childhood, the moral and religious problem of race appeared as miscegenation, the mating or marriage of persons of different races. It was well understood that many slaveholders had forced themselves on slave women, and many people of both races now bear the same family name, due to the children born of this customary rape. The custom had continued between male white employers and their black women employees during the Jim Crow era in more or less public view. Some shame was attached to the more flagrant examples of this practice, especially those that resulted in several children needing provision. The moral problem was not seen as the white man's exploitation or rape, but merely as his weakness of foolish indulgence. These sins of individual weakness and folly had no relevance to faults in the social and economic systems. The laws against miscegenation were intended to maintain the purity of the bloodlines of the white families, not to protect black women.

This dualism of black and white tends to obscure the contemporary importance of the fast-growing third group, Hispanics, and the fourth, Asians. We also pay too little attention to the Native Americans among us, probably out of well-founded shame. But the primary racial division is between black and white Americans. We assume that it is more important to make the distinction between white and black than it is to claim to be Americans together. White Americans collectively have never come to terms with how we have prevented the assimilation into the American economy of the ex-slave culture, as represented by the current black population.

Religion and Limited Community

The call to more inclusive brotherhood, fellowship, or community is a characteristic of religion that is regarded as having high moral value. The Jewish, Christian, and Muslim traditions especially value loving, loyal, devoted spiritual kinship. But, this kinship is exclusively limited to the chosen, the elect, the believers. Typically, outsiders are kept at a specific distance from the boundaries of the defined group. Unity within the group and separation from all outside the group are traditional attitudes. At the commonplace level, these distinctions surface in regulations concerning marriage, employment, and voluntary association. The costs of maintaining separation can be extremely high, so much so that the practical tendencies primarily move in the direction of assimilation. Periodically, earnest spokespersons will arise to lead enthusiastic revivals for separation, along with a "return to the old way," both intended to restore the purity of the group. This passion for separation occurs naturally in religious institutions and will be of passing concern and perhaps some amusement to outsiders. Urban life pulls toward assimilation.

Religious beliefs and institutions are powerful carriers of cultural assumptions. When a religion supports a belief that the essential divisions of humanity include a "we" group who are distinctly human and a different "them" group who are less human or inherently inferior, then the results are tragic for all. Some individuals have the power to impose their belief in this difference and superiority on people who are vulnerable to that power, such as the power of slaveholders over African natives, or Nazi leaders over Jewish citizens. Whatever the individual beliefs of the slaveholders, the religion they taught their slaves supported the idea that humanity is and ought to be divided along a line of racial difference. By believing this idea, the slaves did not think that they deserved respect but that the slave owners did. Forbidden to practice or to mention the religion that they brought from Africa, the slaves learned in its place a religion that chained them to their slavery in hopes of a better life in a heavenly home. They were taught to believe that they would be rewarded in heaven for obedience on earth. Even after legal emancipation, the white culture invented ingenious ways to reinforce the religious message of the degraded status of nonwhites. The seeds of self-distrust were sown so deeply and so viciously that they have been resistant to change down to our own times. We have more to appreciate in the accomplishments of Afro-Americans when we recognize the visible and invisible bonds that have been imposed on them by white men's treachery.

Enlarging Circles of Respect

Religion does not have to support the dividing of humanity into competing groups. It can unite us. This unifying function of religion requires that its believers turn outward toward an inclusive perspective of humanity, rather than inward toward a constricted vision of their own group. This does not require any lessening of the feeling of loyalty to the group itself, but rather the recognition that all people share common values, common needs, and common threats. Indeed, the more we recognize the importance we each have for each other, the better off we will all be. Neighbors share more than sequential addresses: they share responsibility for factors that make a better quality of life possible for all of their neighborhood. A fence between my yard and that of my neighbor may be a useful thing. But if I think I am improving my quality of life by throwing my garbage over that fence, I am surely mistaken. It is good thing to dispose of garbage, but not at the cost of an unnecessary degradation of my close environment, especially when my act also insults someone whose goodwill I need. I have heard it said that our problems of river water quality would be handily solved if every town had to place its own sewage plant upstream from the point in the river at which it takes out its drinking water. This would have the effect of combining our perceived interest in our own well-being with the actual responsibility we have for the well-being of others. We cannot secure our own actual interests if we ignore the interests of others. The reason for this fact of social life is found in the unfamiliar philosophical concept of organism. This concept regards all our separate parts as existing within a single whole, whether that whole is a family, a community, or the cosmos. Our actual human environment, natural and man-made, is an organism. However, our western religions have not adopted this concept and generally do not support any expression of it in their dogmatic or practical activities. The concept of organism that I will call upon has been developed in its modern sense by the late Anglo-American philosopher Alfred North Whitehead (1861–1947), mainly in his book *Process and Reality*. A more contemporary writer in the field of ecology, Dr. Eugene P. Odum, pioneered the organic view in this rapidly growing scientific discipline. Dr. Odum says, "It seems the time has come to develop a *holoeconomics* that includes cultural and environmental factors along with monetary ones."

The philosophy of organism proposes a theory of the structure of relationships between parts and wholes, and between parts and other parts within a common whole. In the concept of organism, all these relationships are held to be internal, or constitutive. In this way, as one organism is considered as an individual entity, such as a person, that organism will be seen as another in the world with other organisms, such as other individual persons. As two people interact, they constitute a complex organism, a miniature society. They act as individuals within their self-determining inner lives. But as they interact, expressing their own internal freedom, they provide each other with the opportunity to develop individuality in unique ways, in a process of mutual nurturing. In such a miniature society of organisms, persons do not lose their individuality in relating to each other but enhance themselves and each other. That is, the relations between the two are internal to both of them, and not external only. This is one of the more crucial points in Whitehead's philosophy of organism. Whitehead overturns the basis of much of materialist philosophy, which insists that each thing has only external relations with other things, so that each thing is expected to develop as it does without regard to the objects that it experiences and to their peculiar individuality. Each of the parts of a whole is interdependent with other parts of that common whole. All parts of a common whole are interdependent with the whole itself.

Our western religions typically exaggerate our differences, rather than enhancing our commonality with our neighbors, close and far. The ideal of protecting the purity of our faith is given as a justification for intensifying separation from those outside the faith. No faith ever maintains purity unless it secludes itself from its surroundings. The natural pull of gravity when living with outsiders is toward assimilation, sharing, and cross-fertilization as interaction takes place in the common pursuits of life. Only by demonizing the outsiders can we preserve the illusion of purity of our group. This path sometimes leads a self-protective faith-group to extreme isolation and self-destruction.

Community or Domination?

It is reported that the United States as a nation lacks any central conception of values and identity, and that a disadvantaged minority faction promotes a low-level class war. Many say that this is a new and negative development, but I have to disagree with the idea that this class warfare is new or is promoted by a faction or is due to minority action. The old reality of class warfare has now become more apparent and more hurtful than it was a few decades ago. We have less civility than we did in past years. More and more confrontations result in active hostility. Anger and rage have stridently emerged in popular discourse. This is more than a reaction to long and oppressive domination; it is also a recognition of the underlying causes of present misery. When people react against what they believe to be suffering born of injustice, they are not likely to approach agents of this injustice with subtlety. The American colonists of the British Empire easily found their collective voice to denounce the arrogant tyranny of George III; yet we do not call the colonists "troublemakers" because of their protests.

The same sense of injustice that motivated the rebellious American colonists now spurs Afro-Americans. Black reaction has now taken on a more strident tone because many black Americans, along with many others disenfranchised throughout the rest of the world, have become a different kind of people in the last few decades. In the past, many suppressed people suffered in silence, having no way to break through the walls of degradation and intimidation that surrounded them. Stridency in reaction was muffled among the American slaves.

Uprisings among the slaves were unreported for many reasons. A "gentlemen's agreement" legal system that accorded no rights to the slaves sanctioned the raping and beating of women and the lynching of men. At the same time, in the North and in the South, bosses who would not allow any hint of union activity exploited working people on farms and in factories. Economic and social pressures quelled dissent or agitation by potential leaders of working-class people. Against tremendous odds at the turn of the century, the sleeping car porters struck and finally won recognition from the Pullman Company. Further labor unrest followed slowly and brought great suffering to miners and textile and other industrial workers. The workers' movement spread slowly in the face of murders and beatings of militant workers and threats to their families.

The silence of the common people lent an aura of "stability" to their working conditions. Tradition decreed that workers take their common lot as the result of fate. A common person just accepted that it was better to endure the worst conditions than to challenge the "stability" that kept things in the accepted order. A few opportunists could amass great wealth and hold sway over religious, political, and educational institutions dedicated to the myth of "progress" while keeping wage earners in feudal dependence. Hierarchy in society placed some in positions of such power as could be mustered and everyone else in positions of dependence upon those in power. Those who dominate have stability as their goal. It has always been in their interest to preserve it, no matter who gets hurt while they enforce their dominance.

The twentieth century has witnessed an unprecedented rise in the power and numbers of working people. These people do the work and bear the troubles in a radically competitive world but seldom share the rewards of the wealthy. Finally, the organizing of labor unions, the rise of cooperative ventures by working people for their own benefit, and the general increase in public education have combined to bring more real power into the hands of the multitude of Americans than had been expected by the most egalitarian thinkers. New voters— the women, the poor, and other previously disadvantaged groups—have challenged and sometimes overwhelmed the slender segment of men whose birth advantages gave them access to the voting booth and thus control of the elective process. These new groups entered the political arena in numbers in the Progressive Era, and their voting power culminated in the antitrust laws, the New Deal, and the Civil Rights Movement. Wage and hour laws, Social Security, collective bargaining laws, and other progressive steps made possible the first real sharing of access to economic and political power that our nation had seen. We will never know for certain what the trajectory of political change might have brought if the Second World War had not intervened and so radically changed the upward political momentum of working people. The Eisenhower Era made it easy to accept the status quo as a respite after the long struggle of war.

In the final decades of the twentieth century memories of such struggles have faded, and a reactionary version of social legislation and financial regulation has surfaced. This new version portrays the free enterprise system as the victim of "liberalism" that set up a "welfare state" and has all but destroyed the American way of life. Regulation of the "free market" reportedly has caused all the troubles affecting the economy. While stressing this renewed triumphalism, reactionaries have overlooked or suppressed the failure of wide-open economic opportunity to provide steady and humane employment. Working people and the environment will just have to take second place to the interests of corporations and their profit reports. Economic democracy is meant for those who can already pay their way into the system, not for those shut out of it in the past. Predatory politicians are set to reverse the progressive gains made in the past and to reinstate a "slash-and-burn" basis for commercial enterprise.

The most vulnerable groups of our society, the poor, the women and children, the migrant workers, and the elderly, are paying the costs of this self-righteous crusade. Thus, the power of authority flaunts the awful fact of dominance. What political advertisements describe as "reform" of welfare and entitlements is actually a show of force intended to remind people as to who really dominates our society, and who has the might and the ruthlessness to use that power to punish those who can resist the least.

This present surge of social deprivation will not likely bring many of its recipients into any worse conditions than they would have known in previous centuries. But now, everyone knows that the deprivation is not the result of blind fate, but is instead the act of those who feel their dominance challenged.

Community and Freedom

How do we get and keep stability in a free and open society? The old guard always sees the threat of anarchy as a part of the common people's rise to power. The moguls who rule by power, through influence or violence, want us never to forget that down through the ages raging mobs have stormed the fortresses and pillaged the farms, upsetting the traditional security of working people. In these years of uncertainty and upheaval among the nations of the world, the power elites try earnestly to get American middle-class voters to turn back the calendar and restore unregulated power to our current crop of moguls to save our way of life. It may happen.

Religious beliefs are deeply involved in all these challenges and reactions. The poor and disadvantaged of the world have relied on such beliefs as a vital resource for enduring hardship. Religious beliefs that place primary value on togetherness, mutual dependence, and reciprocal respect, especially between generations of the family, give strong support to the wholesome socialization of the young. Because of this, many people can live in poverty, degradation, and miserable lack of material things and yet produce continuing generations of young who grow into responsible adults. On the other hand, unmet material needs and blatant temptation by visible but unattainable riches can be corrosive to family health. Religious beliefs can provide crucial support for reciprocal respect; yet adverse public policies can also sap that strength. A religious basis for respect between generations can be a redeeming element. Tragically, many adverse public policies are imposed in the fruitless effort to make poor people over in the image of middle-class people. Marriage loses its attractiveness without a dependable way to pay the bills of ordinary living. Poor young people have the same desires and needs for love and companionship as anyone else. These desires and needs are not quenched by lack of education and employment. Too often, semi-religious decrees, such as mandates for absolute virginity until marriage and marriage in church for all adult companions, foster the judgment that the poor are evil and the middle class are righteous. Thus a variant religion that allows for indulgence and praises responsibility becomes a source of strength for the poor. A conventional religion that requires conformity and permits hypocrisy becomes a source of self-righteous judgment for the middle class. In this way, religion itself becomes part of the cultural barrier between people of different races and social classes who have vital interests in common, but lack reciprocal respect to act with strength for common causes. Although a religion whose primary moral values stress human unity would surmount that barrier, the triumphalist religion of too many Americans reinforces the barrier.

This brief recounting of the complex and baffling record of democracy in action does not intend to answer the technical questions of politics and economics, but rather sets a background for the discussion of our present state of social sickness. We are suffering from an excess of greed and ambition and a lack of cooperation and community. In the process of trying to manage freedom and diversity, we are tearing ourselves to pieces. We labor under the conviction that if some are different, we must be hostile to them, or "we" will be losers and "they" will be winners. The triumphalist religious beliefs discussed in earlier chapters are deeply involved in our beliefs about each other. These religious beliefs that tend to abandon humanity have led us into utterly hostile divisions. We need a different religious approach to the meaning of individuality and society and a richer concept of community.

Community and Nurture

Nothing can supply strength and continuity in a society if community is lacking. The organism of humanity takes its character and strength from the qualities of its individuals, and these components receive strength and character from the social organisms of which they are part. Nurture emerges in the mutuality between the parts and the whole. Humanity lives and thrives this way. No individual can come into full realization without the nurturance of a community, and no community can fully realize itself without its members respecting each other. The Klan or the Nazi community is corrosive and self-destructive because these racists believe that humanity is essentially divided between those who are worthy and those who are unworthy. They define the unworthy in terms of their own fears and hatred. When a communal group bases its existence on the belief that its own value is absolutely more worthy than the value of another group, that community carries the seeds of its own degradation. The Nazis, the Klan, and the Confederacy all achieved high degrees of community at points in their histories, but each suffered the fatal flaw of basing its own identity on the denial of human value to one or more other groups. Many tribes and ethnic and national groups regard themselves as having a unique status in humanity. This attitude is fairly benign until another group presents itself and is either given or denied respect. This element of respect for those outside the immediate community establishes how well the community will serve its own members and thus become a new version of community that includes the outsiders.

Hostility to outsiders breeds hostility within a community. Thus a vital community maintains a healthy respect for those who are outside its immediate group. Overlapping communities will co-exist in a hierarchy based on significance to their members, such as clubs within a school and the school itself. Members of any community will have interests in other groups. In overlapping communities members will move from one to another group and will see their own interests in each community rise and fall. Fathers, mothers, and children will belong to many co-communities in addition to their family. Individuals should feel free to express their interests in the groups that they find valuable. Parents may find it difficult to see their children move away from the primary loyalty to their household. It is a bittersweet experience for a parent to return home after vacationing with a son or daughter, knowing that this will have been the last family excursion to include the offspring. But younger members of the family need to find their own independence among compatible groups. When parents try to prevent their children from selecting associates—especially if the parents' efforts are merely arbitrary and unconvincing—they risk subverting their role as nurturers. Wise parents cultivate in themselves the expectation that their sons and daughters will become self-directing men and women, adults of their own generation.

Barriers to our closeness to other people must be removed if we are to become the individuals that we can and need to be. If we are to become persons in the best sense of the word, we must be free to learn from the examples of others, both when we are attracted to them and when we are repelled by them. We learn to be distinctive persons by responding to clues we get from other people. Far from being simply a copy of the person we emulate, we each become a distinctive individual by the way we adapt for ourselves some part of the other person's stock of characteristics. Our inventory of personal traits rests in those around us. The crucial question of character development is not what we see, but what we do with what we see. One son may see his father's sensitivity as strength and another son may see it as weakness. In either case, both sons are noticing the characteristic of their father and responding to it. Will they both imitate him? Suppose one becomes a sensitive person and the other a brutal person? Is not one adhering to the father's example and the other rejecting it? In both cases they are responding to the same example. Each person relies on an infinite number of examples that have become parts of his own personal inventory, and some traits will be imitated, some will be adapted, and others left out.

Penitentiaries: Anti-Community

Even the best penitentiary exemplifies the diametrical opposite of a human community. We can see something important about communities by examining the kind of environment we might construct if we wanted the worst imaginable case of human togetherness.

The penitentiary is designed to nullify and prevent relationships. Each prisoner bears a number and is dealt with as a totally isolated entity. So far as possible, individuals lose all features of commonality. No kinship, no home or club, no school, no age or occupational ties bind the incarcerated individuals. They are thrown together only through random official reckoning that has nothing to do with the prisoners' identity. When a person becomes a prisoner, he ceases to bear his own identity, as defined by mutual dependency and the support of family and friends. He assumes a new identity based on the power hierarchy in the prison situation. Each prisoner is controlled by fear of those prisoners and guards with more power and, in turn, may be feared by those with less power. The prisoner's power stems from factors of violence and cunning as well as the ranking he and others place on these things. Inside the prison environment, constitutive values of the outside society, such as altruism and fellowship, are alien, if they exist at all. Intimidation is the most common basis for prisoner interaction. The prison system both intentionally and randomly isolates inmates from all past companions and significant others. Prisoners' needs for the warmth, affection, and strength of human touch become degraded to some form of violent or submissive encounter. This is far from an environment in which a community might form. Yet, testimonies that rare, life-changing experiences occur in this kind of environment give tribute to the potential and resilience present as long as human life endures.

The prison situation reverses all that we know about wholesome self-building. We can only imagine how many seeds of harm that are sown in prisons are later reaped in public.

A kindly physician, Benjamin Rush, a Philadelphia contemporary of Benjamin Franklin and a signer of the Declaration of Independence, laid the foundation of the penitentiary system. Rush was appalled at the retributive punishment that was meted out for a wide range of offenses, from failure to pay debts to murder. Flogging, branding, and exile fell just short in severity of the capital punishment that was a common resort in desperate situations. Rush believed in the possibility of restoring lawbreakers to positive citizenship. He believed that the key to this restoration lay in the novel idea that every person has an innate capacity for shame and remorse for evil deeds done. Even the guiltiest person could be salvaged for productive life. Rush shared with many of his fellow Philadelphians the Quaker belief that the "inner light" of God could penetrate and reform the darkened human heart. This reformation could begin only after the evildoer had experienced a season of withdrawal from society during which he could contemplate the evil of his ways, and repent or become penitent for all his wrongs. Rush proposed a stay in the penitentiary as an answer to the problem of antisocial behavior.

Rush had a high opinion of the human conscience, but a poor appreciation for the results of shutting one group of people away under the nearly absolute control of another group. The potential his system had for making amateur criminals into skilled ones must have escaped Rush. He had no reason to predict that the worst among those imprisoned would debase and contaminate the better. Isolation from normal social restraints and healthy relationships combines powerfully to remove from most prisoners whatever remnants of healthy self-building they have known. We cannot be surprised when prisoners become convinced that they are victims of a vicious society that has separated them from everything good in life, largely for hypocritical reasons.

The penitentiary system purports to induce in the prisoner shame and remorse for the evil things that he has done. Perhaps it would do so to a person of Rush's beliefs and attitudes. But applying this procedure to the person who gets involved with our criminal courts—who is likely already among the poorest, least educated, and least cared for—assures the folly of Rush's expectation. Paradoxically, the penitentiary system as Rush saw it would work only when it least needed to, that is, when the prisoner is already habituated to the restraints of conscience. In most cases, prisoners enter the penitentiary system precisely because they have lacked the self-esteem and confidence concomitant to higher levels of conscience, such as moral values and principles.

In prison, all pleasures and pains are structured around the central value of power. This culture of unvarnished, brutal power makes every person the victim or the enemy of every other. The corrosive effect of raw power prevents any healthy social relationships, either between prisoners and guards or between prisoners themselves. Consequently, the prison environment will only support the growth of personal characteristics that facilitate individual gain and will suppress the more socially cohesive traits. As respect for the other person diminishes, so the respect for oneself fades. In prison, the measure of one's self-esteem equates to how much control one can exert over others. The values of respect, fairness, and tolerance are discarded in favor of intimidation, exploitation, and violence.

If the penitentiary system worked, the prison populations would decrease because recidivist prisoners account for a large part of these institutions' population. Whatever brings the prisoners to reformation, Rush's hope for penitential reform applies only to a few. Malcolm Little—later Malcolm X—whose conversion I mentioned previously, was one of those few. He is an extraordinary case of a prisoner who found his direction in life while incarcerated and made a heroic triumph over the degradation around him. Others have done the same thing in less conspicuous ways, but for each of those few, multitudes have traced the spiral downward to its end.

The Way to Community: Reconciliation

In his Sermon on the Mount, Jesus makes some startling departures from the conventional religious beliefs of his time. The Jewish Temple in Jerusalem was built after the return of the Jewish captives from Babylonian exile in 538 B.C.E. The temple lay at the center of religious consciousness of Jews in Jesus' time. Jesus was present in the temple at least twice: when he was said to have impressed the temple elders with his command of the ancient lore, and when he drove from the temple area the money changers who exhorted those who came from other countries to offer sacrifices. But Jesus mentioned the temple in other connections as well and, typically, showed more respect for it than his contemporaries.

Jesus recognized the extraordinary times in which he lived. Roman power had eclipsed the possibility of any independent and authentic temple rituals of repentance and sacrificial prayers for forgiveness. The populace had no way to challenge this oppressive power outwardly. Such rebelliousness went beyond the resources of the Jewish individual. In such a situation, he sought other strategies for serving God and his kinfolk.

Some of Jesus' contemporaries would have set aside Mosaic Law altogether and adopted the Hellenized version of culture that predominated in the Roman Empire. Others sought to accommodate the law to a legalistic code that would capitalize on the governance of trivial behaviors, such as details of Sabbath keeping. Jesus tried to lead his followers in another direction, however much they might misunderstand his intentions or miscarry his plan. Jesus called for a stern and demanding loyalty to Jewish identity and an appeal to the ancient image of God as the loving father of Israel, but his plan also involved the rejection of Roman emperor worship and Greek hedonism. Jesus insisted that the vitality of the Jewish religion lay in its primacy of love and respect for all people, of whatever sort. He taught that the will of his Father God is to unite all his human children in a common practice of compassion and support, especially for those who are in distress.

Jesus saw that the practice of personal and private religious values was always possible, even in the hard political times in which he lived. But this practice meant intense involvement with the daily needs of people close at hand. Absorption in plots to injure or overthrow the Roman rulers or their quisling confederates did not justify standing aside while the victims of economic and political injustice suffered, or while the ruptures in ordinary personal relationships went unhealed. Jesus' radical comrade, John the Baptist, lifted the religion of the Jews above the level of alliances with power and privilege, but Jesus advocated values of the inner life that could mold the outer practices of both Jews and gentiles. He would not narrow his vision to exclude the gentiles from the family of God or lower his vision to accept the goal of outward success in worldly personal affairs as practiced by Jews and gentiles alike. He believed that a life of companionship with people around him was in itself true fulfillment of God's purpose for humanity.

Centuries of institutional existence of Christendom have directly inverted what Jesus taught about the priority of reconciliation over ritual obedience. The triumphalism of the rebellious Jews and the conquering Romans have drawn the

Church into a never-ending contest for superiority, first over competing races and ethnic groups, and then among believers for primacy over one another. The competitive model makes enemies of allies as well as adversaries, because in the end individual success is the highest priority. In a competitive spirit, the efforts that Jesus calls for in service to the dispossessed are instead turned to conquests in his name. The cultivation of social values in pursuit of a common good is lost in the race for individual power and privilege.

Jesus admonished that if any worshiper in the temple can recall hostility between himself and his brother, then the worshiper should leave his gift at the altar and first become reconciled with his brother before offering his gift at the temple. Generally, this message carries the truth about the priority of relationships over ritual observance. There must be a reason why Jesus gave reconciliation priority over this ordained obedience. He saw a vital need for the open and warm response of one person to another, so that the ordinary course of life would not only contain the small interactions of the practical sort, but also so that we would be able to interact with each other in the more profound sense, in those shared experiences that are most essential to our human growth. As individuals, we seem to be detached from one another, but in order to be an individual at all, we must find ourselves in a human community. This community must have its own qualities of respect, tolerance, and fairness if we are to thrive in it as individuals with all the richness of our possibilities.

Jesus also challenges one of the strongest demands of institutional religions: control of access to God, which in western religions is typically regulated in the most exacting and visible detail. Doing or not doing the prescribed ritual things with your voice, your knees, and your hands can open or close the institutional gates to dealing with God. These details of behavior are supposed to be ordained by God and maintained by the authorities.

This religious/moral teaching, preached at the time when Roman law was at its highest peak of official concern, directly challenges the premise of law, both civil and religious: the rules must be kept by all, or chaos will overtake the empire and its institutions. The Romans expected the governors of all its provinces, along with the Jewish puppet governors, to maintain order in their appointed region. The Jewish rulers of Palestine, secular and religious, feared any popular voice of dissent. Any challenge to their authority was also a challenge to Rome. So Jesus' moral teaching of the priority of human relationships over temple observance displayed the behavior that finally sent him to a Roman execution. He usually showed deliberate indifference to Roman authority, certainly less defiance than his cousin John the Baptist. But Jesus' message to his fellow Jews was that God was not satisfied with anything less than the fulfillment of our deepest human capacity, the potential for respectful relationship. This kind of moral teaching does not require the humiliation of the hearer. It does not threaten the hearer who ignores it. It is not a command, in the ordinary sense; rather, it is an admonition to put the healing of broken relationships before all other considerations. Jesus points the moral compass toward the only essential and unexpendable practice that can without qualification increase the stature of a human individual, the offering of oneself to be a companion to another. We grow as persons when we enter and continue in companionship with another, whatever degree of intimacy is involved. And this, we can believe, is Jesus' version of God's will for people. It is also, I believe, the very message that earnest persons need for credible hope in our time.

6

Organic and Atomistic Individuals and Society
The Soviet Realism Exhibit

STALIN IS SAID to have remarked, "All people are just a single screw in the great machines." This opinion was vividly portrayed in a collection of Soviet propagandistic art—posters, statuary, murals from the early decades following the revolution. Those remarkable works presented a vivid portrayal of the atomistic theory as applied to individuals and society. The official Soviet propaganda system had commissioned these works of mass-produced art to impress upon the Russian people the glory of their new role in building a worker's paradise. The power of the visual images carried the message: the revolutionary government was giving the people the kind of life they wanted, and the people should accept it with joy and enthusiasm. This use of visual images to convey official policy lines as pure egalitarian realism is not new or distinctive. All governments use them when they can. The striking thing about the Soviet version was its reliance on strong images of workers and machines as partners in the task.

Most of the pictures had a cartoonlike simplicity. Some showed factory workers happily tending their clean, powerful machines. A harmonious, productive feeling surrounded the whole combination of men and women and steel and steam. Factory workers who viewed these pictures were supposed to see themselves as vastly better off than their ancestors, who had labored in mud and dirt with animals and filth. Industrial life was a novelty to most Russian minds, and the representations were meant to celebrate the victory of the new over the old.

The exhibited pictures prominently featured a mix of genders. Women were shown working side by side with men, doing the same heavy lifting and moving tasks that the men did, with all of the laborers smiling and enjoying themselves. Some semidomestic scenes showed mothers at the end of a long, pleasant day being greeted by smiling children playing at the day-care centers in the shadows of the smokestacks. No traces of grease or fatigue marred the parents' appearance, no soil or tears sullied the children's faces.

The images showed workers moving in concert with the assembly lines and the ponderous machines. Much of the machinery dwarfed the people, but the factory appeared to be a peaceable kingdom, not of lions and lambs, but of steel and muscle. The smoke and vapor from furnaces and cauldrons wound easily upward and vanished conveniently into the blue sky, leaving behind not a hint of bleary eyes or labored breath. Sparks always shot away from workers, overhead and to either side. No worker needed to flinch or dodge an unwelcome spark.

Photos showed proud engineers and architects reviewing schematic drawings of floor plans and building sites, and beaming over the results of their professional efforts to provide a perfect setting in which the worker-heroes could spend joyful hours as appendages to the perfect machines, all part of the ideal industrial apparatus. Those image makers who produced those visualizations did their work well. Soviet citizens saw in them a powerful portrayal of themselves conceived as mechanical objects, collected into a mighty and even beautiful system. This conception must have become an effective bonding agent for those Soviet citizens who participated in the brave, new industrial world.

Whether we look at Soviet propaganda art or the media images that accompanied the American entrance into World War II, we can see the basic value of idealized community, aside from moral or political considerations under which it arises. Each case appeals to the common interest in the national well-being. Social interest becomes distinct from and of greater value than individual interest. Although manipulative private or public persons might have mixed their nefarious schemes into the appeals, the impact the appeals have on their audiences remains strong and invigorating. That a Stalin or a Hitler or an Orwellian Big Brother could subvert the values of their societies through appeals to community does not negate the needs for community appeals and responses. The sins of Stalin and Hitler lay in the violation of their communities by dividing the population, setting some of the perceived individual interests of some groups against the needs and desires of the rest, particularly those most vulnerable. The sin is not in the mass appeal to an uncritical community, however low that tactic is on the leadership scale of value. The greater sin lies in the misuse of power by some at the expense of others. This will always be wrong, whether the vehicle of persuasion is subtle or blatant.

The distorted, mechanistic caricature of humanity portrayed in this traveling art exhibit indicated that the Soviet Union scarcely needed anything else, foreign or domestic, to bring it down. People simply do not thrive in a society that treats them as instruments and suppresses their humanity. Industrial countries, whatever the language or ideology of the society, typically operate in reliance on the assembly line. The use of the conveyor belt makes a universal statement about the place of the human individual in the industrial process. A crafty employer can manipulate his entire work force by secretly finding among the workers a willing ally who will furiously exert himself for a short while for extra pay. The employer can then set the speed of the belt or the line to the pace of his confederate and call that speed "standard." All the workers are then judged by how well they meet that artificial pace.

Given the authoritarian tradition of Mother Russia, the Soviet leadership no doubt had a better chance to maximize the concept of worker-as-appendage than some other countries have had. Many other industrialists would perhaps be glad to adopt the approach of the Soviet realist artists for their own workers' consumption, if the bosses thought that they could get away with it. In the United States, the worker-as-consumer has received the most propaganda emphasis. The mass appeal of media propaganda for advertising and entertainment has encouraged those in the labor force to commit themselves to ever higher levels of consumption and waste, which necessitates ever increasing buying power, made easier through credit buying. These incentives are intended to shackle the working person with guilt and shame for failure to produce and spend at a rate that equals his neighbor's.

Soviet Russia had the dilemma of an organistic theory and an atomistic practice. The theory held that the "masses" rightfully owned the nation's resources and should share in all the riches. In practice, the government treated the people as if they were mechanistic individuals. If the society had truly been regarded as an organism, the interests of all individuals would have been taken into account, and respect would have been given and received as among human equals. But the historical segmentation of Russian society according to hereditary economic lines overshadowed such a humanistic cultural view. The same assumption governed both the "new" Russia and the "old regime": the poor would serve the rich just because that was the way it was meant to be. Under the revised version of this age-old assumption the promise of economic freedom could only mean that a new privileged class would oversee the work of the poor masses in economic serfdom. The factory would replace the farm as the hereditary place of productive labor. The machine and its operation would become the tools the rulers used to organize the laboring class. The worker would become an appendage of the machine.

Organisms and Machines

This dilemma of workers and machines has resolved itself differently in the United States. We have declared that "We the people" will have government "by consent of the governed." This is organically inclusive language, and it conveys the idea of a seamless body of citizens who have the inherent right to respect from one another and from the public. Offsetting this ideal and its various legal expressions, we have the assumption that each individual has the right to property within the framework of the politically enacted economic structure, no matter how that structure might contradict the ideal of equal respect for all individuals. This unlimited right to property under the law gives each individual exclusive right to use his property, however that usage might help or hinder the well-being of other citizens. If the economic structure is to be just, the conflict between inclusive human rights and exclusive property rights must be resolved in a conceptual framework that will satisfy the inherent rights and essential needs of all.

Such a conceptual framework might arise out of two differing, cogent theories: atomism and organism. Both inhere in our "American way of life." Atomism appears in our competitiveness and radical individualism. Organism predominates in our sense of shared values and cooperative spirit. Each of these ideas is deeply imbedded in our concept of who we are as Americans and how we expect to live. I do not suggest that one is good and the other bad, but that we affirm the priority of the organic. They are not absolutes in polar opposition, but correlative ways of relating that are appropriate in ordered sequence: organism primary, mechanism secondary.

We need to examine both ideas and attempt to see how they function: what values, motives, and objectives can they support and enhance? But, most importantly, we need to define ourselves as organic persons in an organic society. Through the lens of organism, we can learn to value competition as a secondary way in which we relate to each other. We need to consider cooperation as our primary way of relating, so that our competition may be symbiotic and constructive instead of parasitic and destructive. Because our society is naturally organic, both cooperation and competition should mesh to bring us all into a healthy and mutually beneficial relationship. By making unlimited competition our standard way of operating, we come dangerously close to spoiling our world for all concerned. Our basic national need is for a sense of the common good, for all Americans and all other people as well.

The philosophical idea and practice of mechanism that so absorbs us come from the ancient theory of atomism. Few of us have any acquaintance with these terms, and there is no reason that we should, except that we need to understand how we have gotten ourselves into such a dilemma of disabling competition. We know that unlimited competition saps our energy, and wears us out needlessly, but we also suspect that it is our most used hedge against boredom.

The power of the human spirit serves as the counterpart to competition between members of a group or between groups. By "spirit" I mean that quality of life that we all possess potentially and that we all exhibit, at least as children. Spirit is the joy of connecting with other people in pleasurable activities. Children can do it in the most unlikely situations or circumstances; everyone can do it when the time, place, and circumstances are just right. I associate "spirituality" with human connections— a "spiritual" experience in isolation is foreign to what I am suggesting. Spiritual experiences have an emotional component, the sharing of joy and mutual appreciation of well-being.

Even though the word "spirit" has been abused by illusory references to something supernatural, "spirit" can still apply to that which is completely human and natural. "Spirituality" can describe a state of mind and heart that is as human and natural as enjoying a social meal with friends or a quiet meditation in a meeting house. But spirit has always connoted powerful activity, whether physical, mental, or emotional. It can be embodied in an athletic event or a dramatic or musical performance. A work of art can evoke a spiritual reaction when we experience a connection with the artist through the expressive object. Human spirit tends to be creative and innovative, because we respond to challenges to say or to do the same old thing in a new and pleasing way. However, a typical athletic competition loses its healthful spirit through the conflict of interest that is inherent in the excessively competitive system.

Many people around the world survive on a fraction of our supply of goods and services. If we compare their provisions with our own, we have to recognize that our frantic competition must serve some other purpose than simply supplying our needs. The impoverished are not trying to seize our food or clothing or our means of livelihood. No one stands waiting for any of us to slacken our efforts so that he or she can snatch our food out of our hands. We would probably not miss many of the things that we have if our incomes were reduced by a third. We compete because everyone else is competing. Otherwise, we would feel that we are missing out on the excitement we crave.

Such talk will not convince us to hustle much less. But by holding the idea of competition up for scrutiny, we might be able to see if it is really as necessary as our mythology tells us. Humanity has reached a point of counterproductive competition and needs to be reminded that cooperation is at least as natural for us, and much more productive. Our problem lies in our mistaken notion of what we as individuals really are, which is living organisms instead of somewhat badly operating machines.

Atomism Applied and Illustrated

The theory of atomism and the theory of organism are two competing philosophical theories of how the basic structure of anything is to be conceived. I will deal with these theories with reference to modern Christianity. We can understand our present predicament only by becoming acquainted with these two philosophical concepts and how they have undergirded the development of modern society and our image of ourselves. Although we do not derive our Christian religion from these or other philosophical theories or concepts, much understanding of our complex world is framed by concepts essentially independent of the religious element. Western civilization is particularly embedded in these two concepts.

The basic ancient theory of atomism has two aspects, mechanism and materialism. Mechanism refers to the ways things act, while materialism refers to how things are constituted. Atomism accounts for both actions and things in a systematic way. The philosophical attraction of this theory is that everything in the description of the actions of things is consistent with the description of the structure of those things. We may question the theory of atomism itself, but we recognize that the theory is internally consistent and that the empirical world it describes can be understood. For example, the atomist does not have to try to explain how atomistic turtles can fly or how atomistic eagles can swim. The atomist's theory accounts for how the eagles of the world fly and the turtles swim. It does not try to account for things outside the empirical world. The atomist does not add anything that is not needed to his explanation of what happens in the commonplace world. For instance, the atomist does not add a halo to a person's head to identify that person as one who does extraordinary things. In the atomist's world, ordinary people do ordinary things, and that activity is enough to account for. The attempt to explain a nonempirical world is not only gratuitous, but even dangerous. To explain things that do not happen removes us from reality and thus subjects us to folly in dealing with what does happen.

Our understanding of ourselves depends on whether we see ourselves and our society on the model of the atom, as matter in motion, or on the model of organisms in process. Let me offer a simple illustration of atomism and then apply it to the human situation.

$$A \text{-----------} B$$

In this example, we will presuppose that the points A and B are independent of each other, so that the inherent characteristics of one are not determined by the other. Each point would exist just as it does even if the other did not exist. The broken line between A and B does not suggest connection or relation, but merely the distance between them, because they are presumed to exist in a common spatial universe and to have spatial locations within that universe. The distance between them indicates where they are with respect to each other. Other such lines would also indicate where they are with respect to any other such points. The distances do not make any difference to the points as such, but are of interest only for purposes of dealing with them. The distance between the points is external only and the only connection they share, if that spatial relation indeed constitutes a connection. The distance between the points could be doubled or halved, or one of the points obliterated, leaving no spatial distance, with no intrinsic change in the remaining point.

Notice that the relation of a bare measure of distance between the physical boundaries of the two points A and B is consistent with the explanation of what the two things are: isolated, independent, self-contained material things. The atomic theory gives us an adequate picture of the world of things, as long as we do not consider the whole world composed of things and persons. If we assume, with the atomist, that all of the material things of the world are alike, whatever we call them, because all those things have the same atomic structure, then atomism taken as a theory only, has little theoretical problem. I do not argue the theoretical basis of atomistic science: that is a problem for philosophers of science. But, I do take issue with the application of atomic theory to persons. I will challenge the idea that this assumption is adequate to account for the novel and personal aspects of our world.

The atomist theory is, I believe, the assumption that underlies and complicates our predominant Western culture, including religion, politics, economics, laws, and so on. If we follow the atomist assumptions about human beings as one kind of thing in the world, then we must try to understand persons, individuals, and groups as though they were like the points and the broken line that indicates the distance between them. Any two or more persons would be considered to be as independent of each other as are the points, with their personal, individual characteristics as free from determination by the other as the points are. Any possible relations between persons would be as fully external to the individuals as are those of the points. All persons would be considered self-contained and inherently isolated from each other. Groups of people, considered as things in the world, would be similarly considered as independent of each other, because only external relations are taken as valid.

The popular mind does not hold the atomist theory as a consciously recognized belief. The atomist theory does not ordinarily get spelled out by the preachers, politicians, or scientists, even though many presuppose it. Scientists, however, have explicitly advanced the assumption and given it the powerful attraction that it has for other areas of our culture. Incorporating mechanistic assumptions has no less powerful results in religion and politics than in science.

The atomist concept goes back at least as far as Democritus, a Greek philosopher of Plato's era. Democritus, and his teacher Leucippus, taught the theory that the cosmos is composed of atoms—those ultimately simple units of matter, each of which is like all the others in structure, but not in particular characteristics. These units are in an eternal boiling motion, and they collide, touching each other, but only on their surfaces. No atom in any way depends on another for its being what it is, but rather each atom is self-contained, complete within itself, and will not be essentially changed by any contact or association with other atoms. This idea of a common structure of all things proved an advance in its time over the speculations of other cosmologists, who held that some element—earth, water, air, or fire—was the origin of all things. The structure-based theory made room for a universal order without limiting the obvious variations among the things of the world. The notion of a universal order that underlies all the diversity of the observed world is perhaps the most significant contribution of the ancient Greek philosophers. The explanation of diversity in an ordered universe and the applications of this concept have constituted the story of our Western scientific tradition.

Democritus' theory defines atoms as indivisible, that is, they cannot be subject to further division. This gives us the picture of a piece of material, such as wood or stone, that has been repeatedly cut in halves until, finally, the last cut has left the halves too small to be further divided: that last, smallest piece is the atom. But this picture misleads us. It is not the size of the atom that prevents it being divided, but its own simple structure. An atom might be the size of a grain of sand, or it might be the size of a planet. The crucial question is not its relative size, but whether or not it stands on its own as a complete entity, with its own characteristics, or whether it is a compound of at least two such entities.

The general characteristics of atoms are their size, their shape, and their texture, all measurable physical quantities. Democritus theorized that in the primordial chaos of moving atoms, there were inevitable contacts between atoms of all sizes, shapes, and structures. When two atoms of sufficient compatibility in some characteristics happened to touch, the atoms would tend to cling together.

The familiar things of the world are combinations of atoms that join into combinations of combinations, and so on and on, until infinitely complex aggregations become identifiable bodies, such as rocks, trees, skies, and seas. Nothing in the physical universe cannot be accounted for by this concept. Anything that we do not apprehend according to its atomic structure, we do not need to explain because it can be considered nonexistent.

The atomist concept is beautiful in its utter simplicity. But this simplicity has been challenged: can this theory account for mind, the thinking thing? Tradition says that when he was presented with this issue, Democritus paused only slightly and answered that the mind-atoms were the "roundest, the smoothest, the fiery atoms."

Democritus' theory is basically a philosophical theory, and subject to the kind of criticism and revision that all philosophical theories undergo. However, it has come to be regarded as a basic element of modern scientific culture. Atomism is scientific not just because of atom bombs and atomic power plants, but because it is the basis for the conduct of modern science. A scientist who decides to study something begins by dividing the subject into its component parts, and looking at the parts first, and then at the parts of the parts, and so on. Thus scientific specialties and subspecialties and compound subspecialties have arisen. This kind of procedure analyzes each part and each subpart, supposedly not ignoring any part. Such a study thoroughly done may yield a result of high credibility. This is the empirical method, and it is certainly superior to a procedure that begins with a predetermined notion of what part is worth looking at, and then scrutinizes that part only, leaving the rest unnoticed. Use of the scientific method generally presupposes atomism. We generally take it for granted that atomism and the scientific method are identical. This is a problem with modern science: it assumes a theory of atomism without acknowledging it. Consequently, we are apt to miss some of the biases that creep into otherwise good scientific work.

Atomism also has its applications in many areas of modern life. Our Western culture has rested increasingly on the atomic model since the sixteenth century, and the rest of the world now assimilates this atomistic model along with the rest of Western culture. Our economics, politics, and human sciences rely on the assumptions of isolated individualism that derive from atomism. In economics, the work of George C. Lodge has called attention to the effects of extreme individualism. Lodge gave one of his books the title *The American Disease,* by which he means the radical individualism that our free enterprise system imposes on our economic life. In a world with this kind of economic system, material things have become for capitalist society what the Holy Grail would have been in an earlier age. The pursuit and possession of things constitute the criteria of a life of achievement. The individual has merit as an economic and political entity according to his possession of things and their surrogates, such as money and credit.

This radical individuality supposedly strengthens the isolated individual for competition with his group, but instead it debilitates him. The intensity of the individual's isolation nullifies his connections to the group and obscures the reactions of the group that would enable him to clarify his identity. He becomes a speaker who can hear no voice but his own and listens only to echoes of himself. The voices of those who hear him and could interpret his words are beyond his hearing. Every word he hears repeats his own thinking, so he listens only to himself.

This description of the individual who hears only his own voice has an all-too-familiar ring to it. Although I did not know it at the time, when I was a triumphalist I was not listening to anyone who did not share my perspective on life. If I had listened to someone who disagreed with me, but had something to say that I badly needed to hear, I would have avoided many serious mistakes. After I realized the fallaciousness of my triumphalist assumptions and beliefs, I could see that I was avoiding information that would have helped me to ask the right questions. My stubborn refusal to hear led to many mistaken decisions. I gradually began to attend to unwelcome messages that came to me, finding it was painful to filter out questions that might challenge my perspective. As an exaggerated corrective, I think that in some cases I hear too much, but that discomfort is a small price to pay for the ability to hear those who have disagreements with me. In my classroom work unsettled students have sometimes directed angry words at me. Student bystanders who overheard these tirades have asked me why I let it go on. Although I am not insensitive to such remarks, I simply cannot turn aside from criticism, which I may well need to hear. If I dismiss what I do not want to hear, I risk closing my mind, a costly mistake that I do not intend to repeat.

In his book *Habits of the Heart*, the American sociologist Robert Bellah examines the personal and social implications of atomism. This insightful book deals with the atomistic concept of individualism in American religion. We tend to look at ourselves and the world we live in as if we are each adrift in a sea of subjectivity, to sink or swim on our own, leaving no essential role for family or associates. At the same time, we feel obliged as parents and teachers to influence our sons, daughters, and students to make decisions, the meaning of which our youth are often incapable of understanding in their full contexts. So, we are in a contradictory position, assuming that we are all essentially independent, isolated individuals, and yet feeling very strongly that we have a responsibility to act in ways that make a real difference in the decisions of those in our care. Is our inclination to care just an illusion and a farce? If all individuals are structured as the atomist theory indicates, with no significant elements that are internal to the lives of other individuals, then we should not be concerned about the well-being of others.

The individual who thinks of himself as an isolated and independent entity will look around and try to find a group that he thinks will offer him the best opportunity for self-enhancement. When he joins that group, he will make those alliances that seem to offer him support for his own autonomy and the means to increase his authority. He will compete to advance over members of the group, and he will compete for connections to outsiders which will increase his value to the group by assuring the group's dependence on him for these connections to the outsiders. His nearest enemies within the group stand directly between him and his upward mobility. He makes alliances within the group based on the intention of nullifying competitors or gaining bargaining status for advancement. This individual uses others for his own purposes and allows himself to be used when it will incur an obligation that will help him in the future. All of this is legal and within the expectations of the commercial system. However, such a user faces difficulty when he gets home and continues his radical individualism in a family system, where organic reality prevails.

Acquisitive American Individualism

This version of individualism has been called "possessive individualism," which seems to be an apt term for the American version of atomism. According to this concept, the individual is defined by his possessions: he becomes who he is by getting for himself whatever he can that he wants, generally the material things that somebody else might acquire. The nonmaterial qualities and values of life that are intrinsic to one's own being are not accounted for by this concept. This is close to what C. B. Macpherson, the late Canadian economist, calls "possessive individualism." Macpherson follows Locke's theory of property rights, in which he finds Locke laying the basis of civil society in the assembling of individuals who possess material goods. Otherwise independent individuals commingle for the purpose of protecting their property and regulating its exchange for other property with their individual peers. The term "acquisitive" is more appropriate to the American version than the term "possessive," because the possession by inheritance or royal favor is less likely in America than the personal acquisition of things. I see no essential advantage in using one term over the other. Both of them establish the meaning of personal identity according to the same priority: having things takes precedence over relating to persons as persons. The activity that "makes a man a man" is acquiring something that someone else might have had, whether it is a tract of land or a "trophy wife."

At this point it is necessary to say again how difficult it is to make our way through the dilemma of individuality and community. I stand by the position that this dilemma is insoluble on the assumption of atomic individuality. When atomism defines individuals as essentially self-contained and independent, it seems almost impossible to combine them into a genuine community, a community whose members are essentially part of one single entity. This may be an unresolvable dilemma, if indeed atomistic individuals and community are taken as absolutes. The problem will be to find a comprehensive way to do justice to both individuals and community.

Organism and Community

Individuality and community are not antagonistic ideas, if we shift our perspective from the theory of atomism to that of organism. Indeed, an atomic individual would certainly be antagonistic to an environment that is compatible with our ordinary concept of community, one that fosters genuine symbiotic relations, such as those that sustain a democratic society. If respecting my neighbor would not lead to his increased respect for me any more than my disrespecting him would, why would we want to share interests and pool efforts? If no parent could forego his own pleasures when necessary to meet his children's needs, who would ever be nurtured into responsible adulthood?

As noted in the previous chapter, Alfred North Whitehead developed organism in our time as the general theory expressed by process philosophy. Whitehead initially gained recognition as the co-author of *Principia Mathematica* (1910-1913), with Bertrand Russell. In 1924 Whitehead accepted an American appointment as Professor of Philosophy at Harvard University. His books of this period, *Science in the Modern World* (1925) and *Religion in the Making* (1926), culminated in the philosophy outlined in *Process and Reality*. As the distinctive and integrative element of his philosophy, Whitehead posited a redefinition of nature—including God and humanity—as the cumulative and ongoing process of emergent new organisms. He denied the separation of mind and matter in natural entities at any level; mind is pervasive throughout nature, and always embodied in some way in all natural objects.

God is part of the mindedness of nature, according to Whitehead. Toward the conclusion of *Process and Reality,* he writes:

> God's role is not in the combat of productive force with productive force, of destructive force with destructive force; it lies in the patient operation of the overpowering rationality of his conceptual harmonization. He does not create the world, he saves it; or, more accurately, he is the poet of the world, with tender patience leading it by his vision of truth, beauty and goodness.

Whitehead yields ground on the absolute attributes of God that the Christian tradition guards so closely. By this means, Whitehead can reasonably believe in God's goodness in an imperfect world. In Whitehead's conception, God is limited in power, but not in goodness. God is not burdened with creating the human world in which we, the most advantaged creatures, can do the terrible things that we do to each other. Those theological absolutists who regard the evil we do as the result of our freedom must still account for an absolute God who created a world in which the gift of freedom is such a tragic and ironic favor. Ironically, divine creation *ex nihilo,* as conceived by the traditional defenders of Christendom, places God's majesty and power in exaggerated contrast to human abasement; yet, that very conception makes the high and mighty God the ultimate source of the evil of human sufferings that occur in the world.

According to Whitehead, God's purpose in the world is to bring all aspects of nature and humanity into a coherence of actualized values. God is not the process, but is an element in the process for maximizing all potentiality for increase in truth, beauty, and goodness. Process philosophy has the goal of explaining all actual organisms according to the widest possible empirical generalization. Nothing can be simply "left out" or glossed over. Although we may not arrive at a rational accounting for every last occurrence, we will acknowledge what is unaccounted for and avoid making generalizations that presuppose that we have accounted for them or that they do not matter. Our moral responsibilities as co-workers with God in the cosmic process require us to select those elements of value that are within our range of potentialities, and to seek to actualize those that lie within the "conceptual harmonization" that God urges upon the world. This is not a utopian dream or a mystical vision, but a purpose that we are able to achieve within our individual potentialities. We are destined to achieve not a perfect world, but a better one.

Human freedom consists in our capacity for decision. We cannot determine the nature of our choices because our world is already advanced in its process, both for better and worse. But we can choose from among the alternatives that are within our grasp at the time. Indeed, we must select from those possibilities that are before us, because we cannot go outside our own world of opportunities to actualize any potential other than our own. God does not impose absolute terms upon our actions or our moral choices, but he does provide the continuity that underlies our own critical and creative choices. Our freedom consists in the decisions we make.

Whitehead does not hold to the conventional description of religion as ritual, emotion and belief, which are all parts of our inherited cultural apparatus. We can involve ourselves in these conventional religious elements without ever reasoning about their particular or general value. In his brief but trenchant book *Religion in the Making,* Whitehead says, "Religion is what the individual does with his solitariness." For some readers these words suggest a gloomy, world-denying mystic in his cave brooding on the secrets of the universe. But within the context of Whitehead's system, this sentence suggests to me a person standing on the crest of the hill, his past behind him and his future ahead of him. He looks to the past behind him and asks, "What has happened to me already to prepare me to move into the future? As I look ahead, what in my past is most worth carrying forward into my future?" Nothing external prompts his answer, but only internal reasons, desires, hopes, and fears that will determine the decision he makes in his solitariness. All the people and events that have touched his life, both for good and for bad, are part of his past. Religion therefore offers credible and responsible hope for achieving symbiotic relations between peoples whose lives coincide.

When we look at the mechanical things we have made, such as waterwheels, clocks, and automobiles, it may be difficult to see any organic structure at all because we have intervened to rearrange and reconstitute the "natural" world, the raw materials, into mechanical things. We have used minerals and metals and plants to make the machines do what we want them to do; in that sense, the machines depend on us, the real organisms, who account for the material things. The machines become what they are through the multiple processes of interrelations of persons and our various functions, physical and mental.

This concept of togetherness makes an essential difference to all of the individuals concerned. It is always easier to see the connections between persons, because we interact more directly and obviously. When a person relates to a machine, it looks like a one-way relation, with the person making all the difference, and the machine doing what the person wants. But the relationship clearly becomes a two-way situation when we notice that the machine paces the person, as in the case of a power-operated treadmill. Surely, someone sets the treadmill at a certain speed, but the person using it will have to keep step with the machine. The more complex the machine, the more significant the interaction becomes. A computer will do only what it is programmed to do, and a person operating it must adhere to just that set of operations. We do not really relate to machines in the same sense that we do to persons. Rather we experience the machine as a surrogate for the persons who made it. But we need to respect the machine for what it is, and ourselves for the persons that we are.

The ways in which we relate to other particular entities—whether persons or machines—and with groups of all kinds determine how we get along in the world. Our dealings with machines must take into account the structures built into the machines. Our encounters with other persons must involve looking at them as individuals with all their subjectivity. On another level, our social environment also shapes our relationships: what does our world tell us about associating with that kind of person? What happens to us as a result of our taking a particular attitude toward one person or another? How can we deal with those expectations that our society places upon us and also create a relationship that is helpful to all who are involved?

These are not specifically religious questions, but fundamental to our understanding and achieving our religious possibilities. In America, at the end of a century full of advances in human relations, we enter another century within which even more progress can be made.

Organism and Relationship

Martin Buber (1858–1965) was a scholar of religion, psychology, and sociology who worked first in Germany and then in Israel. One of the early secular Zionists, Buber associated himself with the "cultural" wing of Zionism, rather than the "political" wing. For his academic dissertation, Buber chose to study the problem of individualism as it appeared in the writings of Nicholas of Cusa (1401–1464) and Jakob Boehme (1575–1624). Both of these early modern mystics examined the "foundation of the very personality ethics" that had inspired the later works of Schleiermacher in Germany and Emerson in America.

Buber's book *I and Thou* (1923, German; 1937, English) won him fame among both scholars and popular readers. This book powerfully influenced Protestant theologians. In the 1940s and 1950s hardly any seminary lacked some instruction in Buber's ideas. An informal subculture developed devoted to Buber's interpretation of the alienation of "modern man" from himself and his world. *I and Thou* can be forbiddingly difficult to read. Secularists commonly think it to be too religious, while religionists consider it too secular. To me, Buber's book concerns God or religion in only a marginal sense. Instead, I think *I and Thou* offers penetrating insight into how people live in a world populated primarily by machines and by people who have come to believe that they and their kin are also a type of machine. Buber, as an authentic prophet, sees into the fallacy of this assumption and seeks to offer an alternative.

These excerpts from his writings briefly summarize some of Buber's ideas.

> MODERN INDUSTRIAL SOCIETY
> Speaker, you speak too late. But a moment ago you might have believed your own speech; now this is no longer possible. For an instant ago you saw no less than I that the state is no longer led: the stokers still pile up coal, but the leaders only seem to rule the racing engines. And in this instant while you, you can hear as well as I how the engine of the economy is beginning to hum in an unwonted manner; the overseers give you a superior smile, but death lurks in their hearts. They tell that they have adjusted the apparatus to modern conditions, but you notice they can only adjust themselves to the apparatus, as long as that permits it. Their spokesmen instruct you that the economy is taking over the heritage of the state; you know that there is nothing to be inherited but the despotism of the proliferating It under which the I, the more and more impotent, is still dreaming that it is in command. ...
>
> Man's will to profit and will to power are natural and legitimate as long as they are tied to the will to human relations and carried by it. There is no evil drive until the drive detaches itself from our being; the drive that is wedded to and determined by our being is the plasm of communal life, while the detached drive spells its disintegration. ...
>
> To be sure, life takes its time about settling the score, and for a while one may still think that one sees a form move where of a long time a mere mechanism has been whirring.

Buber wrote these sentences immediately after the First World War, but they could fittingly have been written now, at the turn of the century. The market state which Buber described has little place for those who are diffident about acquisition of possessions. Individuals participate in the system only as far as they can pay their way. Such a society must be ready to dispose of those who cannot indulge in buying and selling activities. The manipulators of wealth have not accumulated their assets just to watch them siphoned off so that the wealthless can be maintained a little longer. Sooner or later, the obsolete or the never-arrived must be sacrificed so that progress and development can reward the fortunate one who still has some marketable value. Stalin's "single screws in the great machine" must be let go; they are no longer necessary for the operation of the social machine. As surplus machine parts, they are only waste. And, as the machine operators replaced the hand laborers, so a new set of manipulators of wealth will replace the old, who themselves have become obsolete. This mystical development of the market state has lost nothing essentially human because nothing essentially human had ever been part of its world. Only machines and their gears and their screws keeps the system grinding away, as Buber ironically described it.

American culture has so long and so thoroughly assumed that the human individual is naturally constituted on the atomic model that the system has effectively denied and negated an organic concept of society. The atomic–model assumption accentuates the acquisitive purpose of the individual, so that he or she is convinced that no human purpose transcends the gathering and hoarding of things. This motivation suppresses or romanticizes the purpose of achieving health, happiness, and freedom for all individuals. Other-worldly religion allows itself to tolerate possessive individualism because it has no basis for social values in this world. Our major religious tradition even allows itself to support acquisitive individualism and transforms greed into a virtue. Because the tradition posits that God rewards piety and greed with wealth and punishes rebellion and sloth with poverty, the poor and the wealthy are believed to deserve what they get from the economic system. Government exists only to preserve the system and to protect an individual's right to pursue wealth.

Its advocates regard the market-state that developed in Euro-American nations as the one and only proper system for all societies in the world. It is not just an economic system that some societies emulate, but it provides the model for the organization of total societies and imparts its own values to which other societies can conform. The market-states focus on creating a "global economy" on their own values, aware that less-developed and quasi-nations will become market states in time. Whatever organic concepts of individuals and society other people may have inherited from their ancestors, we have decided that they should all be molded into our atomistic image, with the wealthy few in charge of the poorer multitudes.

The world economy is rapidly separating the few with wealth to spare from the many in relentless poverty. Advances in computer technology have done nothing to bring the impoverished into the stream of commercial buyers or producers.

Indeed, unrestrained population increases in poor countries makes it unlikely that they can ever afford the levels of health and education required to bring them into the world of commerce. Current "progress" does not give priority to the inherent value of human individuals. Profit and power come only to those who can pay their way. The system that makes political and cultural assets available screens out the disadvantaged. The system of commerce and industry that promised heaven on earth for all can only provide life jackets for those few on the surface, while the rest are swamped in a foul sea.

The Dynamics of Persons and Things

The organic interactions between individual and individual form the basis of all societies, institutions, and cultures. Each society conceives and creates its economy according to its internal values. Because all societies are organic—whether or not its people know or want it to be so—the modern market state also operates as an organism. When the values associated with materialism and mechanism permeate the market state, the isolation of individuals from each other, the instrumental use of persons as though they were machines, and the subordination of human creativity and productivity to destructive competition take their course. This is what Buber calls the It-world. This world is neither physical nor geographic in itself, such as the animal world or the Asian world. But it is the counterpart to the Thou-world that persons create as they become authentic by means of their dialogue with each other. These two worlds in which people live are parallel structures to the two attitudes in which people can either connect or compete in the most fundamental sense. Buber writes:

> The world is twofold for man in accordance with his twofold attitude.
> The attitude of man is twofold in accordance with the two basic words he can speak.
> The basic words are not single words but word pairs.
> One basic word is the word pair I-Thou.
> The other basic word is the word pair I-It; but this basic word is not changed when He or She takes the place of It.
> Thus the I of man is also twofold.
> For the basic word I-Thou is different from that in the basic word I-It.

Buber believes that the individual has one island of freedom in the human deterministic sea of genetics and environment: the attitude. The person does not create himself or his surroundings, but the attitude he adopts toward others is both his gift and his burden. If he adopts the attitude of I-Thou, in which he respects the other as a human and therefore worthy of ultimate respect, he will engage in relationships with people that bestow the gifts of nurture and companionship. If, however, he adopts the attitude of I-It, he sets up alienation and isolation that can only result in mutual using. This I-It attitude allows the mechanization of humanity to grow and proliferate.

Because all societies are in fact, if not consciously, organic in structure, internal relations within a given society will affect everyone: whatever happens between any of its constituents will reverberate throughout all other members of the society. This is not magic or mysticism, just the commonplace workings of everyday life. The only good in a society comes from the good its people do, and likewise with evil. Societal institutions channel, transmit, and enhance individual and collective attitudes. And societal institutions cross-fertilize each other. There are vast differences between the attitudes adopted and transmitted by individuals and institutions within a society. They exist side-by-side and create tensions as they cooperate and collide. Thou-saying and It-saying may coexist in a family or in a community, because this attitudinal factor is the expression of individual freedom and collective consequences.

The life of dialogue that Buber advocates is the answer to the proliferation of alienated crowds. Dialogue involves people listening to each other with the intention of hearing what is spoken and unspoken and of responding with respect for what is expressed. Alienation, on the other hand, consists of an individual holding back within his or her perceived perimeter of selfhood and reaching out to other persons or things only to use them in ways that will maximize the advantage of that single selfhood.

Reciprocity in Dialogue

Buber writes:

> Relation is reciprocity. My Thou acts on me as I act on it. Our students teach us, our works form us. How we are educated by children, by animals. Inscrutably involved, we live in the currents of universal reciprocity.

…

> The basic word I-Thou can be spoken only with one's whole being. The concentration and fusion into a whole being can never be accomplished by me, can never be accomplished without me. I require a Thou to become; becoming I, I say Thou.
> All actual life is encounter.

This recalls the epigram, "We become like that which we see in others." Buber's conception of dialogue reinforces the truth of this statement. When we listen to the other respectfully, we will hear the overtones and the nuances that are present in that expression. However, when we listen not for the richness of the expression, but for the opportunity to gain some advantage over the speaker, we impoverish ourselves of some potential value. In the first instance, I want to be able to respond to you not superficially, but also beyond that, to the underlying meaning of what you say, so that you might expand your understanding more fully. In the second instance, my purpose is not to understand you, but to use you and what you have to say in some way that will advance my interest separately from yours. In each case, I am going deeper into the attitude that I have adopted. We assimilate into our daily commonplace activities the habits and dispositions that are coherent with our basic attitude. The issue is, What attitude will characterize life as a whole? What manner of being do I carry to others in whatever trivial or significant encounters we have?

But dialogue is only one of our ways of interacting with others. If it were our only way of perceiving, we would miss the objectivity of the other. We do not make the world by perceiving it. If a tree falls in the forest with no one to hear it, it does make a sound. If limbs, branches, and leaves fall to the earth or into the water, the collision of one thing with another will result in sound waves in the air, the raising of dust from the ground, or the making of waves in the water, regardless of whether any ears or eyes perceive those events. So the world around us in its personal and impersonal forms is open to our inspection. The commonplace world must be taken as it comes to us, or we will never know it. The people of our commonplace world must be seen from a distance before we can gain that mediated knowledge that we need of them. Our need for knowledge of people is not different because we habitually take an I-Thou attitude. My attitude does not make an instrument out of the one whom I encounter. But that Other has his or her own identity that I need to know and respect. Knowledge is not the enemy of respect, but is rather the key to the enhancement of the one respected. I need to know the

Other, whom I address as Thou, in order to appreciate the uniqueness and value of that Other.

Alternation of Attitudes

In knowing the Other, in addition to relating to the Other, we need to make use of science in all the ways that we can. We will not be able to serve the person as Thou in a natural and healthy way unless we grasp the details of that person's interconnectedness in the world. Buber writes:

> The unlimited sway of causality in the It-world, which is of fundamental importance for the scientific ordering of nature, is not felt to be oppressive by the man who is not confined to the It-world but free to step out of it again and again into the world of relation. Here I and Thou confront each other freely in a reciprocity that is not involved in or tainted by any causality; here man finds guaranteed the freedom of his being and of being.

The relation of I to Thou can sometimes be like that of a fascinated lover to the newly beloved. When that first bloom of attraction has opened with all its potential for acceptance, pleasure, and excitement, the details of the identity of the beloved are far from the lover's heart. As the relation ripens, there will be the discovery of more and more of the details, which can reinforce the infatuation or squelch it. So with the initial phase of I-Thou relation: no information is needed, only the thrill of mutual recognition. But information flows inevitably, and the fascination that has related with respect and regard for the Other can sort out the information and act in whatever way is appropriate. Sometimes the only way to preserve a profound commitment is to keep it within the bounds that are required by commitments to others. It is no betrayal of the quality of a relationship to observe the limitations that a complicated situation can present. It is indeed a mark of its authenticity when infatuation can mature into deep and lasting friendship.

The quality of the basic word I-It does not by necessity involve evil. It involves evil only when it is presumed to replace relationship with use. The person who serves another in some ways functions in a using capacity. The teacher may "use" a student or a group of students to find the most effective way of introducing difficult material for study. A physician may "use" a patient to test the effectiveness of a new procedure. Within the institutional and legal safeguards that presently exist, there are ethical and legitimate ways of both benefiting the present student or patient and also learning what will benefit others in the future. The test in such cases is whether or not the present student or patient is harmed or put at risk of harm by the procedure. As always the crucial question is the quality and continuity of respect with which the Other is regarded.

No one can function in society in a useful way without alternating between relating to others as persons and also in some way taking the user role with regard to others. We derive benefits and satisfactions from our sons and daughters, and we are tempted to call them "possessions." We exercise control over them as needed for their growth, and we are tempted to rob them of their potentiality for responsibility along the way. The insidious I-It tendency to own and rob persons who are vulnerable to our power and control comes from the social traditions that show us the model of interacting with machines. In the I-It attitude, we practice useful and efficient control over machines and find ourselves treating people, perhaps those who trust us most, as though we owe them no respect as persons of inherent value. We do not need to replace our using of machines with respect for them. We do, however, need to learn how to use machines more effectively to make life better for people who need what the machines can do. Organism is the natural state of humanity. Progressive inclusion of all people, present and future, within the boundaries of respect and nurture is the maturing of humanity. Overcoming barriers to sharing loving concern for all humanity is the function of human spirituality.

7

Religion As Relationship

THE YOUNG MAN I came to know as "Freddy" had been blind since puberty because of congenital syphilis. As a young girl, his mother had gone to a circus where she met a roustabout who seduced, impregnated, and infected her. She died when Freddy was a child because effective treatment was not then available. Freddy's maternal grandfather, a kind but simple man, reared Freddy. His grandfather saw Freddy's blindness as just one of the consequences of his daughter's careless waywardness. Blindness was just the first assault the infection had made on Freddy. The question was, would the rest of his body deteriorate before he lost his mental faculties? Freddy knew well enough that his organs were failing and that the disease had begun destroying his brain, affecting him with dementia.

Freddy and I had little in common superficially, but his intelligence and his skeptic's bravado intrigued me. I was a high school senior and a recent convert to evangelical Christianity. His hero was Robert G. Ingersoll, the notorious agnostic orator of the late-nineteenth century. Freddy devoured semi-serious philosophical literature, which he read in Braille and heard on recorded books. He had a large record collection of the music of Beethoven, his favorite composer. I made my first acquaintance with the "Ode to Joy" in Freddy's dark sitting room, where we sat listening to the choral climax as tears ran down Freddy's cheeks. I don't know whether I was more impressed with the music or with his response to it.

He had no time for despair. His bitterness had run its course. He seemed almost to enjoy the irony of not only being blind and slowly losing his mind, but also knowing that it was happening. I never pitied Freddy, but I admired him, even as he contradicted all of my orthodox religious beliefs. He had heard all the theological sophistry about his situation. He just could not escape the seriousness of it and retreat into an "acceptance of God's will," as religious dogmas would require him to. Somehow, I wanted to be his friend more than I wanted to convert him. My respect for him outweighed my confidence in the evangelical sophistry.

In time, Freddy had to withdraw from public activities, which he always enjoyed. He spent intervals in mental institutions, as his brain eroded. Finally, one day I came home from college and learned that he was in a local hospital, with his organ systems about to give out. I went to see him and sat by his bed. Lucid only at intervals, he would arouse and grasp my hand and say, "Who are you?" I would answer, "I'm Phil."

Then, "And who am I?" "You're Freddy."

Again, "Who are you?" "I'm Phil."

"And who am I?" You're Freddy."

Then silence, and then again and again the same antiphonal identity chant, until my voice yielded to sobs and he quietly drifted off to silence. He died a few days later. I learned that after I left he lay quietly until he died.

I was briefly his source of himself, at that beautiful and terrible moment when he drifted between knowing and unknowing. Weak reed that I was, I was all that he could grasp to believe that he was still himself. I believe that this is very close to the ultimate in the experience of relationship. I was not able to comprehend the total meaning of that event at the time, but I have come to reflect on it with deep appreciation for Freddy and what we meant to each other. All other relational events of my life branch off from that early complex event, because there I experienced an existential moment of identity in relation, the intensity of which has never quite been surpassed. But, the ingredients of mutual respect and trust remain the same in like moments of lesser intensity, whatever the specific significance of the event. I have found that it can happen to anyone who is open to it.

I had never know a blind person before Freddy, so in itself that was a new experience for me. But his personal complexity made his blindness seem almost irrelevant. He had the sharpest mind and the most developed intelligence of anyone I had known. We became friends in an offhanded way. Freddy sold snacks and drinks to the factory mill workers from a refreshment stand sponsored by the state commission for the blind. He earned a small income by his own efforts. I worked in our family business a few hours every morning before school began delivering our bakery goods to his and other such stores. We had a casual relationship before we became well acquainted.

In a short while, it became clear that Freddy and I had much more to talk about than we could ever find time for during our working relationship. So I began to come by after school to take Freddy home from his little store.

I was amazed that he could take such care of his business by himself. I learned that independence was a passion with him. He knew how far he could go on his own, and he accepted help when he needed it. He soon came to appreciate my leaving him alone as much as I did. I was too unfamiliar with blind people to know what to do to try to help him, so I waited for him to tell me. Later, I came to feel that part of his openness to me stemmed from my respect for his independence. I have come to understand him better in retrospect. He maintained his composure for a long while, despite knowing what was happening to his body and mind. I now think that his determination to be as independent as possible kept him focused on his autonomy, and that gave him a purpose in life. His self-control intensified his inner strength and turned his intelligence away from bitterness.

Was Freddy religious? Not that I could recognize. But, was he spiritual? That is a different question, and one not so easily denied. Freddy displayed an authentic spirituality in his qualities of courage, integrity, and regard for others. It was as genuine in its human source as the spirituality of saints, which is generally considered supernatural in origin. Freddy made a creation of his life. He shared his pleasures of body and mind with a wide circle of friends, frequently keeping his associates distant from each other. My time with Freddy rarely overlapped with his visits with others. Freddy seemed to save a comfortable place for me, and I sensed not to pry into other parts of his life. Still, Freddy had a remarkable gift of connecting with a wide range of people. He could discuss books and debate ideas without condescending.

Freddy's remarkable sense of irony and dark humor has come to remind me of the Stoic philosophers, such as Marcus Aurelius. Despite his chaotic life, Freddy maintained the equilibrium of a desert mystic. In his final moments of lucidity, he expressed no bitterness at fate or vengeance against those who had sentenced him to a slow, degrading death. He affirmed life and enjoyed what he could of it. Open to the lives of others, Freddy rejoiced with them in good times and consoled them in bad times. Never mean-spirited or disrespectful to others, he reserved his recriminations for himself.

Can there be genuine spirituality in the absence of religion? Can religion be genuine without spirituality? The many "spiritual aids" advertised in the religious media indicate the popularity of promoting spirituality among the already religious populace. But an abundance of material on spirituality shows little if any affinity for institutionalized religion. S. J. Zinnbauer and K. I. Pargament, lead investigators for a study published in the *Journal for the Scientific Study of Religion,* report a trend toward treating spirituality as independent of or even inimical to Christendom. I tend to treat spirituality very lightly because the current usage of the word has too much ambiguity to make it relevant to me. I see the need for a term that can refer to a human experience of profound and pervasive meaning arising out of human relationships and involving empirical expression of loving care. Our human spirit generates the special quality that emerges in what Martin Buber calls the I-Thou relation.

Imagination can transcend the human spatio-temporal context and make the spiritual connection between one individual and any number of others, near or distant, past or present. Mozart's melodies and Shakespeare's sonnets arise from the same aspect of the human mind that can generate spiritual moments laden with all the superlative values that are conventionally prized as religious. Those who are open to loving care for others will share these experiences, whether or not they think that they emanate from a nonhuman source. The individual human spirit has the inner life and power to find others like itself with whom to share the deeper and wider companionship that fulfills our lives. This is the "communion of like-minded people." Spirituality is neither magical nor mysterious—we can experience it as we cut through the man-made distinctions that separate us. We need to work earnestly and imaginatively to build the structures, systems, and material frameworks that will support, not degrade, the spirituality borne of our humanity.

Two Kinds of Dependency: Darkness and Slavery

At this point, we will compare and contrast the story of the blind and deaf Helen Keller as she emerged from darkness and related it in her autobiography, *The Story of My Life,* with the personal emergence from slavery described by Frederick Douglass in his *Narrative of the Life of Frederick Douglass.* The dependency of Helen upon her teacher, Anne Sullivan, closely parallels the dependency of the slaves upon the slaveholders. In both cases, the dependent one exists in nearly total isolation from the world, except as interpreted by the one depended upon. Helen depends for her understanding of the world upon Anne's hand signals. Similarly, the slave is dependent upon the master to interpret the world to him through the reports that he gives through words and actions. The one depended on provides the conceptual framework in which the other one conceives the world and also develops a self-image. In the case of Helen and Anne, the result was Helen's liberation and thriving as a whole person, and the gradual withering of the dependency. The case of the slave and the master resulted in confusion, terror, and self-degradation for the slave, with continuing dependency long after the slave had become aware of his bondage.

As the one upon whom Helen depended, Anne fulfilled her talent and expertise as a teacher. She charted and directed an educational and personal development regime for Helen that resulted in one of the outstanding triumphs over physical deficiencies ever made in any recorded life. Anne did something that no one had done until her time, and the public recognized her efforts, but mainly she earned the appreciation and honor of her pupil. Anne found a satisfying place in life for herself as she made possible a life for Helen. Helen's dependence upon Anne as compared with the results of the slave's dependence on the slave master contrasts as sharply as dependency's liberating effect upon Helen and the degradation of the slave.

During his dependence on his master, Douglass grew more determined to gain his freedom. Frederick Douglass gives a graphic picture of how dominance affected the wife of his master:

> My mistress, who had kindly commenced to instruct me, had, in compliance with the advise and direction of her husband, not only ceased to instruct, but had set her face against my being instructed by anyone else. It is due, however, to my mistress to say of her, that, she did not adopt this course of treatment immediately. She lacked the depravity indispensable to shutting me up in mental darkness. It was at least necessary for her to have some training in the exercise of irresponsible power, to make her equal to the task of treating me as though I were a brute.
>
> My mistress was, as I have said, a kind and tender-hearted woman; and in the simplicity of her soul she commenced, when I first went to live with her, to treat me as she supposed one human being ought to treat another. In entering upon the duties of a slaveholder, she did not seem to think that I sustained to her the relation of a mere chattel, and that for her to treat me as a human being was not only wrong, but dangerously so. Slavery proved as injurious to her as it did to me. When I went there, she was a pious, warm, and tender-hearted woman. There was no sorrow or suffering for which she did not have a tear. She had bread for the hungry, clothes for the naked, and comfort for every mourner who came within her reach. Slavery soon proved its ability to divest her of these heavenly qualities. Under its influence, the tender heart became stone, and the lamb-like disposition gave way to one of tiger-like fierceness. The first step in her downward course was in her ceasing to instruct me. She now commenced to practice her husband's precepts. She finally became more violent in her opposition than her husband himself. She was not satisfied with simply doing as well as he had commanded; she seemed anxious to do better. Nothing seemed to make her more angry than to see me with a newspaper....She was an apt woman; and a little experience soon demonstrated, to her satisfaction, that education and slavery were incompatible with each other.

Douglass writes his own first-hand perception from the perspective of an escaped victim after he had enjoyed some eight years in freedom. His graphic portrayal grew out of the seven years that he had lived with the wife, who had not been born to the slave system, and her husband, a longtime slaver. Douglass provides a rare glimpse of the degradation of a non-slaveholding white person who develops the more typical vicious character of a brutal slave master. As a result of her subservience to a cruel husband, this poor woman in her relationship to Douglass, her first slave, turns into the mirror opposite of Anne Sullivan in her tutelage of Helen Keller. Helen was dependent on Anne for her escape from darkness and into the world of words and conceptions, and Anne through her achievements finally won liberation from her own past insecurities. Physical and circumstantial limitations had distorted and stunted both of their personalities, but their relationship enabled them to blossom and grow into integrated health. They were free to be themselves and engage with other people creatively, because they were so productively engaged with each other.

As a free young woman, the slaver's wife had made her way in Baltimore as a weaver, and had grown to be the kind of person that Douglass initially describes. Later, however, acting the role of a brutal slave master to a raw and spirited lad, who was coming into his teens with a thirst for learning and freedom, gave her a test she was not able to meet. Douglass had a burning thirst for reading, and she began to teach him to read, until her husband discovered it and forbade her to continue. The resistance that Douglass presented to her fear of his reading next dominated her attention. She invested so much emotional energy in keeping him ignorant, and he persisted so intensely in his motivation to learn, that the adversary relationship eroded her composure. Douglass tells us that during these years he was able to glean and absorb a passing knowledge of language from association with white school boys in the neighborhood. He devised games with them that consisted of picking their brains for the correct spellings and markings to approximate reading and writing. If his mistress had found a way to help him, she might have become a lesser example of Anne Sullivan in her role as a teacher to Helen Keller. But for slavery!

Anne's accomplishments with Helen depended as much on Helen's latent human spirit as on Anne's latent pedagogical skills. What happened to the slave mistress also depended as much on the slave's human spirit as on the master's capacity for cruelty. The master could adopt the plantation ideology as a barrier to recognizing the humanity of the slave. But this did not extinguish the humanity and the thirst for freedom of the slave. The slave-master relationship they were locked in degraded them both. However, the slave had the advantage of being the victim whose resolve became sharpened by his ordeal. As a victim, the slave did not endure the erosion of selfhood at the core of his being. The slave had a life unseen by the master, in which he could nourish the remnants of selfhood without contradiction. What Socrates claimed must be as true for the slave as for anyone: It is better to suffer injustice than to inflict it, because the one who inflicts injustice makes himself unjust, and thus unfit for human respect. The slaves could find in their own people a community that nourished their humanity. Douglass recalled the comradeship that he felt with his fellow slaves:

> It is sometimes said that we slaves do not love and confide in each other. In answer to this assertion, I can say, I never loved any or confided in any people more than my fellow-slaves. ... I believe we would have died for each other. We never undertook to do anything, of any importance, without a mutual consultation. We never moved separately. We were one; and as much so by our tempers and dispositions, as by the mutual hardships to which we were necessarily subjected by our condition as slaves.

The slaves had Sundays free from field work and then generally occupied themselves with personal and family chores. Shortly before his escape to freedom, Frederick Douglass on Sunday afternoons in secret places acted as the only schoolteacher to a class of young friends. They had prevailed upon Douglass to teach them to read, which their masters had forbidden. Frederick Douglass says:

> I had at one time over forty scholars, and those of the right sort, ardently desiring to learn. They were all ages, though mostly men and women. I look back on those Sundays with an amount of pleasure not to be expressed. They were great days to my soul. The work of instructing my fellow-slaves was the sweetest engagement with which I was ever blessed. We loved each other, and to leave them at the close of the Sabbath was a severe cross indeed. ... And I have the happiness to know, that several of those who came to Sabbath school learned how to read; and that one, at least, is now free through my agency.

Brutality did not extinguish the human qualities of compassion and love that these people had for one another. How similar were these people, who were only a few generations away from their African origins, to those who endured death camps in modern Europe? Are there grounds for thinking that one group is very different from the other in moral quality? As in the death camps, so in the slave farms, we have to ask how the torturers can dare to suggest that their victims are the inferior ones and that they, the victims, are not deserving of moral honors?

Community and Nurture in Relationship

Helen and Annie led lives so intertwined that it is difficult to see where each stands alone. This posed a practical problem for people who had the responsibility for evaluating Helen as a scholar. When Helen applied to Radcliffe College, she was examined in Greek, German, Latin, and French, and Greek and Roman history. She answered without Annie's help in translation, but relied on another translator, who had learned the hand alphabet especially for Helen's special need. Annie had not learned all that Helen spoke and wrote through her, but the college took special measures to make sure that it was Helen who was being tested, and not her teacher. Their relationship is a paradigm of how relational values can displace mere instrumental values as life runs its course. They demonstrated how two people can work cooperatively and not competitively in all the petty chores of childhood and womanhood, and also in the refined and mature creative tasks that genius can undertake. They constituted a unique paradigm of community also, having begun their relationship as a journey on an uncharted sea, with the most fragile connection between them. Their mutual voyage together gave them the headings and destinations that they reached together and individually.

Helen's books, letters, and addresses have become part of her legacy, but the personality that she displayed to those who knew her publicly and privately became the more important part of that legacy. She developed into a whole person, becoming integrated as she passed through childhood to adolescence and to maturity. By the time she was twenty-four, she had taken on the responsibility of an adult in a fully sensate world: she had passed through the normal demands of the Radcliffe College curriculum. Anne accompanied her until examinations. The college insisted that she take her exams in conditions as near to ordinary as possible. The only concession the college made was to allow for additional time for the manual translations that had to be made.

In her adulthood, Helen adopted an esoteric religion, Swedenborgianism, and also political socialism, both of which she ardently promoted. Some suspected that others had simply manipulated her into making these commitments, but she wrote her advocacies in such original and lucid language that any subterfuge seems unthinkable. Her major project in life was the education of the impaired, particularly the blind and deaf. As a founder and chief spokesperson for the American Foundation for the Blind, she traveled the continents to persuade people that the impaired need only to be educated to be self-sufficient and productive. Few Americans have done more to bring impaired persons into the mainstream and demonstrate their potential than Helen Keller. She dealt with her problems and integrated those circumstances into her life in such a way as to realize a coherence among the commonplace activities, the intellectual requirements, and the emotional richness of a full life.

Traditionally, organized religions have centered around concepts of God, the morality of obedience, and identity in a belief-sharing group. People do not ordinarily make conscious decisions about their attitudes, and so they do not connect religion with their attitudes. But, because we are free to control our attitudes, we must ask upon what are those attitudes based. Religious beliefs guide and shape the decisions we make about our attitudes and thus help to determine whether we will stand in the relation of person to person, as I-Thou, or person to thing, as I-It. The attitude of person to person engenders a relationship of autonomy and respect, as well as nurture and mutual dependence. This fulfills the religious urge for togetherness and also promotes the valuing of individuals by each other. The relationship of Helen and Anne is a model of the person-to-person attitude. Their relationship gave them both autonomy and dependence. The togetherness they shared made both their lives richer than either would have been alone. No doubt, the process of building up those attitudes was an unconscious process for them. If Anne had seen the rebellious child Helen as demon possessed, the story would have ended quickly and tragically. Apparently Anne's sordid childhood had given her inner strength and sympathy in ample measure that enabled her respect for her pupil. What looks like a miracle from the outside is really an open secret of nature, like that of children speaking the same language as their parents.

Religion As Relationship

Religion understood as relationship will necessarily promote the values involved in sharing everyday life. Two values take prominence: respect and tolerance. These values are appropriate for all the ordinary relationships of life, with other values to be introduced as special relationships require. Any relationship, however transitory or insignificant, will need to be based on respect and tolerance. We cannot achieve a personal relationship with anyone for any purpose, however functional and limited that purpose may be, without mutual respect and tolerance. More specialized and intrinsic relationships may include such values as love and loyalty, but respect and tolerance will still be relevant. These values have wide relevance to all cases of relationship, while other values will be relevant to a narrower range of relationships, such as companionship and familial relations.

The qualities that I am here calling values would be called virtues if I were looking at religion in terms of dominance and submission. But from the perspective of religion as relationship, I will call these values attitudes or habits, because I want to emphasize the commonplace level of the arena in which religious qualities apply to life. I have purposely not used the word "love," because I would reserve that word for something more intimate and distinctive. Besides, are we going to say we "love" all those with whom we pool our votes in elections, whatever our differing interests are? But how crucial that we should manifest respect and tolerance for all these people and groups of people! Is there a better reason for the existence of religious faith than that we may live among people who have respect and tolerance for each other?

I propose that respect and tolerance are more appropriate qualities for our attitudes toward nature and humanity as a whole. It perhaps would be healthy to reserve the word "love" in any connection until we have adequately attuned ourselves to respect and tolerance. Companions, parents, colleagues, neighbors, siblings, all might be better prepared to relate to each other as persons who are good for each other, if we gave more serious concern to these values of respect and tolerance before we say "love" again.

To talk about "loving" our bus driver or letter carrier is fatuous. How much more fatuous is it to say we "love" our neighbors, since many of us are well insulated from them. And are those of another color or class less our neighbors just because they live in another part of town?

Looking back at our relationship example, Helen Keller and Anne Sullivan, we see how respect and tolerance formed the basis for their togetherness, even as that togetherness expanded to fill so much of both their lives. It might be thought that Helen used Anne, although during their early years Anne heard accusations that she was using Helen for her own purposes, for fame and for money. As their lives are recalled by themselves and by others who knew them, it becomes clear that they needed and served each other. Helen needed a teacher like Anne, and Anne needed a pupil like Helen. They shared a unique and significant relationship: unique in that we seldom see two people endure for so long in productive harmony under such strenuous circumstances, and significant in that their relationship shows so clearly and delineates so fully the results of nurturing human interactions.

Neither Helen nor Anne would have said that their relationship was in any sense "religious," and especially nothing mystic or supernatural. But precisely the opposite. The religiousness of their relationship lay in living in harmonious togetherness in a mutually fulfilling relationship. This is a worldly, reality-based religion. No supposed "other" world is involved. No other kind of life is conceived except the gritty, arduous one that Helen and Anne knew so well. They knew each other as persons and lived in exemplary dialogue. For them, and for us, this is the real world.

Relationships happen only between individual living organisms. No machine ever accomplished the creativity that resulted from the relationship between Helen Keller and Anne Sullivan. The striving of the organism to maintain life, and its ability to gather its failing energy into one mighty expression when at the margins of life is a marvelous thing. Freddy was doing that in my last moments with him. I hope he was easy with himself as a result. It would have been fatuous to have tried to talk about "religion" with Freddy at that time. What happened there had the essence of one true version of religion: life's urge to find its very own reflection in the presence of another.

There is another urge, the need to set oneself apart from the other. I reverence them both. Many names have been given to these primal tendencies, and much championing of one against the other. But I believe that in each of these tendencies lies a valid human function. To consciously set oneself apart to make decisions is necessary so that the individual person can be a creator of real personal value, and that this personal value is not merely the reflection of someone else.

The other propensity, to associate with another on the grounds of essential identity, expresses our inherent personal value just as truly as the other. This satisfying urge, or need, for recognition in the eyes of another like ourselves, is one of the fruits of constructive religion. For instance, the Buddhists relate how their Teacher felt himself plunged into an ocean of compassion when he saw for himself the sick and poor and the suffering of his fellow creatures. Jews remember the story of Ruth and Naomi, whose mutual widowhood joined them together in their perpetual dependence on the kindness of their countrymen. When a wealthy man befriended and provided for them, the Mosaic law of the Gleaners brought them a portion of his harvest. In Matthew's Gospel, Jesus taught Christians to "Go and be reconciled to your brother, and then come and make your offering." In all these cases, the religious impulse answers the need for togetherness. God inheres in the relationship of mutual respect and dependence of one on another in human unity.

The triumphalistic form of Christianity places slight value on reconciliation and togetherness. It has become mired in the ancient struggle for salvation in another world, or in a value system that places priority on abstractions. The earthly immediacy of living experience that characterized its origins has been crusted over with mystical formulae for soliciting God's interventions for salvation from divine judgment. This form of Christianity tells people that the same God who created them as prone to the sin of disobedience is also the God who now condemns them for their sins and further is the God who offers them salvation in exchange for obedience. The authority of God's present surrogates rests on revelations based on the claims of the ancient writings. When our ancestors held these religious beliefs as a part of their identity in families and communities, and neither leaders nor followers knew what we know about nature and humanity, this might have been allowable. Now, however, as understanding and assimilation are made possible by recognizing the natural world as the home of humanity, it is different. We have nothing to lose and everything to gain by taking seriously the possibility of religion as a ground for relations between persons. If God is such as the apostles and theologians have said, then there is no reasonable basis for hope for anyone, because they all proclaim their God's vengeance on every one else, which includes all of us. But if God is such as the prophets of compassion and justice proclaim, then our best service to such a God is devotion to one another. In either case, the better course for mortal persons is responsible interdependence. The inherent equality and unity of humanity are the only reasonable basic religious ideals.

Triumphalism or Dialogue?

The human community is a living organism, whether the community is as small as a tribe or a neighborhood, or as large as a nation or empire. The larger the community, the more diverse and the less unified it is likely to be. We usually try to look at communities with respect to both their size and unity but sometimes even the smallest community, such as a family, may be deeply divided, while at some points in its history, a whole nation may have remarkable unity. Whether a community is large or small, a correlation exists between its functional effectiveness and its degree of unity. Although we like to think that a high degree of unity will also mean a high quality of life, this is not necessarily so.

Nazi Germany had a high degree of cultural unity and functional effectiveness. The quality of life for those in highest authority must have seemed to be excellent. Their intellectual level resulted in some remarkable achievements, such as in rocket technology, but plummeted to abysmal depths in other researches, such as the spurious genetic experiments of Dr. Mengele. Technology took precedence over understanding of humanity as the nation maintained itself at the level of a predatory beast. The Nazis did not think that they were simply alienated from Jews; instead, the Nazis believed the Jews, the Romanies (the Gypsies), and other "undesirables" were not human. The Nazis killed Jews not because of differences with the individual Jew, but because of the separation they saw between themselves and all Jews. The Nazi basis for separation was like the separation of whites and blacks into masters and slaves.

The Nazis had a very effective culture for waging genocidal war. That it was almost suicidal in its outcome was not the fault of its military organization. Had the Nazis won, they could have carried out their various programs of territorial expansion and racial purification to a far greater extent. The Southern Confederacy could also have won the Civil War and spread the slave system to the Pacific Ocean and perhaps to Central America. The South's united military culture could possibly have prevailed had it not lacked human and material resources.

Notable historians argue about the macroscopic levels of cultural strengths and weaknesses. I am content to grapple with the ground-level issues of culture, our assumptions about our human and natural environment, and to inquire into the health or sickness of the culture we now inhabit. The increasing distance between the rich and powerful and the poor and powerless in America is based on the belief that there is no foundation for real unity in our society. We can see the self-destructive results of social separation and hyperindependence. The separation is itself a conceptual contradiction. The rich are in fact not separated from the poor, except by a veneer of symbols of wealth and privilege. People who are wealthy are still subject to the poverty of inner life that afflicts others who are less wealthy. Material things cannot substitute for harmonious relationships. The powerful may control some of the outward circumstances governing the lives of the poor, but the poor can learn enough to resist those controls. The rich may resort to violence to control the powerless, but the efforts of the wealthy will become self-defeating if pursued to the end. The poor can destroy the peace of the wealthy with violence and weapons that the wealthy would never think to use.

A family or a tribe or a nation that separates its social whole into fractional parts eventually suffers this fate. If a family or a nation falsely believes that its parts, its individual members or inner groups, are so independent of each other that one can prosper while the others perish, then the delicate fabric that sustains the quality of life of all the parts will be shredded. No amount of activity and vanity can mask the loss of quality that comes with alienation of the parts from each other.

Americans face two major social problems in the future: the alienation of our white majority from the nonwhite minorities and the growing concentration of wealth in the hands of a shrinking percentage of our people. Commercial propaganda exaggerates the correlation of wealth and whiteness, as well as color and poverty; to be white and wealthy is morally good, and to be nonwhite and poor is morally bad. People with comfortable incomes disproportionately hold these views. However, nonwhite people who lack comfortable incomes know from firsthand experience how much difference the money and color questions make to those who do not have those things. It is sheer hypocrisy to downplay the importance of color in attaining positions of wealth and advantage.

Triumphalist Christianity has stood too long and too firmly for the position that the poor are simply undeserving. The scandal of hungry, sick, and poorly housed children, white and nonwhite, in America, remains our family secret. We acknowledge this injustice now no more than our Southern ancestors acknowledged the injustice they did to the slaves or the victims of Jim Crow a century and more ago. Our churches make the salvation of souls a matter of tearful concern, but leave the health of other people's children the sole responsibility of their own parents, no matter what their conditions of life.

Neo-Puritan Christians place high legal costs on sexual dissidence but regard gender discrimination and abuse as a private affair for spouses and employers. Crusades are mounted to promote male dominance and to criminalize abortion and contraception, but education for sexual responsibility and gender equality would be forbidden if the Neo-Puritans gained sufficient political power to do so. Greed and avarice have become virtues instead of vices, with some triumphalist churches offering promises of prosperity in exchange for gifts of money. Tax policy has become a political football with which politicians can promise to return most of "your hard-earned money back to the taxpayers," no matter what requirements of education, health care, and nutrition go underfunded. The Christian Coalition offers voters' guides to triumphalist churches to urge their members to vote for politicians who promise to cut capital gains taxes and reduce welfare spending.

Although the triumphalist cause rides a wave of political and media power, they are not receiving the response that they would get if the general public were favorably impressed with their programs. They make advantageous use of technological communications to simulate a general alarm, but the effect is the "sounding brass and the tinkling cymbal." Most Americans will answer affirmatively if asked generally if we believe in God, but when matters of traditional doctrines that are "fundamentals of the faith" are mentioned, the answers change drastically. Americans do not want homosexuals and unmarried mothers put in stocks and stoned. Nor do we believe that divorce and remarriage should be a bar to public trust and prominence. We believe overwhelmingly that our best chance for an educated populace is public education. We would rather tolerate some salacious entertainment on the margins of our attention than outlaw whatever a narrow definition of decency considers "dirty."

Religion in the next century can be an asset to Americans who want our country to be a society that is a good place for all of us, including our least advantaged. Faith can also inspire those who want nurturing and rewarding relationships, in public and private settings that are compatible with our personal values. Before the tide of triumphalism rises higher, American churches must provide our nation with the "Jesus Solution" to which I referred earlier. The churches owe us that kind of foundation for beliefs that give us hope for the enhancement of our lives and of our society. Within diverse groups and gatherings of wholesome people we can find ground for the common pursuits of our interests. Never before has there been a time of so much opportunity for sharing our ideas and aspirations with people of all sorts, in all places. We can define our "American dream" as the community in which we care for and respect each other and go on to extend our neighborhood to the whole world.

8

Religion and Race

"Why should we save your dirty white skins?"

The words hit me like a bucket of cold water. They came from a young, handsome black minister. His voice was quiet and flat in contrast to his words. He might have been answering my question about where he went to college. I had made what I thought was a very perceptive remark, something like, "It seems to me that American colored people have a great opportunity to tell the new African nations how good democracy has been for you." I expected that he would be pleased that I was aware that the Europeans in the early 1950s had loosened their ties on their African colonies. His words blew a gaping hole in the screen of plantation mentality that had hidden the black world from me. The minister's searing answer has stayed with me as I passed through many stages of growth in my understanding of its meaning.

The attitude behind his unexpected comment has puzzled me. Did he only mean to chide me for presuming that American democracy had been an unmixed blessing for his people? Or, did he have an instant premonition that sometime in the unpredictable future of the world's affairs it would be dangerous to be a white citizen of one of the former colonial powers that have exploited and brutalized dark-skinned people all over the world? Either of these possible interpretations of his reply is very disturbing.

Part of my shock at my black colleague's remark was his startling antagonism toward what I am, a *white* person! I was used to the language that says "white" means the good, the right, the best. Any other use of "white" sounded foreign or, worse, like a curse that no decent person would ever utter. My whole outlook on life was based on the assumption that there are the "real people," meaning those of us who are "white," and then there are the "colored people," who inhabit a different reality from us. The whole culture of my native Southland rested on that use of language. Although at that moment I was sitting in an institution and in a city that was far from that southern culture, it was still deeply embedded in my consciousness, and even more deeply in my subconscious. My shock must have been evident from my silence. I have no memory of any response to him. Yet I have never forgotten what he said.

Many years later in an entirely different context, I had another revelatory encounter about my skin color with a nonwhite person. I was talking about skin tones with a college teacher colleague of Punjabi ancestry, whose parents had migrated from India to America when she was a child. She mentioned that members of her family have several shades of the cafe au lait, a skin tone that gave her remarkable beauty. My colleague revealed that one of her cousins has skin as pink as my own inherited Anglo-Celtic complexion. I suppose that sometime, somewhere, a representative of the British raj had introduced to her ancestors the gene for pink skin, which had shown up in a random instance.

I always considered my inclusion in the Caucasian race as simply a matter of having a particular color skin. Being white in the South carried many connotations, social and racial. I had given little thought to my own whiteness, while I had given long and distressing thought to racism. My East Indian friend said to me: "But you aren't white. You are pink! When you look into a mirror, hold across your face a plain white paper, and you will see that you are not white like the paper at all, but just a rosy pink."

What, me, pink? I could not contradict her and insist that I am simply "white." The next morning, I tried her experiment and, surely enough, I saw skin not "white" like the white piece of paper, but a patch of ruddy, off-pink skin bequeathed to me by my Welsh and Irish ancestors. So, why do we call it white, this skin of ours? And what is this "whiteness" that we happily take so much for granted, but which other people find so maddeningly hateful?

Can it be, I thought, that I really am a person "of color"? Not very much color, and not a very desirable color. Certainly not the rosy pink cheeks that I have seen on my infant sons and daughters. What are you to think when you realize that you have been calling yourself something that you are not? Either you are fooling yourself, or someone is fooling you. At long last, I conclude that it is some of both. I was taught to say "white" when referring to myself and people like me, who talk and live as I do. This did not accurately describe my skin tone, nor did it have anything at all to do with something intrinsic to myself, even as much or as little as my name. Instead, it set me in a category of humanity that marks itself by what it denies to others: privileges, merit, status. My Euro-American ancestors made a social artifact out of "whiteness," and that was what made me who I am. My "whiteness" is shorthand for saying that I belong to a certain group of people, and that I claim my rights on that basis. It means that when another group of people are called "colored," that designation has little to do with the tone of their skin, but everything to do with the way they are deprived of the rights that I claim for myself. Dr.

Vidya Singh Gupta inadvertently afforded me a revelation that day. That revelation, and the consternation that has erupted from it, has revealed to me some of my feelings about skin color, and the meaning of color and privilege, as well as the feeble state of my own moral accountability.

When I try to combine the remarks of my black fellow seminar student and my mocha teacher colleague, I get a special sense of my "whiteness." I have been privileged beyond any calculation by my skin color. It fixes me inevitably as a "white" person in a society in which this is a nearly absolute advantage. But it also establishes me as a part of the group that is accountable for the ideas and beliefs that give me advantages that I do not deserve, and thereby deprive my neighbors of opportunities that they deserve.

I am sure that the social artifact that we call whiteness has been with us for a long time. But I was far along in my lifetime before I became aware of just what it means.

In the class structure of American life, triumphalism presents a sharp contradiction, both sides of which we affirm. On one hand, we claim to be a society of people who are created equal and, on the other, we have a dominant class, the WASPs, who lay claim to the primary privileges. The Merriam-Webster Collegiate Dictionary defines the WASP individual:

> An American of Northern European and especially British ancestry and of Protestant background; a member of the dominant and most privileged class of people in the U.S.

In the triumphalist version, the WASP identity is associated with our "standard" dominant American class, even though in the Constitution, we are committed to the ideal of "We the People." This contradiction was not recognized in our colonial days, but it has become inescapable in modern times. The tension between a dominant WASP class and "We the People" is now being tightened, particularly as the Congress and the courts roll back some of our civil rights gains.

When we call a segment of our population "dominant," we have a false conception that this is a benign dominance, that our white aristocrats, in Jeffersonian spirit, are really looking out for everyone. This conception does not take into account the vast inequalities between the highest and the middle and lowest economic strata of our population. This inequality is no secret to Americans, nor is it unknown that political power follows economic status. There are many books, such as Andrew Hacker's *Money*, devoted to the exposition of these facts. Garrison Keillor made a pregnant suggestion when he remarked in a radio monologue that we are approaching the time when we will be a nation made up of two hundred billionaires and two hundred million peasants. When we assent to the idea that we can be a democracy as consumers at the same time we are a peasantry as earners, we fool no one but ourselves. The rich know how they got that way and how to stay that way: by using their economic advantage to increase their privileges through exploiting the tax laws, the political process, and the public media.

The triumphalist has assumed that some human individuals can achieve victory over all the rest. The "winner" of every engagement is the "one" who prevails in an all-out struggle with the others. Every individual or society strives above all else to do just that. In this spirit the Apostle Paul says, "Do you not know that in a race all the runners compete, but only one receives the prize? So run that you may obtain it"(1 Cor. 9:24).

Such competition is not simply the substance of informal children's or adult games, which can no doubt be invigorating and wholesome. However, we are all aware of the overzealous contests in which people intend to separate one single individual or group from the rest and call that one the "winner," implying that all the rest are "losers." Instead, the real winners in these games are those who have been taught and acculturated to seek to raise the quality of the performance of all the contestants by the test of one against others. This kind of competition can work for the social good, with no denigration of any kind.

However, competition that entails "victory by reduction of the other" works for the debasement of not only those who are not winners, but also those who are winners. The latter lose what others might gain and contribute to the good of all. Those who have lost in one contest may indeed be the very ones who could help those who have won when the situation changes so that a different criterion defines the winners and losers. Being divided into groups as fictitious as "losers" and "winners" works to weaken the very ties that enable individuals and groups to strive for larger accomplishments. Competition is a useful but sharply limited basis for achieving higher performance. It can take on the aura of life-or-death importance when it is elevated above relationship. The triumphalist's attitude in religion seeks to vanquish other religions as though it is in his or her interest to denigrate them.

Social Racism

Racism comes in several forms, but the most powerful form appears in the systemic, pervasive attitude that permeates a culture. My family shared a social racism with our southern ancestors and neighbors. We believed in "racial harmony," which meant that white people were supposed to dominate our world, and colored people were supposed to be submissive in that world. This is a remnant of plantation ideology. The domination of one category of people over another was taken for granted. Men dominate women, priests and preachers dominate laypeople, officials dominate citizens, and white people dominate nonwhite people. These attitudes had been taken as "natural" for generations and for centuries. Only a complete outsider could question the domination of one racial category by another. There is good evidence that this same belief was strong, if not predominant, among nonwhite people. Black people who rose up to question that belief, such as Frederick Douglass and W. E. B. du Bois, found that their greatest difficulty was not in fighting overt white racism, but in trying to rid their black kinsmen of the effects of slavery, and getting their brothers to realize that they had not deserved either slavery or its consequences.

One of my sharper childhood memories concerns the feelings of a young colored woman who "helped" Mother with housework in our modest home, which meant that she did most of it, and all of the more disagreeable parts. One time when I was about four years old, Mother told her to wash me after I came in from playing. She was a kind and gentle young woman, hardly more than a girl, who treated me most cordially. In the course of her washing my arms and legs, I noticed that the color of my skin changed from dark to white, but that the color of her skin remained dark, even though she was being washed by the same soap and water that removed the dirt from me.

I must have referred to the fact that the water didn't seem to change the black of her skin to white, as it did mine. She broke into sobs but tried to continue what she was doing. Mother came to the sink and asked what was wrong. The girl did not respond, so Mother asked me directly and I told her what I had said. Mother took me into another room and explained to me that the girl's skin had a different color from ours, that it was not dirty, and that I should never, ever use the word "black" to her or any other colored person. Tears welled in Mother's eyes as she told me that it hurt their feelings to be called "black," and that she could not bear to have me hurt one of them.

A four-year-old boy absorbs words that bring tears to the eyes of his mother. During the era of "black power" in the United States, I learned to use the word "black" instead of "colored," but at first it deeply pained me to do so. I have since learned to say "black," and I hope in the right times and places.

Many of us who grew up in the Jim Crow South, whether we were on one side or the other, have tried to deal with the implications of racism in all its forms. What we, black and white, have in common is that we did not choose to be born into a racist society, nor did we choose which side we would inhabit. No one "deserves" to be black or white. With rare exceptions, such as light-complected blacks who can be taken for "white," we cannot choose which "color" we are. So, we need to find our best understanding of ourselves and each other, and do what we can with what we have.

Social racism erects an invisible but effective boundary. On one side of that boundary is the "American Dream," a mythic hope and opportunity for improvement in the pursuit of happiness. Traditionally, white people, especially white people of gentile and northern European ancestry, occupy the good and right side of that boundary. The other side of that boundary, the wrong side, is the place for people of mixed and changing categories. African-Americans have almost always been on that side, and at times so have some Jews and Catholics. Orientals were on the wrong side until very recently. Generally, people of dark skin were assumed to be there, along with those white people who had not yet been acculturated to acquire property.

Social racism supports popular approval of the attitude of scorn that is heaped upon those who are on the poorer, weaker side by those who are less poor and weak. This scorn usually arises from a sense of one's own unworthiness and represents a refuge from self-deprecation. "I need someone to look down on" is the unspoken motivation behind the scorner's attitude. But that attitude can linger beyond self-defensiveness and become a well-worn assumption that the poor are really weak and foolish. Although this attitude is almost universally associated with social racism, it affects relationships not only of white toward black by race, but also almost always it affects male feelings toward female and feelings of the wealthy toward poor of all races. Abuse or hurt through exploitation of weakness of whatever kind results in a real enough injury. But when that abuse also expresses scorn, it is doubly hurtful. Ironically, being scorned by a person of superior status usually increases the sense of unworthiness on the part of the person so scorned. It is as though the superior status entitles the scorner to define the victim of his scorn, and to assign blame to that victim for the scorn. And the scorner may be unaware that the victim of his attitude incorporates it as self-hatred and feels it well deserved.

In human dynamics this ramification of scorn represents the other extreme from organic nurture. As the recipient of caring and support of growth replicates these attitudes and inculcates and extends them, so does the victim of shame adopt and extend it among those scorned. Children come to think of themselves as unworthy when raised by scornful parents, women come to think of themselves as responsible for their man's abuse, and those scorned for color or status come to believe that they deserve exclusion from economic and political processes.

People tend to think of themselves according to their parents' status. We absorb the "ways" of our "kind" at home and in the familiar surroundings of childhood. In an oversimplified way, our language, including our colloquial and familial accents, is our destiny. We learn to accept our social status as we do our name and gender. It would be as unlikely for us to feel guilty for being white in a society in which it is bad to be black, as it is would be for us to feel guilty for having our names or genders. How can we feel responsible for being born to whom we are?

Many white people of the South, and of America generally, find it disconcerting whenever they are confronted with a show of black anger, such as that my black classmate displayed. What would it be like to feel guilty about our name or gender? The analogy would be a case of mistaken identity, in which a person bearing my name had wronged someone who then found my address and came to take revenge. I would respond with anger because I was being unjustly accused and threatened for no action of my own. But my response would not lessen the hurt suffered by the person who sought revenge. He might even feel some relief after he had injured me, using me as a substitute for his enemy. Just striking back at some semblance of his attacker might seem in order to him. But, indeed, if I have him arrested and confined, his real enemy will go free, and the victim will suffer again.

The invisibility of social racism makes us all vulnerable to hurt that we do not deserve. Those of us who are white do not see the injustice in the slavery, segregation, and degradation of African-Americans throughout our history. We are not likely to see any connection between our own prosperity and their poverty. We know that poor people exist, and that it hurts to be poor, but we do not feel guilty for our own prosperity, especially when we notice how much trouble we can have despite our supposedly prosperous lives.

Our complacency forms part of the silent, invisible boundary that reinforces our belief that we are on the right side, and that it is not our problem that there are people on the other side. Further, when we learn that there is such a boundary, and that it is not a natural thing like rain but a product of human decision and action, we hear it as an accusation of our guilt. But as yet we feel no guilt—perhaps some minor shame, but little specific guilt.

Slaves Are Not Immigrants

How far does the immigrant experience differ from the slave experience? How much does the system of involuntary servitude, in which every black person is a slave and no white person is a slave, prepare the black person to become an independent, self-supporting person? How is it possible that the descendants of Africans brought to America in chains can have come so far despite such constraints?

Social racism largely results from the persistent white American misperception that black Americans somehow occupy the same position as that of descendants of immigrants like the English, German, or other Europeans. This is not and never was the case. We ask, "Why can the African not do as the others did, and become self-sufficient and independent as did other immigrant groups who came in poor and needy?" The answer is that the Africans who got here before the Civil War were in no sense immigrants, and under the circumstances, could never act as though they were. Immigrants possess some characteristics that slaves could not have, despite the fact that they and their descendants were eventually legally freed.

Immigrants who have populated America have typically been in a very special situation. Most of them have come from Europe or the Middle East, and lately from Asia. In this century, some Africans have entered as immigrants, and not as slaves. During the early centuries of westward movement to America, immigrants had a purposefulness or reasons of their own for wanting to come to America. Some were pushed by bad circumstances in the old country, and some were pulled by expectations of opportunity in the new country. But they had a purpose in making the change, a purpose that they could believe in. They made sacrifices to accomplish the move. Immigrants endured hardships and loneliness in order to find new homes and lives for themselves and their children.

Many immigrants met with disappointments and hostility in their new land. They took their meager resources and found what congenial group of "landsmen" they could to soften the shock of a new and unfamiliar culture. Most immigrants spent a generation in a position that no one else wanted in American society—their housing, jobs, and status were all less desirable than those available to individuals in the American mainstream. Public schools and increasing openness of the American culture made assimilation possible for a second generation. By the third generation, most immigrants had become established as mainstream Americans. Any hostility toward such assimilated immigrants tended to be expressed among ethnic groups in sports and special affinity activities.

The progress of American blacks differs from that of immigrants to the United States primarily because of the vast disparity in opportunities for the education of their children. Most of the immigrants entered the country through eastern seaports that had a deep tradition of public education. Although not all immigrants spent a long time in their ports of entry, many settled in nearby cities and towns. The children of immigrants had incentives and opportunities for assimilation through public schools. Their parents saw school as the doorway to prosperity. The children viewed school as a way to become "American." Although ethnic and class barriers stood in the way of some educational opportunities for immigrant children, children of newly settled immigrants had significantly greater opportunities and incentives than there were for children of the Old South, both black and white. In the South, where most blacks lived, lower economic standards and straitened cultural vitality slowed the development of a viable public education system.

Immigrants always retained at least a shred of hope for the next generation. They could be relieved to know that because of their sacrifices their children would have a better opportunity for a good life than they would have had in the old country. Most Americans can relate family legends about the silent, patient work and hardship borne by men and women who, without the sound of a familiar language or the sights of well-known faces, persevered in their labors in a factory or on a farm to keep their children focused on an upward path in life.

White Americans look back at the hard lot of their immigrant ancestors with admiration and sympathy. We regard ourselves as somehow deserving of the good possibilities that they secured for us. Our heritage is a source of pride and status. We think of ourselves as keepers of a sacred trust in the values of freedom and democracy. When we realize the vast and complex disparity between the way white people got to America and the way black people got here, it becomes inescapable that we white people need to make some humbling admissions about our responsibilities.

The slave experience differed greatly from the immigrant experience. Because he or she was a native of Africa, the slave had no knowledge of the American slavery system that brought him to a strange land. Whatever comfort or suffering he experienced in his native world, it was his own world: his own family, his own society, and his own culture from birth. As a slave he entered a new world of physical hardship and cruelty and psychological stresses and torments, such as hostility, alienation, and frustration of all hopes and expectations.

The new world told the overpowered African that he lived among a race that could hurt him without measure or restraint. Everyone like himself was powerless to control any part of his life. The most elemental concerns of his youth, adulthood, and old age rested completely in the hands of people who somehow could buy, breed, and dispose of him and his offspring. He never saw a person of his color who stood on equal ground with a person of the other color. Any challenge he made on his own behalf was met with terror.

No decision that the slave made could change his life for the better, unless he chose to submit more humbly to the rule of those over him. This white man's world simply made no sense. The white man's value system required a black mother and her child to be separated for life if one or the other were for sale, as if that were just a natural occurrence. The African did not know what that value system was, but he knew that it had no place for him as a human being. Although he recognized that he was not an animal, the best that anyone could tell him—if he dared to ask—was that he was a perpetual child, to be subject his whole life to a white person of whatever age. The African could believe that he was more a child than a man and could find that identity more tolerable than the animal status given him under the white man's tacit value system.

From Christendom to Plantation Ideology

The plantation ideology was designed to force the African into a complete abandonment of his self worth. The slave owner inflicted punishments on him to prevent his causing trouble and rationalized the maltreatment by claiming that the victim needed discipline because of his evil nature. White Americans who did not believe in slavery itself still tended to believe that the Africans caused the racial problems. President Abraham Lincoln expressed this sentiment at a meeting with a group of Negroes during the Civil War:

> See our present condition—the country engaged in war, our white men cutting one another's throats, and then consider what we know to be the truth. But for your race among us there would be no war, although many men engaged on either side do not care for you one way or the other.

So it was the black man's fault that the white man was a slaveholder, and it was somehow the white man's sorry lot to have to deal with slavery! This level of reasoning was hardly suitable for the wartime president who had made decisions that had cost the lives of hundreds of thousands of people. In spite of the eloquence and wisdom that Lincoln might have reached at Gettysburg, in this statement he seems to have descended to the depths of social racism. He was no doubt distraught and overwhelmed by the reports of casualties on both sides. But to assert blame for the war on those Afro-Americans who had come to him as patriotic Americans, seeking to have their ethnic brothers allowed into the Union Army to fight and die to help rescue their brothers from slavery, seems to me to exemplify plantation ideology at its worst. Fortunately for Lincoln's reputation, this is a fairly overlooked event. But unfortunately for historical understanding, this obscurity deprives white Americans of a look into the mirror of our true minds.

As time passes, as generations accumulate, a social actuality such as the white man's domination takes on the facade of natural reality. The slave comes to terms with his condition by partially accepting the myth that he should be blamed for his status as a slave. He accepts the basic premise that his master should dominate and he should submit. He even accepts the characteristic degraded, quiet acquiescence in submission that his master rewards in his slaves.

Whether the plantation ideology was consciously contrived, or whether it was simply a derivative of the circumstances in which it arose does not matter. Perhaps, if we can understand the ideology underlying slavery, we will be able to see how our beliefs and attitudes relate to our present racial problems.

Like other social and economic innovations in the New World, the system of slavery in the American South arose out of the tradition of Christendom of the Old World. There was also a more modern element. The modern element was the assumption that the right to property is fundamental and nearly absolute, overshadowing the right to personal freedom and privacy. The right to property was *de jure* in the Constitution, and the absolute right to property was rising as the operative assumption, at least among the ownership class. Slaveholders found it easy to persuade themselves and their northern property-owning counterparts that their right to their property, the African natives who had been delivered to them in bonds, transcended the slaves' rights to their persons and privacy. This key element in the legal and social arguments undergirded the plantation ideology, that construction of political, religious, and legal claims that developed during the "tenancy" of slaveholding. A twentieth-century exponent of plantation ideology, James J. Kilpatrick, describes its dynamics:

> Yet the myth persists. There is the Old South Legend of the white-columned plantation, the hoopskirted belles, the hot-blooded men. In the foreground, beneath the magnolia trees, the darkies are plucking banjos; in the background, rows upon rows of cotton, and off to one side, a steamboat coming around the bend. Master loves the Negroes, and the Negroes love old Master.

In a different vein, Kilpatrick continues:

> The reality the South has had to cope with most constantly, beyond the realities of defeat and poverty, is the reality of the Southern Negro....the Irish fought their way up, on merit and ambition and hard work. No such reality has been visible in the South. Instead of ambition (I speak in general terms), we have witnessed indolence, instead of skill, ineptitude, instead of talent, an inability to learn.

Kilpatrick, then editor of the *Richmond NewsLeader*, wrote his book in 1962 in a gallant attempt to soften and delay the imposition of school desegregation in the aftermath of the *Brown v. Board of Education* Federal Supreme Court decision of 1954. He remained a leading voice of resistance to the demise of the Jim Crow system. Kilpatrick does not overstate the case of the plantation ideology. If he could have found reasonable justification for perpetuation of the slave system, he would not have had to appeal to the mythical view of it as he did. He tried to defend what he saw as a flawed remnant of a decent world whose time was past.

Another scholarly view of slavery points out the weakness of Kilpatrick's case for a benign view of slavery. Max Lerner, in his book, *America as a Civilization*, writes:

> The abolitionists who saw slavery in the image of its worst examples had hold of a deep truth: the cancer of slavery...was the idea of slavery itself—of one man owning another and in the fact that there was nothing to keep the worst type of white man from owning and exploiting those who were better than himself. The slave died young. His women were often taken sexually by the overseer and the master's sons, whether out of passion or out of sport, as the record of racial mixture shows. Yet since the slaves were valuable property they were usually treated with some care, and a rough affection on both sides. Discipline was maintained; if the slave protested he was whipped; if he sought to escape he was tracked down. He lived in ignorance but in a bare kind of comfort....too many Christian churchgoers considered him outside the scope of their charity, compassion, and militancy.

The plantation ideology contained but obscured the contradiction inherent in the slave system between the democratic principles of self-government enunciated in the Constitution and the aristocratic elitism of the triumphalist Christian dichotomy of humanity, which specifies an "elect" part and a "lost" part. The American ideal of democracy involves a concept of a common humanity that all inhabitants possess equally. The state cannot endow these rights, because all men already possess them; nor can the state withhold them, except by unjust force. These rights inhere in the meaning of human life. If a dichotomy is introduced into this concept, that dichotomy will undermine the rights. The Founding Fathers did not believe that they could win the independence of the people by force as such, but that they must appeal to the conscience of mankind to evaluate the essential justice of their claim. This claim could only be made by demonstrating that all the people could show respect for the rights of all. If some of the people refused to respect the inherent rights of others, then the whole day was lost, and the nation was back to despotism and force.

Christendom proclaimed a doctrine contrary to this claim of common human nature. The Church taught a divinely ordained dichotomy of humanity that resulted from Adam and Eve's Fall into sin in the Garden, and the subsequent selection of a portion of fallen humanity that would be "saved" from that sin. Only the "chosen people" would find salvation and favor with God. These elect alone had access to truth and righteousness by which the whole of humanity could be rightly ruled. Through this dogma Christendom lent malignant support to the slavery that the South needed to sustain its labor-intensive cotton economy.

In the third century, Augustine, bishop of Hippo, laid the foundations of the worldview by which Christians would see themselves as the "elect" of God for salvation. In his manifesto for Christendom, *The City of God,* Augustine taught that the world is composed of the City of God, practically synonymous with the church, and the City of Man, which accounts for everyone else. The Southern churches claimed to be the "elect," those whom God has chosen to save from hell. The ecclesiastical authorities used the terms "church" and "Christians" to claim for themselves a legitimate line of descent from the apostles.

The system of slavery needed to distinguish individuals on the basis of skin color, the operational evidence of race. And race, interpreted as skin color, determined where on either side of the divide each person stood. The "free Negro" intruded into the racially ordered society: he could become a slave simply by lacking proof that he was not a slave. If he offended a white person in any one of many ways, the free Negro received the lawful punishment of being sold as a slave, with the proceeds from his sale going to the state. For instance, a "free Negro" who worked as a crewman on a ship docking into a southern port had to stay on board that ship or risk being hauled off to prison and the auction block, unless there was ready advocacy by the ship's officer. Every "free Negro" had to have a white sponsor who could attest to his status and testify on his behalf in court, which all persons of color could not do for themselves.

In the plantation version of the Christian doctrine, divine election made a place for the slaves. Not only were they covered by the general doctrine that includes all of fallen humanity, but they also had divinely appointed status as slaves. Episcopal Bishop Meade of Virginia gave this instruction for slaves as part of their religious indoctrination:

> Almighty God hath been pleased to make you slaves here, and to give you nothing but labor and poverty in this world, which you are obliged to submit to, as it is his will that you should do so....Do all for God himself.

The triumphalist gospel that was preached to the slaves told them that their only hope lay in an afterlife that would give them comfort and peace. They could find this relief from their degraded existence by avoiding any hint of disrespect for their masters, and by welcoming any correction they received as a scourging of those earthly impurities that would prevent their finally entering God's presence. The slaves were forced to reject any desire for the wealth, ease, and pleasure of their masters and to approve the master's scourging of any slaves who were overtaken with a rebellious spirit.

Christians in the orthodox triumphalist tradition had learned to think of themselves as needing the suffering of sickness, toil, and sorrow for the purification of unworthy souls. The pilgrim progressing to the Promised Land endured these conditions as a means to attaining the heavenly city. Aristocratic Christians expected to experience their share of this world's woes in more esoteric "spiritual" trials than in actual physical experiences that could be avoided by wealth. But the ancient patriarch Job who underwent suffering and humiliation to learn "patience" served as a readily available model to explain to the slave why his life is rightly spent in enforced purgation of pride and self-will. The slave-master therefore acted as an agent of God in teaching the slave humility.

Today Americans have to take seriously these pernicious religious beliefs, along with the question of how we perpetuate our unspoken assumption that "racial harmony" means that whites dominate and blacks submit. That assumption is deeply embedded in the Southern culture and has been effectively worked into American culture at large.

As a boy of twelve I went to a courtroom for the first time. Joe, a black lad a few years older than myself, was charged with shoplifting a box of sugar from a neighborhood grocer. I listened as the grocer told his story from the witness stand. He said that Joe had taken the sugar out of the store without paying for it. As I sat and listened to the story being told about Joe, I remembered a story about myself that had never been told. Once, out of curiosity and boredom, I had accidentally set fire to a junked truck in a vacant lot. I ran and hid while the firemen came and put it out. I never told anyone that I was responsible, but I never forgot it either. I doubt that anyone knew of my guilt until now.

At the end of Joe's trial, the judge pronounced this black defendant guilty and sentenced him to a term on the county-road work gang. I left the courtroom with a heavy heart because I realized that I had done a worse thing than Joe: he had been punished and I had not.

According to Joe's mother, he had told the grocer that she wanted the sugar charged to her account, which she paid by the week. Joe thought that the grocer had recognized what he had said and agreed to it, as was his custom. The first Joe knew otherwise was when the police came later that day to arrest him and take him to jail.

No one thought it necessary to question either Joe or his mother in the "trial," nor did he have the representation of a lawyer. It was assumed that neither he nor any other black person would ever contradict a white person, and that he was guilty as charged. He and his mother traded tearful kisses as he was led off to serve his sentence. Later, when he came back to work, he seemed not at all surprised at what had happened to him. Many of his male friends and relatives had been in prison at least once, and they expected it to happen. Little stigma was attached to it, because white people assumed that blacks were incapable of self-control.

Joe's trial and sentencing taught me a bitter truth about the world of racial segregation and oppression that lay hidden behind the facade of the "Southern way of life." I knew at the time that if I had been brought into court for burning the truck, I would have had different treatment and punishment than Joe had.

Jefferson's Dilemma

Thomas Jefferson saved some of his best skewers for his last-known letter, written on June 24, 1826, before he died on July 4, 1826, the fiftieth anniversary of the official signing of the Declaration of Independence. In that letter, he said of that document:

> May it be to the world, what I believe it will be, (to some parts sooner, to others later, but finally to all,) the signal of arousing men to burst the

chains under which monkish ignorance and superstition had persuaded them to bind themselves, and to assume the blessings and security of self-government. That form that we have substituted restores the free right to the unbounded exercise of reason and freedom of opinion. All eyes are opened, or opening, to the rights of man. The general spread of the light of science has already laid open to every view the palpable truth, that the mass of mankind has not been born with saddles on their backs, nor a favored few booted and spurred, ready to ride them legitimately, by the grace of God.

Jefferson expressed a revolutionary idea for his time. The French Revolution had inspired fear and hope all over Europe. The palaces of kings resounded with fear that the ideas of liberty, fraternity, and equality would infect the common people who docilely accepted the changes that had taken place in the previous centuries of Enlightenment. In many places, the common people hoped that the boots and spurs that Jefferson mentions could be swept away and the mass of men could be unsaddled of the burdens of unequal shares of productive labor. In our time, some still think themselves entitled to ride on the backs of the mass of humanity and have not arrived at Jefferson's insight, in spite of the advances in reason and science in two centuries. However, even Jefferson seems to have had gaps in his own otherwise admirable insight into the better way of self-government.

In an earlier day, when the question of emancipation of slaves came under debate, Jefferson expressed his tentative views to "A Foreigner of Distinction" in the "Queries" that are among his papers. Jefferson seems to have connected emancipation with repatriation, the freeing of Africans from slavery, and the sponsoring of their return to Africa or to another "place as the circumstances of the time should render most proper." He considered emancipation impractical without repatriation, which most Americans of his day considered unworkable. Although an enlightened student of scientific inquiry, Jefferson found abundant "evidence" of the natural and essential inferiority of black people to white people, at least in those matters that are necessary for what he would call "civilized society." He said:

> It is not their condition then, but nature, which has produced the distinction.—Whether further observation will or will not verify the conjecture, that nature has been less bountiful to them in the endowments of the head, I believe that in those of the heart she will be found to have done them justice.

In this passage Jefferson denies that the "condition" of the enslaved Africans is responsible for their comparative lack of "endowments of the head," or intelligence. Their natural limitations set them apart from his fellow white men. He attributes to the blacks a just portion of "heart," by which I think he means richness of emotional life. This describes the inferiority he saw in the people around him on his plantation in a charitable and sensitive way. Jefferson's countrymen shared his low estimate of black intelligence, if not his high regard for the blacks' capacity for feelings.

If Jefferson or anyone else in the Continental Congress intended their Declaration of Independence to include any females or nonwhite people among those who were expected to give consent to the government, there is no record of it. To the contrary, it was possible to get the inclusive language in the Declaration adopted only by excluding any negative mention of slavery. Subsequently, the Constitution as written a decade later made specific provision for the institution of slavery and gave that institution tacit moral approval. So, the colonists claimed the right to be free of domination by the British Crown and establishment, but they recognized no similar right for either women or the Negroes in bondage to participate in their own governance.

That contradiction cast only a verbal shadow in 1776, barely visible in the strong light of liberty. But how could the Founding Fathers declare that "all men are created equal" and then reserve that equality to free, white men like themselves? Did they set aside their appeal to the "opinions of mankind" when they excluded those whose humanity they found it distasteful and unprofitable to recognize? What, indeed, is the meaning of "liberty" or "freedom" if those concepts apply only when no one dares to withhold consent? If they, the proclaimers of liberty were created free of bondage, then what could be the origin—-by creation or otherwise—of those who they now claim are legally born in perpetual and positive bondage? If governments derive their "just powers from the consent of the governed," what kind of powers do they impose on their slaves, who are governed but have no consent to give or withhold? If they demand representation in the councils that impose taxes upon their goods and trade, which come and go by the day, how can they withhold representation from their slaves? Not only do they exact a total tax upon the fruits their slaves' labor, but they commandeer the very children of their bodies.

Jefferson accepted the principle that the right to property was a corollary of the right to self-government. The individual has a right to life and the possession of certain things that are necessary for the continuance of life. These things become an extension of the person who possesses them and whose life they sustain. Therefore, the individual must have the right to own property for private use and profit. The monarch, in theory as the surrogate of God, owned everything, even the lives of his subjects. But the new secular world of democracy and science would offer an abundance of things, and each individual would have the right to possess what he could. Making the rules by which property rights would be adjudicated among equals was part of the business of democratic governments.

Jefferson's experience blended these ideals, the patriarchal and the liberal. He inherited land and slaves from his father and his father in-law and took his place among other gentleman rulers over his lands, family, and servants. He believed in the aristocracy of intelligence, on the model of Plato's guardians of the state. According to this model, all future leaders of the state were to rise to power by intellectual excellence alone, without any possibility of inherited privilege. The actual rulers lived in voluntary poverty and without identified progeny and served the state out of benevolence alone. They were secular priests who worshiped only goodness, truth, and beauty.

Jefferson's role in the writing of the Declaration of Independence followed naturally from his reputation as the foremost theoretician of the colonial cause. His treasonous dissertation, "A Summary View of the Rights of British America," had been published by his Virginian friends in Philadelphia and in England. Later, the Continental Congress appointed a committee to write a document that would explain the reasons behind the movement for independence. The task fell to Jefferson and other members of the auspicious committee, including Franklin and Adams. So at the age of thirty-three, Jefferson wrote his best-known work. His draft did not perfectly suit the temper of the Congress, but congressional amendments shaped it into the founding document. Jefferson included a denunciation of human slavery in the Declaration, but the group would not accept it.

Jefferson was a child of the European Renaissance and the Enlightenment. His education and tastes made him the most fully classical thinker, writer, and practitioner of humanistic theory in the colonies, if not in the world in his time. His education had been steeped in the elegant teachings of Plato, and he absorbed Plato's passion for order and excellence. He must have pondered the concept of justice, as Plato himself did, when he depicted Socrates searching for an acceptable understanding of justice in *The Republic*. Plato regarded justice as the virtue of virtues, the summation of political wisdom, and the only proper goal of all who rule. Justice became the most powerful element of the liberal secular creed, as the new nation was founded.

But the term "justice" is strangely absent from Jefferson's Declaration. Jefferson repeatedly uses the words "liberty" and "rights." He refers to the idea of justice only to qualify the "just" powers of government, which he says rest on the consent of the governed. If the committee had approved, the Declaration would no doubt have contained a section condemning slavery. Jefferson had written such a section into his original draft, and the committee appointed by Congress removed it from the draft that they reported and that was adopted. This led Jefferson to believe that if the Continental Congress had condemned slavery, there would have been no Declaration of Independence, no Union, and no United States.

The contradiction of slavery in a self-governing society hung like a cloud on the horizon when Jefferson wrote the Declaration of Independence. The warm, moist climate and level land made cotton easy to grow in the South. The worldwide demand for the fabric, and cotton's ability to withstand frost, shrinkage, and rot when kept under good conditions added to the crop's desirability. Unlike food crops, it could be stored over from a low-price year to a high-price year without loss. However, until Eli Whitney invented the cotton gin in 1793, cotton bore the status of a minor crop in the South because of the labor-intensive work involved in removing its seeds from the raw lint by hand. The cotton gin rendered the time-consuming, tedious work of harvesting the crop relatively easy, so cotton became a staple in the agricultural life of the South. "King Cotton" became the master and provider of wealth for the plantation owners. It also called for the enormous expansion of the slave population. The planters' dependence on cotton also made them dependent on more and more slaves. The surplus wealth of the planters allowed them to live like royalty and to influence those in political power. Jefferson could never have foreseen this world; his dream of democracy rested on a society of free and politically mature agrarian yeomen. Nor could Jefferson have foreseen the entrenchment of slavery in our national life as an antagonist to free labor and democratic government.

Born into the slaveholding culture, Jefferson also owned slaves all his life. He criticized the system throughout his public career and lobbied against it whenever he could. He seems to have expected the death of that "peculiar institution" until 1820, when the Missouri Compromise rang the "firebell in the night" that warned him that the Union was in mortal danger. He realized too late that the men of 1776 had doomed their descendants to an impossible contradiction.

Jefferson presents us with an intellectual dilemma. He knew more about the world than many of his contemporaries, and he made bold use of that knowledge. He recognized that humanity is not a servile product of a vengeful cosmic potentate, so that self-rule is the only rationally defensible human state. He also knew that education is the only road to attaining self-rule, and that the achievement of a level of education sufficient to self-rule is a slow and arduous for humanity. His knowledge must have led him to desperate questions. How long do people have to learn and practice self-control and tolerance of others while ruling themselves, before they can harmoniously experience the values of those virtues? And how long does it take for a self-ruling people to realize that tolerance for other self-ruling people yields greater gain than dominance over them? And so, is there time for that process to take hold before the whole mass of people reverts to a precivilized state of self-defeating competition?

Jefferson did not believe that the two races could ever co-exist or become assimilated. Jefferson had seen the affinity whites had for the European style of culture, economy, and civil society, and an aversion toward that culture by blacks. He put the entire moral fault on the slave stealers, who had so carelessly and greedily brought the two races into proximity without regard for their incompatibility. The stolen Africans were not immigrants, like the Europeans who had chosen to come to America. Slaves had no natural reason to adapt to the Euro-American culture of work, thrift, and rational self-control. The national government's restriction on the spread of slavery and the withering away of the labor-intensive agricultural system of the South left no way for the races ever to come to any peaceful future. In his "firebell" letter mentioned previously, Jefferson seems to regard the mandatory abolition of slavery as suicidal folly.

Jefferson felt concerned for both principle and political and social necessity, as he saw them. The principle of self-government—by the consent of the governed—had to apply to black as well as the white, whenever the blacks were ready to seize it. But the differences between black and white capabilities for reasoned and dispassionate action would, he believed, preclude the possibility that the two races could ever be combined in one political system. The one, being more naturally capable of foresight and self-interested planning, could always dominate the other, with no semblance of fairness. Political union with whites would always leave the blacks at the mercy of some manner of unjust exploitation. Whites could not be trusted to govern blacks fairly in a political union.

Jefferson demonstrates some wisdom, despite his lack of a thorough understanding of "racial" divisions of humanity. He saw white peoples' potential for mendacity in exploiting blacks. After three centuries of slavery and a century and a half of racially motivated social domination, we have yet to see a white American government dealing effectively and equitably with black Americans over the long term.

Jefferson seems to have seen, better than his contemporaries or most twentieth-century white and black Americans, how deeply the racial division is embedded in the social consciousness. Jefferson was mistaken about the inherent cause of the African's status. We have learned that the Africans' functional deficiency in living and competing in Euro-American culture is a cultural by-product of the African slave experience, in contrast to the immigrant experience of typical Euro-Americans. However, Jefferson also better grasped the tragic case that because of the Africans' inherited disadvantage, the existence of a single, biracial society would be virtually impossible. We have yet to prove him wrong in that estimation, against the hopes of many of us.

Jefferson's judgment about the differences of whites and blacks in adaptability to Euro-American culture was not unusual for his day, or for ours. In the Jim Crow era in the South, it was conventional wisdom openly to justify the condition of black schools, housing, and employment on that basis. Black people were compared to perpetual children. They were not to be hurt, unless their better tutelage required it, but they were not to be expected to live as "we" did. Popular wisdom held that to invest money in their education would only add to their frustration because they could never expect to enjoy the rewards of a kind of life for which they had no capacity. Better to confine their expectations to the menial arena in which they would operate. Our parents believed it, we believed it, and I think many blacks believed it.

Jefferson was as blinded to the intellectual quality of black humanity as we have been in the South. Our blindness results partly from snobbery and partly from self-defensiveness. It serves our tastes, our status, and our money to refuse to see what is in front of our eyes. The civilization that we have inherited from Christendom and the Puritans has insulated us from the reality of our common humanity with our black neighbors. Some more enlightened among them have rejected this view, but they are marginalized. Others among us were ashamed of the hating spirit that we shared but scarcely made a noise about it. Most of us, the more "decent" of us, acted patronizingly and charitably toward individual blacks whom we thought "deserving" of our good will and occasional benefits. We would not join the lynching party, but we would not oppose the elected officials who allowed it.

Most of us have been profoundly ignorant, or in denial, or both when faced with the depth of our separation, which Jefferson saw. Speaking truth about race in America is rarely easy: whether it is to the powerful who still do not accept responsibility for perpetuating the effects of slavery and racism, or to the uninformed of both races, who still suffer those awful effects with little ability to change them.

We even incur risk when we speak the truth to the powerless who are black and who may still believe the white man's myth that they deserve to be powerless and are destined to stay powerless. If these people are weak, it is because the racism of white people has made them weak. The truth is that their ancestors have bequeathed to them a strong heritage of struggle, survival, and adaptability which will transform their powerlessness.

Today, the way to the future of racial harmony is through the past. If we understand the past experience of both black and white Americans, we can better see how far we need to go for reconciliation. We can earn the respect for one another that we need and deserve. But we cannot do that if we deny the past.

Jefferson believed in the reasons he had penned for the rights of the colonists to set up their own government. He did not spin his arguments like monastics speculating on the attributes of angels. He was just as sure of constancy in the affairs of humanity that corresponds to a cosmic order as he was of a constancy by which the stars follow their assigned paths. Jefferson the planter and patriarch controlled his passions and his pleasures with tolerable discipline, but he did not think that he had license to enhance himself by denying the humanity of people of a different complexion from himself. He could compromise a good principle for the sake of a better one for political expediency, but he did not believe that he could put curved sides on a square.

Jefferson's dilemma leaves us with a double burden. First, American principles elucidate the undeniable commitment to an essential equality of human life in all tribes and sorts of people. There is no separating humanity into one group which is due to participate fully in "the consent of the governed" and another group which is not. If this right does not belong to all, it cannot be self-evident that it belongs to any. Only the raw power of uncivilized tyrants, of whatever name, stands on the other side from this inclusive democracy.

Second, economically and socially powerful white-skinned Americans have dominated colored-skinned Americans and treated them as second-class citizens. In an America governed by a kind of justice superior to the actual present case, there would be no color-based domination. The denial of economic and cultural privileges has reinforced this domination, and it has withstood a bloody war, a promised emancipation, a legal demarcation by color, and a struggle against poverty and prejudice. In spite of progress, a residual shadow falls over the hopes of the child and youth of color, and that shadow says, "You can see what your white brothers and sisters can have, but you need not try to have it for yourself." Looking inwardly as well as outwardly, Jefferson saw all too well, that white hearts were not prepared to be open to the full humanity of people of color. As a nation, America still has to cope with that indictment.

Those who have the dominant status find advantages in holding such beliefs as the right to money, pride, leisure, and power through intimidation of those who are the "lower" race. And these advantages offer a powerful incentive to perpetuate the system. The awful truth is there to be seen, but we have had no eyes to see it. Is it not a marvel that a person who will make reasonable judgments about his own talents and abilities, as compared to that of other people, will become unreasonable in his judgment when the complexion of the other person differs from his own?

9

Religion, Politics, and Economics
Separations Within Communities

THE TRIUMPHALISTS MAY BE protesting too much again. The Puritans did it when they hanged four Quakers, Mary Dyer and three men on Boston Common in 1660, and again in 1692 when they killed at least twenty people in the witch-hunt craze. After the Puritans had accused the wife of Governor William Phips of witchcraft, the English king stopped their killing of religious dissidents and other victims of wild suspicion by denying Puritan courts the power to carry out sentences that were not legal in England.

Zealots of hatred usually press their causes of righteous vengeance so far that more sensible people recoil in revulsion at the excess. Contemporary Neo-Puritans of the twentieth century show their triumphalist credentials in their demands that the nation enforce their truncated version of morality upon the populace. They demand that their own version of religious literalism and belligerence be made into public policy. They would drive out of public life all who do not conform to their simplistic notions of sin and righteousness.

The Neo-Puritans use slogans to reinforce their claims and charges. They can find some public support for these formula abstractions, such as "unborn child," or "partial birth abortion," so long as they are not called on to explain their assumptions. The anti-abortion crusade rests on the assumption that an embryo or a fetus is a fully functioning person. This assumption is hard to disprove, because it assumes the conclusion that the term "embryo" or "fetus" refers to an intact person, one equal to any other person. The assertion lacks any credibility outside the simple claim that they believe it is so. Circular reasoning does not bother the triumphalist because he has already based his belief system on his willingness to submit to God, instead of on any coherent basis. The triumphalists insist that national policies be made to fit their Neo-Puritan assumptions that are unarguable as stated.

That women are denied freedom to control their bodies and the implications for parenthood are forced on unwilling people are of no concern to the triumphalists, when they can claim that the "life" of an "unborn child" is at stake. Whatever the cause or argument, Neo-Puritans will reduce their claims to slogans and repeat them until they become "known facts," readily acceded to by an impressionable public. But those shrill claims and slogans also leave the impression of excess and generate backlash.

Authoritarian religion has served as a facade for greed and arrogance throughout the ages, and contemporary triumphalist religion is highly susceptible to perpetrating this duplicity. In the United States we have tasted social compassion in the New Deal and in the Civil Rights movement. These have whetted our appetite for enlightened social policies, but at this time we are urged to revert to Puritan ways of punishing the dispossessed.

The concepts of atomism and mechanism and the division of humanity into races and classes led ineluctably to the stratifications inherent in Puritan thinking. The religion of reconciliation shows how these separations can be overcome by recognizing the injustice and exploitation of past centuries. A diversity of ethnic groups can enrich society when respect for one another prevails.

Our social environment places us in the It-World, in Buber's terms, and we enter the Thou-World when we as individuals make the move to relationship with other individuals. The two spheres of economy and politics dominate our interests and activities by their sheer overwhelming presence. In the It-World, fear and the need for assimilation predispose us to become like the things and groups that we use and that use us. The things that we possess and the possessions that we lack establish our status among other such people as ourselves. Authentic existence is waiting to be achieved and to flourish. The gospel of care and respect provides the pattern of authentic relationship, and the religion of community.

In the triumphalist scheme of things, those individuals who lack the things that are currently valued receive the status of dispossession. Dispossession means removal from the scene of activity in which things are made and exchanged. Those who already have some possessions exploit the economy and are ready to participate in exchanging things with other people. People who are not able to pay their way in exchange for the possessions of others have no set place in this schema. Our current political system is prepared to let the dispossessed sink or swim as the tides of sympathetic feeling rise and fall. Such sympathy for the dispossessed gets meager support from the religion of triumphalism, because that religion is based on the belief that rewards of wealth are for those who are divinely favored. The distinction between the saved and the unsaved is the model for the separation of those who are worthy of the rewards of earthly wealth from those who are not.

The religion of the gospel of love that Jesus taught and exemplified has a different basis. It begins with the concept of respectful and respected persons who are united in the activities of life. In this caring world, we find ourselves mirrored in the humanity of people we meet and hear. Our connecting with them provides the nourishment that we need for growth and thriving. Things are in the world as a harvest of nature and the results of human effort and inventiveness. The fruit of the earth is food by which our bodies become flesh and bone and blood. We are all partners together in the production and enjoyment of the earth. Our physical bodies together provide sustenance for future generations to continue this enjoyment. Our spirits receive nourishment through our common efforts and inventiveness, making our world one of beauty, truth, and goodness as we mutually enrich ourselves, each other, and all of humanity.

The Engines and Pathology of Envy

Envy is defined in the *Merriam-Webster Collegiate Dictionary* as "painful or resentful awareness of an advantage enjoyed by another joined with a desire to possess the same advantage." Envy has become a driving force in American life along with the proliferation of our materialism and commercialization. The ability of American business to produce great quantities of things of all sorts has made us the envy of most of the rest of the world. We now quantify our "standard of living" by use of consumer terms, referring not so much to what we have as to what we want and will spend time and resources to get. It is an open question whether our mass production of things or our advertising and merchandising of those things is more impressive. Both of these have become major influences within our culture. The terrible consequence of our pervasive culture of consumerism, aside from its distracting us from better pursuits, is the limited ability of some to consume due to hereditary economic disadvantage. One-fourth of our children lives in poverty. This does not mean that they lack access to television commercials, but that their world is defined by the images of and the desire for things they only see and cannot have.

The role of envy magnifies when great and conspicuous differences exist between the statuses of members of families, communities, or nations. In many ways, our modern American society excels in the vicious production of pathological envy. Although the masses of Americans could live with satisfaction on modest means or less in colonial and pre-Civil War times, in our time the great differences between the wealthy few and the unwealthy many that we now witness are eroding our social fabric. Why do so many people of currently working families now say that they were poor when they were growing up, but that they did not seem to know it? These working people compare what they had back then with the possessions of people now who consider themselves poor and feel a resentment close to anger toward today's poor. They remember that poverty was thought to be tolerable when they were children, and they wonder why they are now expected to help support people who have more things than their families ever had.

Their question is more rhetorical than actually resentful. People do not really want children to be hungry and sick when help is available. Individuals realize that having a television and a boom box does not make hunger any less hurtful. And they know that because of their extended families they were probably more protected from the worst aspects of poverty than are current poor families who are isolated in rural areas or in cities. Despite these subjective insights, the question of relative wealth does bear on the awareness factor in envy.

This great economic difference fuels the social unrest that currently plagues us and most of the world's people. Whatever degree of economic prosperity or economic decline any society may enjoy or suffer, we now see more perceptible difference than ever before in human history. The expansion of communication media, and their nearly universal saturation of the world, has made more people aware of the great differences between themselves and "others." The "others" may well be actors who are depicted enjoying something as trivial as a Pepsi Cola or as rare as a luxury yacht—but it does not matter. Whether the actors may or may not be able to afford what they are depicted as enjoying does not matter. Indeed, the depiction may be an animated cartoon, so that no one who is depicted actually enjoys anything. The perception that someone is enjoying something that the perceiver cannot ever expect to enjoy incites envy.

So much real deprivation exists in the world, through civil wars and ethnic strife, and so much hunger and dislocation caused by population pressures and man-made disasters, that it is almost blasphemous to talk about envy of mere possession of things. But the stark reality is that the perception of deprivation can be as psychologically destructive as actual privations. Not all of that destructiveness is obvious. Inner wounds are slow to heal when the conspicuous consumption for which we are famous as a nation exaggerates the perception of deprivation.

In the riots that swept many American cities in the wake of the assassination of Martin Luther King, Jr., acts of arson destroyed many homes and businesses that were badly needed by the very people who were setting the fires. Those needy people still lack some of those homes, businesses, and jobs. But the looting did not result just from juvenile pranks. It demonstrated the pent-up rage of people who had been tantalized by years of viewing things and enjoyment that they were unable to get. In many cases the looters descended from slaves who had lived in the cruelest poverty that the nation has ever seen. But the looters, generations after the end of slavery, had seen and heard the sights and sounds of prosperity and plenty, but still could not hold that prosperity and plenty in their hands.

The person in the second highest position in a neighborhood or company can be eaten alive with envy of the person in the highest position. The stress of this envy itself causes the corrosion of mind and spirit that afflicts so many of us. The school and workplace killings we have witnessed in the past few years are almost all committed by people who were or are well paid and not poor at all. These killers hold a grudge against someone whom they perceive has deprived them of something. Their envy has become a passion impelling them to throw away whatever they have left of life in one grand gesture of revenge, because they usually commit suicide after wreaking whatever vengeance can.

But the most destructive envy results from small, multiple, and tantalizing displays of advantages and enjoyments that lie beyond the realization of those who constantly witness them. The price of viewing an entertaining television show will inevitably entail watching a commercial in which eating, wearing, or driving something seems the rightful enjoyment of everyone. Advertisers know that they must continually make those displays attractive to the widest possible audiences, even though the vendors also know that a large number of people who see the commercials can never afford the products. How many of us have felt mild discomfort when we see an ice cream commercial, knowing that we are not going to indulge ourselves in an extra dessert? But how many children will see those same commercials and wonder—even if they no longer ask—why they cannot have some of what they see other children enjoying?

What is wrong with our social system, with its politics and economics and education and religion that makes envy so powerful and so corrosive? Would it be better if we confined the portrayals of the life of ease and plenty to some enclaves in which the advantaged could enjoy their luxuries out of sight of ordinary people? Was it better when people really believed that a cosmic justice governs the distribution of goods, when the Puritans taught that God rewards the righteous with abundance and punishes the wicked with poverty? Is blind and cruel fate easier to accept as an explanation for the difference of status than to suffer from unbridled envy?

Our assumptions of isolated and independent individualism lie at the core of much of our envy. The essence of envy is the locus of desire, which is the singular individual. We cannot separate desire from a self who desires. But the way the self orients itself toward its desires and their satisfactions makes a difference. I cannot ask individuals to give up their desires unless I am willing to say that those individuals are not worthy persons. If that were so, they could be treated as means to some other ends, but not as ends in themselves. So the question becomes, "What is the satisfaction that best suits the desiring person, treated as an end and not as a means only?"

That question can only be asked of the individual, and no one else can answer for him or her. Each person is an organic individual, with many and complex desires, none of which can be truly satisfying in isolation from all others. Equally important is the individual's status as a part of a complex organic community, family or whatever. The satisfaction of individual desires must be viewed and respected in the context of those communities. With creative and earnest effort, I believe that we can all decrease the extent and power of our envy and increase the breadth and significance of our satisfactions. Satisfaction should be comprehensive and coherent if it is to extend and endure. Otherwise, it will turn sour to the individual and corrosive to others.

"The mass of men lead lives of quiet desperation." This terse jewel of wisdom appears in *Walden* by Henry David Thoreau. It illustrates Thoreau's deep and impassioned sorrow over the majority of humanity's inability to realize any more than a portion of its potential as human beings. Thoreau devoted his own life to winnowing the precious grains of truth from the fields of chaff that surround us and dull our conscious regard for our real powers. Although frequently referred to as America's quintessential individualist, Thoreau seems to exemplify the truly organic individual whose life is deliberately interwoven with that of his family and friends and ultimately with the whole of nature and humanity.

Thoreau's attitude toward material possession contrasts sharply with the envy and greed for possessions that dominates so much of American society. His words scissor through the abstractions of economics and commercialism: "…the cost of a thing is the amount of what I will call life which is required to be given in exchange for it, immediately or in the long run." Thoreau framed that definition in the midst of a life far removed from most of what we call the "American standard of living." He regarded possessions as suspect until proven necessary in the laboratory of solitary life. However, his whole life through, Thoreau rigorously observed his obligations to his parents and siblings, while he at the same time refused to commit himself to other normal domestic demands. He had made his own personal commitment to seek and to serve truth and fulfilled it in the writings in his *Journal* and other works and in his personal dedication to freedom and justice for all people.

Henry David Thoreau grew up in a financially modest but cultured family in the historic village of Concord, Massachusetts. His mother's family were Tories who left their considerable property in the colonies to settle in Canada during the Revolution. The family never recovered from that move. Thoreau's father failed at being a storekeeper but found a way to earn a modest living for his family by making pencils and selling them in wholesale trade. Henry was said to lack ambition, yet he considered himself well employed because he worked just enough to sustain himself and to buy the paper and ink that he needed for writing. He and his brother graduated from Harvard College, where they prepared themselves to operate a private school. One year of teaching other people's children was enough for the Thoreau brothers. John died a tragic and painful death of tetanus just the next year, leaving Henry to live a solitary life in his family and community.

Henry went to the cabin at Walden Pond to discover what he really wanted in life, so that he would not arrive at death's door and find that he had lived his life without gaining comprehensive and coherent satisfactions. He was trying to find out for himself what was worth having, and thus worth wanting. He once said that his chief talent was to want but little. By that he meant that if he wanted to be free to pursue what he valued most, he would have to forego wanting whatever was contrary to his achieving his goal.

Thoreau was reluctant to name his major occupation directly, but I think he wanted to serve humanity through writing. Because of what he learned at the pond, he organized his life so that his commitments remained confined to a limited context in which he could be free to think about what he had to say, and to write just what he meant to say. In practical terms, he dedicated himself to the pursuit of justice. He spent his famous "night in jail" as punishment for his refusal to pay the "head tax" that was levied on all male citizens of Massachusetts. His tax protest grew out of his objection to the Mexican War, in which the United States forcibly annexed a large part of Mexico. His best-known essay, "Civil Disobedience," also emerged out of his disapproval of that war. In later years, Thoreau campaigned against slavery and supported John Brown of Kansas and Harper's Ferry fame.

On his last journey Thoreau traveled to Minnesota. He briefly visited an Indian site and met some of the people who would be involved in the altercation that resulted in the mass execution of Indians there by the United States later in 1862. He seemed to be well disposed to the Indians he saw and to think that their grievances against the government were justified. One of Thoreau's last audible words spoken before he died the next year was "Indians." I believe that if Thoreau had had more good years of health, he would have upheld the cause of Indian justice in the same way that he had so long campaigned for justice for enslaved Afro-Americans.

Thoreau once said that the most important thing to do is to simplify life. He did not want to make himself dependent on other people in ways he could avoid by simply doing for himself. Far from being a recluse, he centered his life on his mother's home, even during the twenty-eight months that he lived in the cabin at Walden Pond. He knew the path through the woods from Walden Pond to her door so well that he could walk the path in the dark without touching a bush or limb on either side. He reveled in the dining table and living room talk with relatives and friends who were guests from time to time. Thoreau also enjoyed visitors at the cabin and visited his neighbors regularly. When he became an invalid and wasted away from tuberculosis, his sister and other relatives and friends cared for him at home. When near the end an evangelical aunt came to see him and asked him if he had made his peace with God, Thoreau is said to have replied, "I am not aware that we have quarreled."

Thoreau believed that his stay at Walden Pond taught him important lessons:

> I learned this, at least, by my experiment; that if one advances confidently in the direction of his dreams, and endeavors to live the life which he has imagined, he will meet with a success unexpected in common hours. He will put some things behind, and will pass an invisible boundary; new, universal and more liberal laws will begin to establish themselves around and within him; the old laws will be expanded, and interpreted in his favor in a more liberal sense, and he will live with the license of a higher order of beings. In proportion as he simplifies his life, the laws of the universe will appear less complex, and solitude will not be solitude, nor poverty poverty, nor weakness weakness. If you have built castles in the air, your work need not be lost; that is where they should be. Now put the foundations under them.

Did Thoreau realize his dream of writing? He boasted of his library of nearly one thousand books, over nine hundred of which he had written himself. The publisher of *Walden* had printed the book at Thoreau's expense and delivered the copies to him. He probably never recovered the cost of the writing that he did during his lifetime. However, he is probably one of the most frequently encountered writers in the language, if all the reprints and anthologies containing *Walden* and "Civil Disobedience" are counted. His work influenced Tolstoy, who influenced Ghandi, who influenced Martin Luther King, Jr. The challenges that people face result in a cycle of interest, if not devotion, to Thoreau's writing. Thoreau never becomes obsolete; instead, people need time to realize his depth.

Our society has become fragmented into an infinite number of isolated centers of desire. The system itself sets interest against interest, forcing individuals to struggle madly to get what they desire without knowing whether or not what is desired will satisfy them. Our desires clash and collide in such chaos that we do not recognize what might give us satisfaction. As a result, we can lose control of our desires and waste the better parts of our lives scattering our efforts. Our system of getting and having things overwhelms us and breeds envy that drives us apart, when our real goals should be in the relationships that nourish us and provide the context in which we can best understand and fulfill our most productive desires.

We live at the mini-economic level of desires and satisfactions and at the level of wages, prices, and taxes, not at the macro-economic, abstract, and ephemeral level of fiscal and monetary policies. Wage and price issues are best handled when individual desires and satisfactions are understood and placed in order. We as individuals need to place our desires within the context of relationships and partnerships so that our desires will not control us. Religion of the kind that I have called the gospel of love, which is related to the teachings and example of Jesus, helps to build those relationships. The religion of fear and separation, which I have associated with triumphalistic Christendom, is more likely to deter relationships and partnerships than to support them.

Individuals in Politics and Economy

Overspecialization in economics and politics has fragmented these social sciences, like the physical sciences, into ever more rarified spheres of knowledge. This fragmentation of knowledge has made it hard to understand our contemporary national situation. People who graduated from college only a decade ago may already be badly out of touch with issues that arise from the "globalizing" of our commerce and industries. When we try to understand politics, we have to take into account a much more complex set of determinants than existed when most of our laws and regulations were set up. Factors such as exploitation of labor and pollution, which were fairly invisible elements a century ago, have become problematic with the industrialization of formerly subsistence agrarian societies. For instance, we have ceded our place in world industry as the chief producer/exporter of heavy machines and electronic instruments so that we are now primarily an exporter of raw food and materials.

Political policies regarding environmental and safety regulation, taxation, and corporate competition have, until now, been influenced—if not controlled—by those with the greatest economic stake in their outcomes. This shaping process of influence and control has always emanated from domestic interests. However, now many non-American interests have a large stake in our national policies and are willing to protect their future profits by investing in our political processes. Any legal barriers to their million-dollar contributions to electoral candidates have more holes than fish nets. When politicians need to raise enormous amounts of money to win reelection, they rely on those whose interests coincide with crucial policy decisions for much, if not most, of the political campaign money. From the standpoint of large corporations, it is just a good investment—and good business—to make large contributions to all viable politicians; that way, whoever wins will remember where the campaign money came from.

This does not necessarily result from greed only. It is also follows inevitably from the sheer domination of life by the economic process. We are an economic state in which everything functions by means of economic interest. This "economic interest" differs from what it was in the old days. When our nation was founded, people could manage very well without financial institutions or much involvement in an economic system. Many people alive today still remember when it was possible to get along without a bank account. The post office used to be a favorite savings repository: it was easily accessible and far less intimidating than the bank. Many businesses operated through the "hip pocket" and handshake money system.

As corporate business has grown to dominate life during the last three centuries, all societies have needed a way to cope with the sheer size of the combined weight of financial interests. For instance, the laws governing the structure of corporations provide for stockholders to invest in enterprises and to profit through the operations of the company without encountering financial liability if the company runs up debts that it cannot pay. However, if a sole owner or partners were the only investors, and they held all the ownership of the company, then they would be legally required to pay the bad debts of their company. This is an enormous favor to the holders of stock shares and to the entrepreneurs who float stock offerings. Most of us would not invest if we knew that we might have to sell our homes to pay off the incurred debts of a failed enterprise. Similarly, as one study states. "For venture capitalists, limitation of liability was (and remains) distinctly desirable and quite possibly essential."

Today's corporate world hangs suspended on that single legal provision. No modern industrial country would exist without it. Although it is a good law, it operates too much to the advantage of people with excess capital to invest, with too little responsibility for the social good. Once, applicants for a corporate charter had to demonstrate that they would serve a social good and purpose if they obtained a corporate charter. This idea would be considered quaint by present day Wall Street. Our present culture, based on the assumption of radical individualism, disregards the concept of "social good." The decline of the potent belief in "social good" in the Euro-American culture, as it was expressed in "We the people," and the rise of the more powerful notion of unrestrained individualism, which I have called the "atomic model" of persons, constitute a major shift in American society that has occurred since our founding as a nation. This version of individualism is a strong component of the WASP identity, and both are supported by the attitude of triumphalism.

In much the same way that triumphalism shaped the institution of slavery and the acceptance of greed as a public virtue, religion has suppressed the morality of equality among citizens. We have little sense of the place of the poor and dispossessed in our society. The provision for the landless in the Hebrew Scriptures, the Law of the Gleaners, is incomprehensible to commercial consciousness. The way today's triumphalist Christians promote policies of cutting back public support for housing, health care, food, and schools for the poor, we would think that their God had traded Jesus for Judas.

Balancing the economic power of wealthy people with the social good falls to local, state, and federal governments. Few business people think that we would be better off with "more government." My father feared for the future of his little business when a new federal law in the thirties required that products carry labels listing the ingredients contained in the product. Because this law applied only to those products packaged for wholesale delivery in interstate commerce, our baked goods would need to satisfy the requirement. My father seriously considered abandoning the modest sales that he had in Virginia at that time, so he could avoid the law. He believed that he could not do business under such stringent conditions. He was not an exception in his fear of governmental regulation. Doesn't every businessperson think that he or she needs just a little more profit, just enough to keep pace with the next round of increases in the costs of doing business? The business that makes enough money has not yet appeared. Our company always had to keep making more sales, because somewhere, someone was going to stop buying our products, and we had to replace those potential losses, whether or not we knew when they would happen or why. Standing still meant losing ground.

A gravitational pull seems to draw us toward looking to individual sins or personal failures for the solution to our economic and political problems. When a business fails, we suppose that the owners are responsible, at fault, or wanting in some respect. If the one in charge had been a better person in some way—more industrious, intelligent, or crafty—then the business would have succeeded. We seldom think that something in the economic system itself might have contributed to the failure. Instead, we tend to look for negative causes at the point where we think a difference might have been made: at the level of individual effort. This assumption favors those who are succeeding at the time, since again the system does not come under scrutiny.

We live in an organic universe, and nothing really lies outside the system of systems. The "economic and political system" refers to that organic entity of which we are all part. As much as we contrive to envision our society as a vast machine, composed of complex and replaceable parts, in reality it is composed of interdependent and mutually limiting and supporting parts. However, all of our overt contemporary definitions of society are based on the concept of atomic individualism. Nevertheless, we remain connected to each other as systems and subsystems, affecting each other intrinsically as well as superficially. Our economic and political connections are believed to serve individual, rather than public, interests; thus, they degrade our public interests and work in favor of some privileged individuals' interests. In this way we neglect and ignore our more basic interests, which we all share, and the common satisfactions for which we depend on one another.

There are always differences in the significance of the specific cases of our interdependence. Some connections have trivial significance, such as those between motorists using the same highway to commute to work. We drive along one at a time and have little care or concern for the other drivers, so long as they stay out of our way. But if decisions need to be made about rerouting the highway, we find the significance of our connection with other drivers on that piece of highway suddenly escalates. A controversial school bond issue can bring out the mutual interests of parents who had never seen, nor cared to see, each other before. When my children were young, my neighbor and I shared cordial and very helpful relations until the proposal of a school bond issue that would have increased property taxes somewhat and provided enrichment for the school programs. Our neighbor had neither children nor grandchildren. He opposed the bond issue as vigorously as we supported it. Our former amicable relations barely survived the strain of the referendum. In the end, I promised to support an effort to pass a tax relief measure that would limit the increases in any home owner's tax bill, including special assessments. Reason prevailed and tranquility was restored.

The Invisibility and Inevitability of Systems

Americans proudly think that the free enterprise economy and democratic politics provide the best model for a nation that the world has ever seen. We feel that all nations should operate according to the American model. But we strongly resist the idea that just a segment of the population actually controls the system at work here. We are wedded to the idea that this well-operated nation runs on the combined efforts of millions of individuals, all freely looking after their own economic and political interests—the "invisible hand," that Adam Smith wrote about two centuries ago. He said that when individuals are all free to compete with each other, the result is an improvement in everyone's economic situation, as if an invisible but entirely efficient and beneficent hand worked to secure the social good. We deplore the thought that the system at work enables one segment of the population to manipulate the economy for its own interests, regardless of the social good. Talking about our system is somewhat subversive, because it implies that one group of people can control things "behind the scenes." We fear that open discussion of our system in this way might be taken too seriously, and this would introduce class conflict into our otherwise democratic and egalitarian society.

The American "Disease"

A Harvard Business School professor, George C. Lodge, has written a book he entitled *The American Disease*. Lodge summarizes his concept this way:

> There are today two dominant ideologies in the world: individualism and communitarianism.... The traditional ideology of the United States is an individualistic one. The community, as Locke would see it, is no more than the sum of individuals within it. The values of self-fulfillment and self-respect are realized through an essentially lonely struggle. The fit survive; if you do not survive, it is because you were somehow unfit.

Thus John Locke (1632–1704) is rightly saddled with bringing radical individualism into the American consciousness. In addition, the Puritan theology of individualized salvation fits into this notion of each individual having a destiny apart from all others. By this reckoning the "thrifty" become well provided for and the "have-nots" are undeserving of such providence.

Lodge's "American Disease" refers to our fixation with economic radical individualism. Americans espousing it hold to the most rigid and intransigent version of persons and property, despite the concept of organic community that many other nations embrace for themselves. Consequently, American businesses remain tied to the model of all-out competition with each other, while other developed nations, Japan particularly, can make enterprises work jointly and successfully by cooperation and central planning. Lodge does not suppose that individualism itself is the disease, rather he believes our rigid ideological commitment to individualism is the malady. This is not my view. I see individualism as a basic misconception of reality, and further that it yields a net deficit because we have lost more by the distortions of social fracturing than we have gained by individual competitive efforts.

Our American priorities in the way we regard persons and property are problematic. Part of this problem may stem from the changing uses of the term "property." In the beginning of the modern age of highly defined property rights, as embodied in the work of Thomas Hobbes and John Locke, the use of the term applied to a range of rights, such as the right to the exclusive use of one's own person and labor, as well as the right to enjoy commonly held possessions, i.e., the air, the oceans, and common lands, such as the Boston Common or Central Park in New York. But the possession of property also involved the exclusive personal right to the use and control of some material thing, including the right to bargain with it, to sell it at will, or to refuse to sell it at all. The term "property" has taken on a regressively narrow meaning in the centuries since the seventeenth and now refers almost exclusively to the ownership of material things. I venture the possibility that the Civil War at some level resulted from the working out of the contradiction between the old meaning of property as possessing the right to use and control labor, and the newer meaning as the exclusive possession of a material thing. By implication, by owning the right to the labor of another person, a slaveholder also transformed the slave from a human being into a *de facto* material thing.

The disputes over the older, expanded version of property and persons and the newer, restricted version omit a significant consideration. This is the difference in the assumptions about individualism held first by the medieval world that legitimated property, and then by the present world that makes exclusive reference to material things. The citizen of Locke's world, which was still in the last days of medievalism, was appropriately bound by limits on the available goods that an individual could take from the world as private property. Locke said:

> As much as anyone can make use of to any advantage of life before it spoils, so much may he by his labor fix a property in; whatever is beyond this, is more than his share, and belongs to others....He that leaves as much as another can make use of, does as good as taking nothing at all....He has

only to look that he used them before they spoiled, else he took more than his share, and robbed others; and indeed, it was a foolish thing, as well as dishonest.

Locke set his limitation on the right to property at the point at which the individual took more of the fruits of the earth than he could use before those fruits began to spoil. The limitation arose not because of harm to the earth or to the tree that bore the fruit, or even to the fruit that might spoil uneaten. The thievery affected that unfortunate individual—representative of the remainder of hungry humanity—who would come upon that tree and find it bare and thus be unable to eat and be nourished. Each hungry individual was one of an infinitely long line of individuals who would come to that universal tree and depend upon it for food and ultimately for survival. The last person in line had as much right to the fruit as the first, because they all depended upon it for food and survival. This inclusive version of human society, just as the universal category of humanity, predated any formalized economic structure. The individuals in human society have an equal right to access the natural supply of needed goods, a right equivalent to the right of any individual to claim possession of anything upon which he labors. But Locke also insists that each individual has an equitable right to the common natural resource. This involves a limitation on how much any individual can take without infringing upon the equitable right of one who comes last. That an individual arrives last does not reduce the validity of his claim for the respect of the earlier arrivals. Because Locke assumes that the common resource "tree" has an adequate supply of fruit to satisfy the survival needs of all comers, those who come early have no competitive advantage. The situation is not one of essential competition, but of mutual respect. Locke calls all abridgments of this respect robbery and dishonesty, essentially violations of moral values honored by civil society. This quaint analogy suggests the general limit of present necessity, in recognition of the same necessity on the part of others who are as yet not present.

Locke emerged from a tradition that accepted lordship and serfdom as legitimate class states with different responsibilities and privileges. He must have known that whatever the philosophical and legal definition of private property, ownership would preponderate in one class and be almost absent from the other. Locke was nurtured in a culture that claimed it had a moral basis in the moral and civil order because it recognized a higher value than power. Locke's era defined that higher power as the power of people to govern themselves. The rights of people to be governed by their own consent had begun to supersede the ancient powers of arbitrary might and coercion. If the right to self-government inheres in the human society as such, then no nonarbitrary point exists that sets apart consenting and nonconsenting people. Either all have the right to self-government, or none has that right. And either there is respect for the principle of self-government, or there is no recourse against raw power, however disguised by sophistic discourse.

The Shock of Recognition of Systems

The recognition of the reality of systems is a heavy but necessary burden of knowledge that represents a breakthrough that challenges the system itself. In recognizing the economic system for what it is, we confront a new set of assumptions. Our culture tells us we are all individuals in the world, and that whatever happens to us is what we deserve. This presumption seems to be a product of the idea of individual salvation that is part of the Apostolic gospel: each of us is a lost soul who can be saved only through his or her own isolated faith; no one except the self can make the "decision" that will bring that self into salvation; we can begin the Christian life, but whether or not we endure to the end depends on whether we can win against the satanic forces arrayed against us. Thus, we suffer in accordance with our own lack of faith or failure to conform to God's will. The system uses the weapons of fear and guilt to hold us in our submissive place. To break free of this submission, we must recognize that there *is* a system, and not just a multitude of individuals working in self-interest, but a self-perpetuating system by which power is allocated in a hierarchical fashion, that treats us as a piece of the machinery. This is what Buber calls the It-World.

This recognition brings with it a dark and sinister fear that tells us that we have betrayed our superiors, our benefactors. Frederick Douglass felt this terror when he realized that he was a slave, and that the slave owners' system had concocted the slave system and designed it to keep him ignorant of his true condition. They had told him that he was created to be a slave, and that to earn his salvation he must be a good and obedient slave.

Douglass knew this system because he had learned to read. He could now read the words that named the evil that bound him as an animal, but he realized that because no animal can read, he must not be an animal but a human person. When the evil was nameless, it was invisible to him, and so he thought his condition was natural. But the same blessing that opened the world to him also became a curse that told him how monstrous was the evil that bound him. He refused to yield to that evil the power to destroy him. He pledged to himself that he would transcend it, if necessary by dying, in the attempt to be free. He vowed that he would not die in a state of submission to slavery.

American slavery was an example of the It-World that Buber describes. It was a marvelously efficient economic mechanistic system, capable of keeping a multitude of causes and effects moving, colliding, and somehow surviving to move and collide again. For a person to believe that slavery was simply a collection of individual elements in random motion, that the slaveholders and slaves fit merely as individuals into the cause-and-effect churnings, and that they all deserved what they got as part of the machinery, is the same as submitting to this system. But to recognize slavery for what it was, an ancient institution like other such institutions that have survived the ravages of time and change, requires that we stand back and see it in perspective. The system has neither god nor devil in it, just the distilled essence of generations of users and used who have found how to repeat the motions that keep it on its course. From this perspective, we need not succumb to the principles of It-World as such. Instead, we can set out priorities in this It-World according to our knowledge of the Thou-World. Our relationships in our chosen and prized communal world can become the basis of life as a whole. The religion of relationship does not separate us from the empirical world, but gives us a sensible reason for connecting to it, a reason that serves our purposes.

Thoreau did not tie his writings in a bundle and throw them off the pier at Provincetown, to be carried out—possibly—to the continents by the tide. He took them to a printer and made them available to generations who would buy them and devour them. He did not change the system that made inferior writers and thinkers famous authors, while he himself remained known to a select few people. Instead, he related himself to that system in such a way that his talent and personality might someday come to energize multitudes of people to think, read, and write for themselves.

In a commercial enterprise, one of the easier ways to increase profit is to discover a potential change and to use it in your favor. For instance, if you can get a better depreciation plan on a piece of machinery, you might accrue monetary savings that would otherwise require a large increase in sales to accomplish. This is why CPAs and corporate lawyers are so well paid. And it is also why society badly needs to have a vigorous and strong governmental system to uphold social interests in the face of the vigorous, strong commercial system that we both need and want but also have to control.

Organic Society and Its Political and Economic Functions

We need to think of our society as an organic whole in which all systems of politics and economics are parts. As such, our society must run the government as a way to control business so that business operates in the interest of everyone. Over the past two centuries, the legal status of corporate enterprises has changed: formerly, a business had to serve a public interest directly; now, anyone can operate a business for private interest, with less or even no regard for public good. However, it does not simply follow that whatever makes a dollar for one person and leads to another person's earning a dollar is sure to enrich the society. A hot-dog-stand operator who saves money by not screening his windows may profit by a dollar or two, but society suffers ill health from the flies because of his greed. Multiply this a million times, if you will.

An organic entity such as a national society can possibly operate under a set of ideas and concepts that define that society as a mechanism. Indeed, when a society's leaders focus on making the system function as a machine should work, they will have a society, but a sick and fragmented one. The sickness of our society is not just a plague of personal sins. Neither personal sins nor personal virtues alone make our society sick or healthy. We have a sick society in the way that an organism can be sick but a mechanism cannot; our system is fragmented, dysfunctional. Our social fragmentation occurs in those areas of life still affected by sickness from the compounded mistakes and ignorance of the past.

Our next American religion may help to overcome these political and economic fragmentations. We need a religion that supports the community good, the general welfare, and social interests. It can do so by restraining triumphalism and promoting partnership, fairness, and respect. We must shape our religion into something that will reflect more of the reality of Jesus and less of the ideas of Apostle Paul and the Puritans.

Our American ancestors did much that was good and noble, but also much that was misguided. Some of their activities were downright cruel. The persistence of legal slavery, the failure of Reconstruction to give freed slaves a basis for the exercise of citizenship, and then the imposition of Jim Crow laws have made of us *Two Nations, Separate and Unequal,* as Andrew Hacker noted in his book about our racial fragmentation.

In spite of the strains that our fragmentations place on the reality of a "single society," we must work at understanding the causes of our separation. For instance, one of our major problems in the past, present, and future is how to actually apply our constitutional values of equal citizenship to those members of our society who are on the margins of its economic, political, and social structures. We have to recognize that some of our citizens lack realistic access to those structures. That recognition will prepare us to face the problem squarely and to find solutions to solve it. I believe that a creative and progressive religious culture can contribute significantly to those solutions.

The wider context of current religious issues calls for examination in light of the plausibility of the theory of organism. Perhaps the shattered condition of our society, based as it is on individualistic assumptions, raises doubt about even the provisional assumption of organicism. Nevertheless, this shattered condition demands that we find some plausible alternative to the bankrupt theory of radical individualism that has so miserably failed to sustain our society in these times of drastic change.

Provisional Organic Society

The term "provisional" here will indicate that this is an attempt to approximate a conceptual version of an organic society in the process of transition from a mechanistic world. Some doubt exists that a world such as we know our material world to be could or should operate on the principle of an organic society. Buber confronts this issue directly and says:

> Man cannot dispense with communal life any more than he can discard the It-world—over which the presence of the Thou floats like the spirit over the face of the waters. Man's will to profit and will to power are natural and legitimate as long as they are tied to the will to human relations and carried by it. There is no evil drive until the drive detaches itself from our being; the drive that is wedded to and determined by our being is the plasma of communal life, while the detached drive spells its disintegration. The economy as the house of the will to profit and the state as the house of the will to power participate in life so long as they participate in the spirit. If they abjure the spirit, they abjure life....The statesman or the businessman who serves the spirit is no dilettante. He knows well that he cannot simply confront the people with whom he has to deal as so many carriers of the Thou, without undoing his own work....He does not become a babbling enthusiast; he serves the truth which, though supra-rational, does not disown reason but holds it in her lap. What he does in communal life is no different from what is done in personal life by a man who knows that he cannot actualize the spirit in some pure fashion but who nevertheless bears witness of it daily to the It, defining the limit every day

anew, according to the right and measure of that day—discovering the limit anew.

The person who lives in the communal world of other persons by nature possesses enough creativity to navigate in the It-world and to find the right relationship to the whole world. As long as an individual respects the Other as a person, as one who is to be treated as an end only and never as a means to some other end, an infinite array of possible operations becomes available in carrying out mutual interests.

A society functioning along these guidelines would be a provisional operating organic society. Buber gives no specific guidance on how to organize political and economic principles for such a society. However, a contemporary American philosopher, John Rawls, is a noted theorist on philosophical principles of rights. His book, *A Theory of Justice,* gained recognition as a benchmark in innovative social theory. Rawls's explicitly aims to avoid the perils of utilitarianism and perfectionism. He eschews utilitarianism because it would allow the injury of one or a few persons in order to secure the benefit for many. Utilitarianism provides for empirical measures of good, but it also outlines a calculus of benefits and harms, seeking always to assure that the benefits provided to some will overbalance the harm caused to some others: How good for how many is weighed against how harmful to how many. Rawls also eschews perfectionism, which requires a specific conception of the good that is "Taken as the realization of human excellence in various forms of culture." This idea insists that to assure achievement of the highest level of human attainment of one single individual, it is worth placing on the satisfactions of all other individuals whatever limitations are necessary for that attainment. This principle has great appeal for certain imaginative souls who envision an ideal member of society who achieves a possible level of attainment and who, from his glorified height, presumably rains down surrogate satisfactions for all other members of the society. In this case, all would agree that perfectionism is a suitable principle of social policy, except those who sacrifice their own satisfactions in more lowly attainments. No doubt, a strong show of authority backed by force would be needed to provide such an arrangement. Some have suggested that slavery is the best way to get enough people to forego freedom to support the one or few who are pursuing some form of perfection.

Rawls' work has received criticism most notably for his method and his terminology. He claims that he wants to reverse much misguided social ethical theory. He seeks a method that will not quash personal interest but rather utilize it.

Rawls allows that altruism is an inconstant quality at best; at worst it can constitute a facade for veniality. Although almost everyone will achieve some degree of unselfishness in his decisions, for Rawls it is not a dependable motive. He holds that the altruistic motive can be manipulated so that the more suggestible among us will most often give up self-interest. Rawls claims that the recognition of self-interest has the advantage of getting an issue on the table so that it can be assessed and an account can be taken of what aspect of the issue each person considers in his or her own self-interest. Then, not only can the competing interests of others be considered, but a real examination can also be made of the validity of what each has stated as self-interest.

As an example of how to mix self-interest with fairness, let me suggest the method of securing equal shares in the absence of conveniently divisible numbers. For example, five people each have paid an equal amount for a share of a round pizza, and each person desires an equal portion of the food. How to accomplish the equal distribution? Because the pizza is getting colder by the minute, and most people prefer hot pizza, the situation requires a timely practical solution, not a theoretical analysis. I suggest a simple procedure that will most likely divide the pizza into five equal portions: Specify that the person chosen to slice the pizza will get the last piece, after each of the others has made his choice. The person in charge of slicing must exercise great care in order to get a fair share and to ensure that the last piece is as large as it can be, knowing that if any piece is noticeably larger than the others, it will surely be taken before he gets his own portion. Hence, in this mundane example, self-interest is placed in the service of fairness.

This approximates in crude terms what Rawls says in elegant terms. He uses the phrase "veil of ignorance" as a metaphor for the "Original position"— that standpoint that lacks rules for distribution of goods and precedes the establishment of those rules. My undergraduate students express amazement that an astute writer such as Rawls uses such a misleading phrase as "veil of ignorance." He does not mean that any decisions as to the distribution of advantages are to be made in the absence of knowledge; but rather he desires that each person simulate ignorance of his or her own interests in determining the outcome of the decision-making process. It is as though I place my own status and interests behind a "veil of ignorance" while I participate in consideration of the rules. For this purpose, I am to suppose that my status as an employer or as an employee is unknown when I consider the kind of rules I will endorse for the treatment of employees. I am to suppose that if I do not know what my financial status will be under the rules in question, what rules will I select to govern the exercise of property rights? Insofar as we could simulate a suspension of specific knowledge of our several self-interests, we could enact rules as fair and just as our imaginations and consciences could produce. Rawls's position provides for both personal and social priorities. His strategy answers some of the difficulties raised by the axiom, "Do unto others as you would have them do unto you."

Rawls's meticulous work defies summarization. His work on ethics is arguably the most extensive since that of Immanuel Kant. This is one of his summary statements:

> GENERAL CONCEPTION
> All social primary goods—liberty and opportunity, income and wealth, and the bases of self-respect—are to be distributed equally unless an unequal distribution of any or all of these goods is to the advantage of the least favored.

Rawls offers an exhaustive rationale for this position, and I will venture just two comments. Notice that Rawls's takes into account people of all sorts. He recognizes that there are those who are "least favored." Based on his principle we can say inclusively, "We the people," with a clear breath. But, the unequal distribution of goods will still happen when it is in the interest of all, particularly the least favored in the past, and who are therefore less able to bargain for themselves. For instance, the preparation of those who educate the public will require that they have the opportunity for formal study by which to prepare themselves so that the public can be educated. And so with those who will provide health care and so on. This does not militate against the opportunity of individuals to pay for education in private institutions, religious or secular. But it does provide that the opportunity for education of social value will be open to all who can use it. Rawls's "General Conception" does not prohibit the expenditure of personal funds for oneself or one's dependents, but it does provide a theoretical basis for the return of wealth to the public treasury for the useful promotion of social services. Rawls's formulation recognizes that every society is a whole composed of many parts, and all are interdependent together.

In Rawls's philosophy, the owner of an enterprise, the consumers of the products he makes, and the employees who produce them are all part of the social fabric. Liberty to pursue one's own ambitions and goals is assured as long as it does not prohibit someone else the exercise of his like liberty. Rights of speech and association are assured so long as the exercise of those rights does not prohibit someone else the same rights.

This theory has been called a socialist scheme, and Rawls does not object to this characterization. His plan certainly denies the validity of an advantaged position such as that of the American WASP class. The cause of justice concerns the WASP only when the use of public resources for individual profit is allowed by public policy. The WASP presupposes the existence of a settled set of personal advantages from which he can increasingly accumulate wealth within a legal system that is designed to promote that accumulation. The WASP individual masters this system and devotes his considerable talents to the purpose of applying this system in all aspects of society. The WASP system only excludes benefits to those who have been slighted by the system itself. This non-WASP portion of society has been effectively barred from receiving the benefits of the system while its contributions to the continued operation of the system have been utilized to the maximum. The hand-to-mouth plight of those tentatively placed at inferior status within the system is exploited for the benefit of those just above them. A requisite talent for the WASP to achieve status is the knack for using those just below on the ladder, and the capacity to accept being used by those just above.

Let us now mix and separate some concepts. Buber says that both the Thou-world and It-world have validity in our total world system. This would mean that the person who has settled into Thou relations still lives in the world of It-usage. The whole person is involved in the whole world, with primary practical roles alternating from one realm to the other. The value of all persons in the total world calls for the maximum attention to justice for each. No one deserves to be denied justice because of his or her involvement in either the Thou or It realm. The point of Thou-life is not to separate from the It-realm of persons, but rather to join them better in an authentic relationship. Thus, our blending together with all sorts of people will serve all of our interests, no matter where we are on the way to greater immersion in the Thou.

Life is more than just one thing, and attempting to settle into a fixed mold offers a poor beginning. Our lives are always in a state of tentative cohesion. Both as individuals and as a society, we need to have a sense of proportion in where we are now, and where we want to be in the future. Buber and Rawls provide very good conceptual frameworks in which to see both the personal and the public roles and concerns that we have. Each philosopher deals with different dimensions of life, but their concepts are compatible. Each respects the individual and the society as real priorities, neither of which is reducible to the other.

Religion Within Economic and Political Society

So far in this chapter I have avoided emphasis on religion. This is not because I consider economics and politics immune to religious interests. On the contrary, I wanted to deal with some issues on practical grounds and in secular terms, so that I can now consider those issues as religion bears upon them.

I mentioned the causes and effects of envy, especially as regards possessions, at the outset of this chapter. Now I wish to return to the discussion of motives and actions as religious factors in our personal and public relationships, particularly in those aspects dealing with possessions. Professor Richard Ely, who taught political economics at the University of Wisconsin at the turn of the century, said:

> We find this,—that things exist for the sake of persons; we find established a human control over things. But the essence of property is more than this. *The essence of property is in the relations among men arising out of their relations to things.*

To treat a person as a means to an end, such as a political or economic purpose, is overtly to violate that person's intrinsic worth and covertly to violate the worth of humanity. The user devalues himself as well as the one he uses. So the pursuit of the possession of things and the imitation of that pursuit of things in our use of persons violates the religious principle of the priority of the person. The religion of triumphalism promotes this violation, but the gospel of love reveals its harm. Respect for persons as such is a religious principle that engenders the belief in fairness, justice, and actions that increase those values in society.

That is precisely the role of religion in a secular democratic society: to provide beliefs and motives for action that will incite people to work for the increase of justice and fairness in society as a whole. We need coherent content in our principles and our beliefs, as well as inspiration that will help us accomplish what needs to be done in accordance with them. Religion has served humanity well when it has called upon people to make sense of their beliefs and to act upon that sense. Religion does not tell people only what makes them afraid and guilty and thereby prevent their doing what they can to improve their world. But people must be discriminating and critical of their religion if it is to support improvement rather than harm. The hard work of careful inquiry can enable us to find the better resources in our past and present that can inform our hopes for the future.

Although we need a religious prophet such as Martin Luther King, Jr., to function among us at the start of the century, we are already subject to too much spurious predictive prophecy. It does not help humanity's progress to have accidents, natural disasters, and terrorism portrayed as the precursors of the wrath of an angry and vengeful God. These tragedies have occurred throughout the ages, and they will continue to happen in the future. To stir fear and guilt among the populace simply because of the changing millennium is criminal irresponsibility. We do not need that kind of religious demagoguery.

Responsible and intelligent prophets of religious life and thought need to distance themselves from these purveyors of fear and guilt, and to inspire their people to produce works of art and engage in action that will open up our present world to new religious visions for the future. Every generation needs prophetic insight into the deeper meanings of its times and events that will encourage reactions and responses from people. Poets, artists, and writers can portray truth and beauty that the rest of us can recognize only when the gifts of insight are provided for us. But, the call for prophetic actions in our times is as great as the need for insight. Religion has often served as one of the powerhouses behind great movements for freedom, justice, and human transformation. The rise of humanistic science and philosophy does not lessen the role of religion, but strengthens it by ridding it of dross.

This book has provided selective criticism of traditional religion, but it does not intend to undermine the faith of people who find religion to be a resource for good in their lives. I have not attempted to promote or to degrade religion, but to hold it up to the best light that I know. My own passage through the minefields of ancient dogmatic error and modern fundamentalist distortions does not lead me to think that I have all the answers. I have much to learn, and nothing to present as beyond question.

This is my faith, then. It is a chosen faith, not a revealed one or a commanded one. If I believe in this capacity of humanity to be reconciled, I will act as though it is true and make my commitments in that light. To the extent that this belief is acted upon and humanity works to bring it about, then it will become true. It is not my faith alone, but it is mine because I have inherited from the past those resources that make it possible. It has become a live option for me, so I choose it as my priority. Reconciliation may never come to be, but it is more worthy of belief and hope than anything else I know.

10

America's Next Religion
A Champion Triumphalist

THOMAS N. CARVER, a Professor of Sociology at Harvard University in the early twentieth century, was an unconventionally candid commentator on religious issues of his time. As a secular scholar, he went beyond the usual limits of polite theological or sectarian discussion. His sophistication enabled him to take a detached and dispassionate view of religion in all its forms. His book, *Religion Worth Having,* rebutted those of his time who insisted that an educated person could not support the continued existence of organized religious institutions. Some charged that to support any organized religion now was to act like the cathedral builders of the Dark Ages, who are said to have put needed resources into inefficient uses. To the contrary, Carver insisted that one religion could be better than all the others:

> What is the best religion? That is the best religion which (1) acts most powerfully as a spur to energy, and (2) directs that energy most productively.

Thus, Carver takes an uncritical but utilitarian view toward what some insist is a matter of mystical meanings and beliefs. If there has ever been a secular spokesperson for the triumphalist view of progress and its benefits, it must be Carver. After describing the Spartan discipline and rigorous order of his ideal "church," Carver says:

> This church would be founded upon the rock of economic efficiency, and the gates of hell should not prevail against it....Such a church could not help becoming a rich men's church, because it would be making its people rich and prosperous. Not to become a rich men's church in this sense is a disgrace and an evidence of failure.

Carver's book, published in 1912, seems to be much in tune with the era of "manifest destiny" and "progress onward and upward forever." His approach makes little appeal to psychological subtlety but calls for sacrificial action for the greater glory of white Protestant America—and woe to all who miss the call.

> Again, the Fellowship of the Productive Life is a new conception of the Church militant for the conquest of the world. In season and out of season it is the call to be made for men to abandon the unproductive and take on the productive life. No human being is to be regarded as beyond the reach of this call. But, they who do not respond to it but persist in their unproductiveness, are doomed, which means damned. They refuse to conform to the universal laws of success, and nature damns them.

The scope of the effort Carver predicts for a Christian America involves nothing less than final global conquest:

> If Christians make themselves worthy to receive the world by making themselves more productive than others—able to use the resources of the world to better advantage than others—then the world will be actually delivered into their hands, not by some sudden and miraculous intervention, that is, by some sudden and unusual manifestation of divine power, but by the sure process of economic law, which is, properly understood, the regular, uniform, everyday manifestation of divine power.

Those who heed Carver's call to this kind of religion will find themselves "participating in the building of the Kingdom of God."

Although Carver's book is so much in keeping with the predominant popular mind of the time, his work is still relatively obscure. Carver could have joined the company of saints who presided over Wall Street before the crash of 1929, or the postwar boom of the Eisenhower era, or certainly the Reagan "trickle-down" years. If I had not grown up in the twilight of the era of unlimited faith in progress, I would find Carver naive and simplistic. But America, despite the Great Depression, still had faith in progress. I recall visiting the "City of Tomorrow," the Trylon, and the Perisphere at the 1939 New York World's Fair. They presented a vision of an uncluttered future, one so ordinary that it was as familiar as the streets of one's hometown. But to my boy's mind, the startling innovation was the fanciful vehicles of the future, composite cars and airplanes that seemed to buzz around in profusion without any danger of colliding. It looked so familiar and unthreatening, and yet so different. The producers had cleverly taken our ordinary world and filled it with familiar things that were portrayed as doing fantastic things. Airplanes took off vertically and needed less space than that in the typical suburban backyard to get aloft. That was the intent of the exhibit: to depict a world everyone knew and loved and make it nicer and easier to use. We were not supposed to see the built-in complications that trade-offs with developments always involve. As with the designers of the "City of Tomorrow," Carver seems to have been as unaware of the underlying complexities of modern urban life as most of the educated people of his time. Some people could see the smoke on the horizon, but they tended to be the people who politically espoused fringe areas of racial, intellectual, and gender issues, and who were thus not taken very seriously by the public.

Carver represented a wide and pervasive American mainstream. Few people of his time consciously connected their triumphalist religion with the greed for wealth that Carver approved and promoted. Authoritarianism predominated in the family, churches, and schools of American society, even though some early progressive challenges had emerged. The people were actually being grossly and systematically exploited, but not many were aware of that fact. Few among the exploited groups had the necessary knowledge and courage to speak out about that exploitation. The labor movement had made striking gains in a few lines of work, but employers and police alike had brutalized those in the labor movement. One employer's statement, "I can hire half of my workers to kill the other half," seems to sum up the business-class attitude of the time. The typical American, which Carver represented, was conservative and reactionary. He or she also believed in Social Darwinism, the value of colonialism, and the inevitable triumph of the free-enterprise system. Confidence in America's role as the colossus of the West remained unchallenged. America was seen as what the Puritans had intended it to be: a divinely chartered state that would teach the rest of the world how God meant for humanity to live.

Carver's thinking about religion made some important advancements over that of his orthodox Christian contemporaries. Carver makes a Copernican-type shift by moving the center of religious gravity from the "other world" of heaven to this world of rocks and trees, skies and seas, and his own vision of humanity. He disregards the former burning evangelical issues of "Where will you spend eternity, either in hell or in paradise?" What Carver considers good must be good here and now, not somewhere, sometime. Carver's God does not hang haloes on pious, sentimental spiritual dilettantes. His image of God well approximates the deist's divinity, a creator of nature who has set things on course so well that we have only to get in line. In all this, Carver is an age ahead of the Puritans and their surviving "revivalist" followers who constitute contemporary fundamentalism.

Carver retained all the generalized assumptions that the earlier deists had proposed. Not only did he assume that the deists were right about God, but he also seems to have believed—at least partly on the basis of their assumptions—that the deists would have agreed to absolutize the capitalist, free-enterprise system that had grown up since their time. Carver seemed to assume, as do his current counterparts among the Christian Coalition and their political allies, that there is only one game in America: everyone has to play the game by the same rules, but those favored by birth get a head start.

This triumphalist concept of equality of opportunity works somewhat like a try-out for an imaginary baseball team. Let us suppose that everyone who wants to play will have the same opportunity to prove what he or she can do in a contest in Yankee Stadium. Each hopeful candidate gets a swing of the bat, one chance to hit the ball thrown by a fast-ball pitcher such as Nolan Ryan. If the batter hits a home run, he makes the team. Imagine one young person, fresh out of a triumphant high school or college athletic career, who competes against another youth whose lack of coordination since childhood kept him from being picked for any team. This version of "equal opportunity" makes no allowances for whether the batter has ever seen a baseball before in his life or has ever held a bat. He is expected to stand in the batter's box while the pitcher throws the ball at a hundred miles an hour within a few inches of his head. Of course, they all have the same chance: one pitch, one swing, and either a home run or a failure. This system of equality of opportunity favors its chosen ones and mocks the rest.

The situation is similar among the current competitors for places in our economic system. Some have the momentum of many generations of successful ancestors on their side. They have grown up in families that could give them early exposure to the ethos of business and the professions. Dinner-table conversation and interaction with their parents' social circles further reinforced the education and culture of these privileged ones. Such youth were destined to follow in the footsteps of those who had gone before them to achieve wealth and success.

Political arguments against such social programs as Head Start and affirmative action initiatives presuppose that all the prospective candidates for places in the economy already encounter a level playing field. Those who have never lived in a home with an adult who has held a regular, lifelong job nevertheless are presumed to stand on the level with the privileged. Those who have suffered malnourishment and deprivation from birth are supposed to have bodies and minds that thrive as well as those of the middle and upper classes. It is unrealistic to expect the one-fourth of our American children who live in poverty to compete on an equal basis with those of us who grew up in comfortable circumstances. I became aware of this inequality when I spoke about the unfortunate eroding of Affirmative Action in a class on Business Ethics. My Euro-American students could hardly be convinced that in my own youth I had undeserved advantages over my Afro-American peers when I competed for job placement. The Euro-American students seemed convinced that they suffered a disadvantage because special considerations placed women and minority candidates in competition with them.

Carver, a Harvard professor and thoroughly secular believer, is more akin to members of the Christian Coalition than many a priest or bishop in his thinking about religion in our time. His "ideal religion" is roughly equivalent to a marketplace version of Christendom, with buyer decisions made on the basis of the self-aggrandizing and advertising powers of the competing movements, ministries, and media. The Crystal Cathedral in the Los Angeles area stands as a most garish example of a monument to self-glorification among church-type enterprises. The congregation's leader, Robert Schuller, is among the most notorious of the "prosperity gospel" purveyors in both religious and secular settings. The media and mail-order empire of Pat Robertson seems to have gained ascendancy over even the long-running Billy Graham establishment in the crusade and electronic media enterprises.

These and similar groups will differ on the minutiae of doctrine and practice, but unlike Carver, they are all basically wedded to the creationist world-view and to the hope for heavenly rewards. They make the same appeals to the appetites of the privileged white-male majority and those who aspire to join them. They advocate a certain amount of "charity" for victims of disasters and sin-related troubles combined with appeals to return public life to Victorian standards of sexual and work ethics. These religions regularly reassert male and heterosexual dominance and the sanctity of the "free market" as it operates for the benefit of profit-oriented corporations. Such churches preach moral absolutes invariably based on individual effort and decisions and define all moral values in terms of obedience to or violation of holy laws. They never suggest that a flaw in any traditional or majority structure might be responsible for any personal or social problems.

The era following the Second World War ushered in an elevation of the socioeconomic status of the working class, which represents the numerical core constituency of the neo-conservative majority. This new prosperity eroded working-class support for trade unions and sanctified radical individualism among workers during the Reagan-Bush years. This new financial status resulted in a strange marriage of working-class incomes with executive-class interests. Workers have held their sheer independence, or "freedom," as an article of faith, even when simultaneously these same workers find their wages reduced, their benefits withdrawn, and the factories in which they worked transplanted in the pursuit for cheap labor. A "conservative" politician can identify with "family values," e.g., male dominance and homophobia, and get working-class support for his program to cut the taxes of the wealthiest Americans.

Carver: Halfway Home

Thomas Carver deserves credit for reorienting his religious center of gravity from the other world to this present one. He is to be commended for realizing that "religion worth having" should be directed toward the problems and opportunities that exist here and now. He forthrightly claims that the aspirations of Christendom for taking over the world's devotional life are wrong, and that the right aspiration would involve governance over practical affairs. These ideas must have sounded heretical to traditional theologians and preachers of his time. But because these traditionalists had their hands full fighting with the evolutionists and the modernists within their ranks, they did not see how Carter disparaged their heavenly fiefdom.

However, Carver had traveled only halfway to the destination. He still carried much of the baggage of triumphalism left over from earlier times. He kept American religion exclusive, dividing "us" from "them" as though we are indeed the chosen people who are divinely destined to rule the "lesser breeds without the law." Carter's formulation retains and extends the WASP philosophy, perhaps adding the proviso that recent immigrants can be included among the chosen people if they become productive and wealthy. Carver exaggerates the materialist assumption that the increased production of things alone enriches the person and society.

Carver assumes that the production of more and more things will clearly and certainly benefit the nation. This assumption rests upon, but perverts, the obvious perception that individual and social benefits accrue more frequently in a nation that makes adequate provision for the physical and mental needs of its people. But we notice the great gulf that exists between the provision of basic needs, on one hand and, on the other, the profound enrichment of life through nurturing relationships within a community of caring and productive people. It is unwise to expect that the community can thrive and endure in the absence of the former, but it is equally unwise and naïve to think that the latter can be reduced to the former. The two empirical conditions are complementary: an adequate supply of goods supports the achievement of relationships between cooperative people, and thriving individuals in a mutually supportive community will be more likely to utilize work and materials in producing things that are genuinely needed, and not merely marketable incentives to envy and competition.

Carver not only perpetuates the fragmentation of the community, but he increases the confusion of persons with things. This confusion does not appear to Carver, because he remains encapsulated within the mechanistic point of view. He sees the American citizen only in terms of his usage of other people, foreign and domestic. Carver rightly reads the system of commerce on its own terms, but he fails to see the limitations of this system as a basis for living. If we could enclose aspects of life into airtight compartments, we might be able to get away with using without being used. We cannot adequately manage the using to get all its benefits without any of its cost. The problem is that "simple using" is incompatible with the structure of the community, which is inevitably organic, and not mechanical. "Simple using" differs from "mutual using" in this respect: we all function reciprocally with others in a complex version of "mutual using" that is grounded in the organic unity of humanity. "Simple using" is characteristic of an It-World or a spurious mechanistic universe.

Carver made commendable progress in taking an empirical approach to religion, but his theory does not go far enough. Can Carver's empirical step that relocated the Holy of Holies from the other world to this world be extended to the areas of values and purposes? We need to consider some concrete examples of the situation in which we find ourselves at this time.

Triumphalism Today

The religion that Billy Graham has promoted in America has generally perpetuated the major themes of the triumphalists. However, he has leaned toward a certain amount of change in racial integration. He went to Birmingham, Alabama, in 1964, to hold an arena service with an integrated crowd, reputedly the largest racially mixed event ever held in that city up to that time. Graham had distanced himself from the major efforts and accomplishments of Martin Luther King, Jr., and the Civil Rights movement. Ralph Reed, the one-time Christian Coalition leader, quotes Graham as saying:

> I must admit that in all those years it didn't cross my mind that segregation and its consequences for the human family were evil. I was blind to that reality.

Although Graham has since repudiated the racist position, some of the fundamentalists see a worse problem in Graham's words than just his insistence on preaching to an integrated audience in Birmingham. His open and sometimes unseemly mixing of the "old-time religion" with modern ecumenism, which brings famous and powerful nonfundamentalist people into his company, makes his standing ambiguous. Apparently, an invitation from Billy Graham is too important to refuse. From time to time, presidents, cardinals, and crowned heads appeared at his rallies like trophies. It is ludicrous to think that some of those people sympathized at all with his message of the angry God, but he traded reflected glory with the celebrities and capitalized on it with the public. Graham has been the white-collar icon of triumphalism. He claims that he is offering people "good news," but the assumptions of that message are that they must deal with an angry God, and that Graham will tell them just how to do it. But Graham's day has passed, and he is now being replaced by more abrasive vicars of God.

Triumphalists have prevailed in American history despite the steady increase in the presence of diverse classes, races, and genders in public life. Paradoxically, progressive political and religious leaders sometimes made ambiguous use of proscriptive rhetoric in their efforts to accomplish significant progress in the causes of justice and freedom. Jefferson relied on the language of ancient scripture in his statement, "All men are created equal and are endowed by their Creator," but omitted any reference to the topics of sin and salvation, heaven or hell, creeds or rituals, which the Puritans used liberally. Martin Luther King, Jr., confronted dual problems: first, he needed to inspire white people to work for Afro-American justice; and, second, he needed to motivate black people to risk themselves for a cause they might well lose. King had to inspire and to activate the ordinary American people whose major value system was based in scripture, and in American idealism. He used the common traditional religious rhetoric, "Let my people go" and "I've seen the Promised Land," but simultaneously resorted to the nonviolent disobedience tactics of Gandhi. Then, he departed from the traditions of both black and white by teaching and exemplifying nonviolent resistance and love for enemies rather than stressing the forceful tactics of Nat Turner, leader of a slave revolt, and John Brown of Kansas and Harper's Ferry.

Although King's appeal was contrary to American triumphalism, his labors brought into the Civil Rights movement white Americans who believed in the cause of justice, but still felt concerned about obedience to local laws. King's exhortations gave these Americans the authoritative justification that they needed to resist established conventions. Jesus had also preached and practiced nonviolent resistance; his example provided Americans with the rationale to follow King, even though it meant going against their well-entrenched habit of conforming to convention.

King's strategic use of both prescriptive religious rhetoric, as in the "Let my people go" example, and also the unconventional prophetic religious ideal of "turning the other cheek," sheds light on the possible course of future American religion. King managed to mobilize both black and white people to reject strong local racial conventions and to withstand criticism from those other black and white people who had entrenched interests in maintaining racial separation and discrimination. Although other factors, such as the GI Bill of Rights that gave many black men and women access to education, and the emotionally powerful assassination of President Kennedy, contributed to those victories for civil rights legislation, King's leadership served as the catalyst for unprecedented social change. Future progressive leaders will need to utilize both prophetic and proscriptive rhetoric to inspire sacrificial human service.

Triumphalists have so effectively preempted the rhetoric of Christendom that the language of our common religion has lost much of its power to motivate well-meaning citizens toward sacrificial service for empirical human values. Fundamentalists have made such strident and arrogant use of their proscriptive language in their abuse of poor, female, and nonwhite people that their talk of love and righteousness is more repugnant than inspiring. Cases of this acrimonious abuse of language appear in the fundamentalist crusades against contraception and abortion. These crusades rest on beliefs about religious teachings that deny the realities of contemporary life. The fundamentalists assign the same moral and legal status to a newly conceived zygote or a fetus at one month of gestation as they do to the offspring of a woman and man with responsibilities for and commitments to a presently living, growing family. These crusaders assign equivalent moral standing to a microscopic group of cells in the first few days after the union of ovum and sperm, before it is implanted into the wall of the uterus, as to a full-term fetus. In both cases, they claim that interrupting gestation is always the same as the murder of a person. However contrary to fact this claim may be, the fundamentalist bases his belief on an absolutist interpretation of certain sayings in the ancient scriptures; he summarily disregards the context of the scriptural citations that do not assign equal value to both the conceptus and a fully evolved person.

Fundamentalists believe that all human sexuality is a mystical affair between God and the creatures He has defined as consumed with lust and carnality. Fundamentalists believe that this deity will not approve any experience that can distract from adoration of the deity himself. Hence, because the deity has ordained sexual experiences as necessary for the continuance of humanity, procreation and not pleasure must be the only reason for indulging in sexual practices. What might be the moral status of a man and wife who engage in sexual intercourse during her early pregnancy, when they know her to be pregnant and so cannot become any more pregnant whatever they do? One experienced advocate of the fundamentalist position replied: "They can go ahead and do it, but they just shouldn't enjoy it." Although he seemed to enjoy the humor in his answer, he not surprisingly considered the question facetious and evidence of a bad spirit.

Progressive Inspiration

Future progressive leaders and teachers of religion face a serious question: What sources of inspiration for human service will be available and effective within the scope of credible assumptions about the empirical world? The examples of Jefferson and King show that because the audience already believed in a mystical view of the world, the leader used rhetoric that was easily compatible with that view, while subsequently moving beyond the conventionally held truths to more empirically comprehensive assumptions. Jefferson did not ask white Americans to tell black Americans that God loved them and would welcome them to heaven equally with the whites themselves. Instead, he based the American ideal of a democratic and just society on the principle of government by the consent of the governed. That principle carries the inescapable implication that all Americans who are governed by the laws of the nation, whether slave or free at the time, have full rights to participate in the governing process. In the same way, King did not ask that the white churches close down the black churches and let black people join the whites in worship. Instead, he asked for recognition of black people as worthy of full rights of citizenship and for the end of official and social denial of justice for his people.

The America of the twenty-first century will not be the America of the past. Education and enhanced experience of the world has extended comprehensive empiricism among the populace, and this new knowledge will inevitably require that religious leaders and teachers speak and act on assumptions different from those of our ancestors. Sex can no longer be treated as a mystical concern between the ordained surrogates of God and their subject people. People will increasingly demand freedom to control their sexual activities for their mutual satisfaction and their parenting responsibilities. Comprehensive empirical principles will need to replace abstract rules and prohibitions. We already know much about human sexuality as it is understood and practiced by people all over the world, and this knowledge will not allow us to observe ancient religious commands as though our culture defines right and wrong for everyone on earth.

We still face the question of how best to shape our appeals for human service so that they reflect the new assumptions. Our answer should be analogous to our ways of communicating in other areas concerning motivation for nurture in a world of new and challenging assumptions. For instance, new knowledge of genetic and environmental causes of debilitation and disease is revolutionizing health care, and making it distinct from our previous understanding of infection and malnutrition as exclusive causes of health problems. If we are to benefit from this additional empirical understanding, we will have to find ways of motivating people to act on it in their own behalf. In the past we were cautioned to wash our hands and to eat our fruits and grains. In the future, we will need to demand governmental monitoring and regulation of corporations that deal with genetic and environmental benefits and hazards, along with educational programs that raise the population's awareness of the effects of these manipulations.

How can we inspire our young people to take responsibility for the new meaning of social good, when that good has been redefined according to the ideals of comprehensive empirical values? The pivotal question for the coming generation should be "Who gets hurt and who gets helped by the proposed public action, and by what factors of quality and quantity?" We need to recognize that only those who have received deliberate and structured nurture while they were young will be able to respond to such values. Then we will realize that we need to make provision for nurture so that we can instill a sense of caring purpose in our social activities. I do not profess to have the answers to these questions, but I believe that we need religious leadership that will respect the need for inspiration that can combine our nostalgic attachments to language and symbols of the past with values based on an empirical understanding in tune with the future. Simple and easy answers will not do. But I believe that one method can offer hope for the difficult task, the method of pragmatism.

Pragmatism: the Alternative to Dogmatism

John Dewey (1859–1952) pioneered the laboratory study of the learning process in children. He tried to discover what actually happens when a child learns. Dewey found that the learner is the primary agent in the learning activity. In effect, learning takes place not because of the activity of the teacher as a giver of information, but rather because of the activity of the student as a creator of personal knowledge.

Dewey believed that intelligence arises from human nature, as the human organism exercises its most unique function, that of rational construction of knowledge. Learning is a process of meeting the challenges of natural existence. Most of an individual's learning derives from the learning experiences of other people, not from each individual's firsthand experience. We all learn within "our world," which is constructed by the combined and extended learning experiences of our ancestors. Just as we do not need to dig a well every time we want a drink of water, we do not invent a whole world in order to learn about the one we live in. What comes first in learning, questions or answers? The old style of education assumed that teachers had the correct and final answers, and the students had to learn to repeat the responses that the teachers had taught them.

The pragmatic approach places primary pedagogical and logical importance on the questions. That is, the individual thinker will encounter problematic situations in life and have to find satisfactory solutions to those practical problems. The problematic world calls for us to think about our actions. Education does not prepare us to go into the world knowing the answers to all the questions that may arise. We go into the world with a method of dealing with the problems that we meet. No teacher could anticipate all the answers that a pupil will need, nor can the teacher go along with the student to provide answers to questions as they arise. However, the teacher can act as an example to the learner and can provide a method by which the pupil can confront the questions that challenge him.

Pragmatism is the method of science. In the scientific method Dewey found the closest approximation to an absolute. An absolute is that which depends upon itself alone and requires no explanation outside itself. The scientific method therefore is a functional absolute, if not a metaphysical one. As an illustration of this functional absolute, assume that we were to find the scientific method inadequate to deal with a problem: how would we best deal with that finding? Is there a better way to solve that problem than to apply scientific method to it? That is, in order to replace the scientific method, we would have to use the method itself to find a better one. We would examine the problem, gather evidence from our observation, propose a hypothesis to account for that evidence, and then find a way to test that hypothesis. Notice that there is no prior assumption about what the answer must be. This denial of unquestionable assumptions is the sticking point for most enemies of pragmatism.

Philosophical pragmatism provides a foundation for inspiration and motivation because it enables us to see the organic connections between ourselves and other human beings. We can then experience an upsurge of compassion and an incentive to do what is good for others on the basis of that organic connection alone. The power of humanistic inspiration can direct people onto paths where their efforts can make a difference for others, instead of into areas where their individual interests benefit only themselves. This kind of inspiration motivated and sustained such individuals as Jefferson, Thoreau, Douglass, and Keller. They were not considered saints in any conventional sense. Their sources of inspiration sprang from sources as diverse as their paths to personal development. But they all shared a deep belief that humanity is a whole which is undivided in essential worth, and thus due respect and nurturance. They used different talents and methods to bring their visions to bear upon a society recalcitrant in its atomistic individuality.

A unique human spirituality compels such people to find and enlarge upon those potential connections between people that make life better and the world more coherent. Although they were not "pragmatists" in the technical sense of the word, Jefferson, Thoreau, Douglass, and Keller shared a belief with pragmatists such as Dewey that humanity is at home in nature, and that all of us have an equal right to natural satisfactions and benefits. Such people are examples of those who seek after wholeness and goodness in nature, and who do not appeal to anything supernatural to validate human values. Theirs is a spirituality that denies that some of us have an essential worth that others lack. Those weak and disfigured in mind or body may not find their rightful share of the benefits of nature and society, but they deserve to find them, and fairness requires that none of us exploit their condition. Such spirituality seeks to strengthen and extend the processes of nurture for all people. Such spirituality has neither vision nor hope for perfection in the sacred or secular ideals of humanity, but it envisions and produces improvements in the conditions of people as individuals and as a society.

A pragmatist is a humanist and a consequentialist. As a humanist, he or she believes that authentic values are inherent in the human situation, and not in anything beyond humanity and its workings. As a consequentialist, he or she is concerned with the distant and comprehensive results of an action, as well as results that are obvious and immediate. All human decisions must be seen in the light of the larger and future outcomes of that decision. For example, if we would help someone in crisis, we need to avoid incurring another, more serious crisis in the process. The pragmatists recognize that we are in an organic world. All webs of circumstances are interconnected so that we can never do just one thing. So long as that one thing makes any difference at all, it may also bring about some differences that we did not intend. Whatever change comes about because of our intention and sight, other changes, unforeseen and beyond our present vision and intentions, may also arise. The pragmatist needs to remember the ubiquitous question in all moral problems, "If I do this, which I think is good, then what?"

Pragmatism rejects traditional absolutes such as unquestionable revelations and supra-natural beings. As scientific method is its rational "absolute," so nature is its "absolute" reality. Humanity as a part of nature is our original position. We find ourselves in the midst of a world of beauty and problems. It is our normal function to appreciate this beauty and to deal with those problems. The pragmatist believes that we are naturally equipped to do so. All else flows from these assumptions, and these assumptions are arguable among all inquirers. There are no privileged positions or truths, no unquestionable assumptions.

Before John Dewey became a pragmatist he was concerned about education in the public schools of America. He was fortunate to be raised in the small town of Burlington, Vermont, which was also the seat of the University of Vermont. After graduation from college, he taught in the public high school of Oil City, Pennsylvania, for two years. There he was exposed to the rough and seamy side of public education in a nation that had little interest in its young people spending time with books rather than with the chores of adult work. Public education was still in its formative stage, and rural and poor youth were more out of school than in. After doing his graduate work in philosophy at Johns Hopkins University, Dewey went to the University of Chicago in 1894 where he established the Laboratory School. There he and his colleagues actually watched and listened to children being taught by means of various educational procedures and used those observations as the basis of their theoretical work on education and their recommendations for education of teachers.

Dewey's group first gathered relevant information by which to formulate questions and answers. By observation, he ascertained how children learn and what conditions promote that learning. This became the starting point for his inquiry into the question of what are the best teaching practices. The results of Dewey's approach became known and popularized as "progressive education." This pedagogical theory and practice emerged during the early decades of the twentieth century, when much of American public education began taking direction. Dewey and thousands of other teachers thought about and fought for a concept of education that makes the child central to the process. This theory and practice are relevant factors in the actual schoolroom. Sometimes they have yielded great success; sometimes unprepared people or unfavorable circumstances have bungled Dewey's method of progressive education. On the whole, pragmatism has served the American educational process well. The solution to the present problems of American education is to be found in more pragmatism, not less.

By contrast, triumphalist ecclesiastical institutions and leaders take an approach that has so little relevance to actual problems of social morality and public needs as to be virtually from another world. People who live in thrall to dogmatic religion have a restricted view of the world around them. The ancient dogmas they believe and defend limit the believers' perspective. Because their beliefs define the world for them, problems find certain solutions among the prescriptions of dogma, almost without regard to the actual situation. Consequently, the sexual regulations of Augustine and the Puritans are useless in the real human situation. Abstinence outside marriage, absolute heterosexuality, and the holiness of virginity and celibacy, with all prohibitions that come from those ideals, just do not answer real human problems. In earlier times, such admonitions as those might have been effective, especially when reinforced by the controls exercised by village and elder oversight of behavior in a closely knit group. But as those older, closely knit groups have disappeared and as many of us live not only in urban isolation but also in crowded poverty, the regulations required by the old dogmas have little relevance. We need another set of values to inculcate sexual responsibility in maturing adolescents and adults. Puritan times and our times differ in the access our children and pubescent youth have to sexual initiation and stimulation, especially in a culture steeped in "using" relationships. In addition, we live in a culture permeated by violence perpetrated against minds and bodies and saturated with media advertising and entertainment. As a result, our world has become a world of escalating hurting and being hurt.

Our American obsession with relations that are primarily instrumental rather than nurturing has poisoned our efforts to provide help to people who need it. A grudgingly patronizing attitude too often accompanies our charity and welfare. Because we lack respect for the humanity of those who need help, we treat them as if they had failed to earn the economic wherewithal to exchange for what they lack. Our efforts to help them are intended to correct this failure and to fit them into the system. We have no way to see both them and ourselves in our actual situation, a situation in which our lack of mutually respecting relationships has stunted us all in our growth as persons. We all lose when we treat each other as means rather than ends.

The awful tragedy of current American religion is its irrelevance to this current plague of people hurting people. The answers to the epidemic must come from some other source than mere dogmatism from the ancient past. I suggest that the better source lies in adopting a more pragmatic approach to the actual conditions that we have allowed to overtake us. This involves respect for the scientific competence of those to whom we turn for understanding of the problems. Science has no magic solutions; indeed, some assumptions of current scientists need reformulation, such as the materialistic individualism that makes nature a system of usable things only, as well as the male dominance that reduces respect for women as scientists. But we cannot go forward by abandoning science. We can go forward only with more and better science.

The attacks on the pragmatist's position on morality remind me sadly of the attacks on Socrates in Athens of 399 B.C.E. Plato tells the story in his dialogue *The Apology*. Socrates is not guilty of atheism, as his enemies charged, because he does indeed invoke divine guidance in his philosophical inquiries. His only offense is that he believes that the gods are at least as good as good men, and Socrates' accusers believe that the gods are neither moral nor immoral but are not subject to moral judgment. So his defamers executed Socrates because he held a better opinion of the gods than the people of Athens themselves had held. Still, some Athenians wanted their city to claim the patronage of deities who acted immorally in mortal terms. Socrates did not accept this version of the character of the gods, even if it were the conventional belief. The pragmatic view does not allow for a deity who purportedly subjects humanity to cruel fate, but who is beyond moral accountability. A deity who stands outside human morality and still intervenes capriciously in human affairs contradicts the best we can know of reality, as the pragmatist sees it. The pragmatist thus holds a higher standard of morality for the universe than the triumphalist does.

A Basic Question of Social Morality

The next American religion will have to address moral questions involving the allocation of our national resources for nurturing or destructive purposes. This is a moral question because it is based on value assumptions and on the issue of inclusion or exclusion of marginal citizens. On the evening of January 17, 1961, President Dwight D. Eisenhower urged the American populace to exercise moral responsibility in this regard in his "farewell address" on the eve of his successor's inauguration. This American general had spent his career in the military establishment, but in his last words to the people who had elected him almost by acclamation, he issued a prophetic message. It did not concern global economics, or "family values"; it concerned the priority of nurture.

President Eisenhower warned his country against the system that he had helped build, the military-industrial complex. He did not suggest that we dismantle that monstrous machine of destructive power. But he did warn against losing our sense of priorities. Among other things, he compared the cost of an aircraft carrier with the public's investment in schools. He urged the people—not the politicians or the military-industrial moguls, but the citizens of the United States—to realize that they could not buy safety from foreign threats by depriving their children of nurture and opportunity. The possible misapplication of priorities posed as great a threat as that of all potential enemies. Eisenhower concluded his address with an earnest plea that "all peoples will come to live together in a peace guaranteed by the binding force of mutual respect and love."

The noble, elder warrior-statesman could hardly have known that somewhere in the vicinity of the White House from which he spoke, his youthful successor prepared another speech that would initiate a new round of the process that the outgoing president warned against. In his inaugural-day speech, John F. Kennedy promised that Americans would enforce "freedom" worldwide, "Going anywhere, paying any price." Soon, the "Bay of Pigs" became part of our vocabulary, and then Vietnam, and Nicaragua, and so on and on. Not only did we pour our resources at forced-draft speed into everything from hand grenades to hydrogen bombs, and from walkie-talkies to "Star-Wars" technology, but we also extended our space program into a national crusade, a thinly disguised assault on Russian claims to missile superiority.

A story from Cape Canaveral reported a meeting between the head of the man-on-the-moon program and a representative of the Civil Rights movement, Dr. Ralph Abernathy. He claimed that millions of poor Americans needed the resources of our nation for nurture and opportunity, and those were measured against the enormous expenditure for the space program. Dr. Thomas O. Paine, the head of the installation, acknowledged those claims and said:

> If it were possible for us not to push the button tomorrow and solve the problems with which you are concerned, we would not push the button.

Paine asserts that he agreed with the assessment of the priorities. He confessed that if he thought that the money being spent on the lunar program would instead be spent on human needs, he would call off the launch. Abernathy had put forward concrete enough needs: schools, hospitals, and housing for poor children and families. The availability of money was obvious from the lavish expenditures on the long-range and hypothetical usefulness of the moon program. But Paine concluded that no such transfer would be made. The nation would not invest its resources into human needs but it would support scientific experimentation bountifully.

Paine's comments displayed remarkable candor and insight. With less frankness but more hubris, politicians, scientists, and preachers had endorsed the moon explorations as a triumph for humanity and especially for America. Only advocates of economic and racial justice raised a voice at the violation of Eisenhower's warning. I believe that the roots of American urban degradation and civil chaos grew out of the misplaced priorities represented by the moon business, even though many religious leaders would say that the space program gave the American people a great psychological boost, and that it was necessary to our winning the Cold War by outspending the Russians. Those who would take this position prove my point: America needs religious beliefs which challenge the moral values of a society that leaves human needs unmet, but instead indulges itself in grandiose ego-tripping. American society in 1969 was not so challenged. This failure to confront hubris corrodes our national fabric as surely as any chemical addictions or narcotic dependencies.

Can we tolerate the prospect of a society that continues to provide more and more frivolous entertainment and expendable products to a majority, yet leaves a growing minority bereft of necessities? This seems to be the direction that our economic policies will now take for the short-term future, at least. As long as we willingly act on the premise that a market-driven system must involve absolute freedom to amass profits, with no regard for social or contextual consequences, then we cannot expect to gain much ground in the race between population and starvation. A market-driven economy will invest in research primarily because of its concern for profit, that is, how much will its supported research return in dollars. The knowledge crucial to the problems of worldwide crowding, hunger, racial and gender equity, and more basic environmental problems will not be attained by adding more channels to the television offerings, or by connecting everyone whose world is illuminated by light bulbs to a network of electronic transmitters. The final flaw of market-driven capitalism might not be its runaway competition, but its siphoning of the intelligence of humanity into irrelevant pursuits.

Self-Interest With Cooperation

Many want to what know what we can do to achieve the benefits of cooperation when we are so deeply entrenched in a culture of competition. This is more a problem of appearance than of reality. We need to address the question of how we can properly determine where competition is appropriate and where cooperation is inappropriate. I have critiqued competition on the assumption that its unlimited exercise is contrary to our essential connectedness. The essential, common organic life that we share makes the good of all increase the good of each and, conversely, the good of each individual increases the good for all others. This occurs whether we compete in some parts of life or not. When our competition disproportionally hurts one seriously and helps another marginally, then it should be curbed. When our competition can enhance the growth of some important and helpful factor for many of us, then it should be encouraged. An example of the former would be an employer who drives an employee at a pace that destroys his health in order to save a small cost in production. An example of the latter would be a government contract to purchase a large quantity of low-emission trucks from the company that first develops the needed technology.

Competition must be adjusted according to the larger need for cooperation. This requires an adjustment of the perception of self-interest in the light of the larger perception of interdependent interests. If I am running a business in a small town, I will see myself competing with other town business and property owners for public funds to improve the streets around my enterprise. But, if I monopolize those funds so that the rest of the town is left in shambles, my own business prospects will suffer through the loss of incentives for people to live and trade in my town and the resulting loss of purchasing power.

Is There Hope in Humanity?

The future is always in the hands of people like us. It has to be, because that is all there is: more generations of people like us, with our hopes and fears and faults. At one time Galileo had never seriously looked at the stars, Newton had not thought about the motions of the planets, Shakespeare had never written a line of dialogue or poetry, Beethoven had never touched a keyboard, and Rachel Carson had never listened to a bird song. How then did our world get to be what it is? Those people, in childhood, youth, or adulthood, started from where they were, took what they had, and created something of lasting worth out of all their abilities and potentialities. They were not ordinary people in the sense that most of us are ordinary, but what we mean by "ordinary" is that we do not rise to our potential. Those people were extraordinary because they made much more of what they had than do most of us. We never know in advance what can happen if someone takes what he or she has and makes with it something that is lasting. How many natural gifts are lying dormant, waiting for someone to help them blossom, as Anne Sullivan did for Helen Keller?

Hope must be made out of possibilities; otherwise, if it were already an actuality, there would be no need for making improvements. The past and its realized potentials give us our possibilities. All the creative people we have mentioned might have done one different thing that could have changed his or her life. Suppose one day in long-ago Vienna, someone had said, "Herr Beethoven, you have written eight beautiful symphonies. Surely you do not need to write just another one. Why not try your hand at some nice polkas?" Might Beethoven then have left his "one more symphony" unwritten? But Beethoven had the music inside his head and mind and heart and gave the world his special version of the music of the triumph of spirit over frustration, limitation, and despair.

In a recent short book on environmental issues, Bill McKibben's *Hope, Human and Wild: True Stories of Living Lightly on the Earth,* the author calls our time "a hard time for hope." McKibben had written earlier about the sadness of humans in parts of our earthly habitat; subsequently he had the opportunity to visit Curitiba, a city in Brazil, and Karela, a state in India. These places in the world today defy the stereotypes of undeveloped societies. Curitiba is in the same country as Rio de Janeiro and has grown along with the rest of Brazil, yet unlike other large Hispanic cities, its citizens take pride in its accomplishments. Karela is poor by any standards, yet enviable in its quality of life.

Unlike Rio and most of the rest of the cities in the western hemisphere, whose growth has proved toxic to man and nature, Curitiba has enlarged and improved on its past. In the last forty years, it has become a city in which people want to live, and one they do not want to leave. It may be the only city we can find that gets better for people to live in as it absorbs and assimilates newcomers in large numbers.

The Curitiba style was inaugurated when a new mayor, Jaime Lerner, decided to thwart an old plan to devastate the central street with an overpass. To circumvent that loss to the heart of the city, Lerner replaced the street with a pedestrian mall. When the opposition, led by the local automobile club, threatened to reclaim the street by means of a massive motorcade, Lerner and his supporters responded. On the appointed day, the motorcade arrived and found that Lerner had not called out the police, but had city workers lay down strips of paper the length of the mall. When the auto club arrived, its members found dozens of children sitting in the former street painting pictures. The transformation of Curitiba had begun.

McKibben quotes some other visitors to Curitiba:

> Yuri Gagarin: "I feel as if I have just disembarked on another planet, not earth."

André Malraux: "A murmur of glory accompanies the pounding of your anvils that salute your audacity, your faith, and the destiny of Brazil, as the Capital of Hope surges on."

Frank Kapra, the movie director, thought Curitiba the eighth wonder of the world. McKibben sums up his estimate of what makes Curitiba different:

> But the most impressive transformation may be the willingness of the people to support social programs. In a city widely described as conservative, I met no one who thought the city was spending too much money helping the poor: the mixing and contact spurred by all of Lerner's schemes, and the fact that the schemes work, seems to have lessened the fear and contempt that hobbles such work in other places.

The point is so clear: When citizens realize that their social efforts are helping to assimilate newcomers into their city and so ensure their good life in the city, those longtime citizens realize that their own lives will be better for it. In how many American cities have older residents decided that the newcomers, many poor people and/or people of a different color or origin, are going to ruin the city, and so move to some suburb where they will be newcomers who are resented by the old residents? Separation instead of assimilation takes place all over. That "fear and contempt" that Curitiba avoided is rampant at all levels of American life. Curitiba demonstrates that it need not be so. Assimilation can be achieved if there is fairness, tolerance, and respect on all sides. Those qualities must be nurtured because the seeds of "fear and contempt" are ready to sprout wherever great differences exist in the extent of control that old and new citizens have over the situation. The newcomers do not make the atmosphere of the city—it is there when they arrive. If their trust is not secured through sincere and active assistance programs, then their distrust will inhibit the effectiveness of whatever piecemeal help might be offered later.

In both Curitiba and in Karela, McKibben found that even under the most unlikely circumstances, the trust between those in control and those in most desperate need formed the basis of social progress in raising the quality of life. In the old colonial days, Karela had humane landlords who became convinced that their control over the lives of their serfs was nearing an end. An *awareness* of the social values of cooperation grew among both the wealthy and the poor in Karela. McKibben says:

> Such awareness—some new level of understanding where self-interest and public interest intersect to leave behind a new attitude and a changed

> behavior—is clearly essential about such issues as mass transit and conservation and living lightly. The Keralite experience indicates such awareness comes through widespread, self-reinforcing change. People have fewer children in this pocket of India because life is safer, fairer, more decent. Because they have fewer children, life should be safer, fairer and more decent in the future.

The "developed world" often pays too little attention to the humanity of the people of the "undeveloped world," treating them as only a blur of faces without individual and familial identity. We simply cannot see them. This was a feature of the plantation culture, as well as the world of Jim Crow. We just did not see the people whose ancestors were slaves or their homes or schools or churches. It was not part of the world that came into our focus, which had been fixed by our mythology about the utter "otherness" of colored people. As long as we did not see them, we did not have to ask, "How do you suppose it would feel to live like that?" We would not allow ourselves to admit that they must feel very much the same way that we would feel if we were in their place. We would not admit that if it would hurt us, it surely must hurt them just as much. That is our danger now: that we will continue to dehumanize people whose circumstances have given them so little and to suppose that it doesn't really matter as much to them as it would to us.

McKibben addresses the American fear at the thought of being dragged down to the level of the Third World:

> Karela offers a pair of messages to the First World. One is that sharing works. Redistribution has made Karela a decent place to live, even without much economic growth. The second, and even more important, lesson is that some of our fears about simpler living are unjustified. It is not a choice between suburban America and dying at thirty-five, between Wal-Mart and hunger, between 500 channels of television and ignorance. Karela is a fact on the ground, both inspiring and discomfiting. The average American income is seventy times the average Karelite one—there is some latitude for change.

What Christianity Owes America

This brings us to the juncture of the next American religion and our destiny, along with the impact that our destiny has on the rest of the world. The distance that we keep between ourselves and others, at home and otherwise, breeds the "contempt and fear" that prevents our participating in a fairer and more decent world.

The dualism of the western religious view of humanity to a large extent creates and supports that distance. According to this view, on one side of the duality are the worthy and, on the other side, the unworthy. We Euro-Americans have learned through centuries to regard ourselves as worthy and everyone else as unworthy in the grossest, most overgeneralized terms.

This now translates into a contemptuous unwillingness to see anything wrong with the differences in the way humanity shares the goods of the planet. McKibben points to the proportions:

> Remember what this world is like: the richest fifth of the world's people in 1989 had fifty-nine times the income of the poorest fifth—up from a mere thirty times in 1960. Fifty-nine times the income!...And there is no reason—of morality or environment or economics—that people across Karela couldn't double or triple their "standard of living."...And no reason they couldn't have more without harming the environment—if we had less.

This last phrase is the sticking point: *"if we had less."* What will it take to break through the "fear and contempt" that drives us into our fortresses of security and separation in residential suburbs? What will broaden our vision of the humanity of all the people of the world? What will heighten our pursuit of justice among the children of earth? What will inspire us to seek respect for ourselves as we show respect for our brothers and sisters over the earth? A religion that nurtures humanity instead of abandoning it will do all these things. The gospel of Jesus is such a religion, even if the churches promote triumphalism instead.

Is There Humanity in God, or God in Humanity?

The next religion will arise from the same historical sources that all the others have come from and combine these roots with the new hopes, ideas, and combinations of old and new that people can imagine. The old idea proposes that although humanity is made in the image of an exclusively male God, humanity is nevertheless irrevocably male and female. This old idea also entails the doctrine of incarnation, that is, that God takes on human life; "The Word was made flesh," with all its implications. Jesus is said to be God incarnate, but still limited by and subject to human nature, although not subject to inherited sin. This doctrine is important because Jesus has to be genuinely human in order to substitute for humanity in the sacrifice to God for sin. Christian thought has centered on Jesus as the Man-God, because if Jesus were not God, he could not be sinless, and if he were not man, he could not die for human sin. Traditional Christian intellectual energy has been devoted to promoting a deified Jesus, but it seems to me that this Man-God idea also humanizes God. For instance, it opens the way to ask about how genders in humanity suggest genders in God. The goddess idea is a very conspicuous emerging topic in our time.

One particular new idea has become available through the work of Riane Eisler, a scholar of wide-ranging interests who wrote *The Chalice and the Blade*. This scholarly exposition examines the predominant tradition of male domination and aggression that has come down through the millennia in all historical civilizations. Eisler reviews the research, mostly anthropological, that has recovered some traces of other kinds of civilizations in the Mediterranean area and in "Old Europe." These civilizations often practiced goddess veneration and were not dominated by deities of a single gender. These societies were overcome by the rise of aggressive and male-dominated societies that operated according to the current mode of territorial exclusiveness, with cities and towns as centerpieces.

In Eisler's book, these aggressive societies are represented by the "blade," and the earlier, nonaggressive ones by "the chalice." The book works toward the concept of gender partnership rather than domination by males and submission by females. This concept is a corollary of the nurturing relationship referred to earlier. Eisler says:

> Although this suppressive-dominator approach to conflict still overwhelmingly prevails, the success of less violent and more "feminine" or "passive" approaches to conflict resolution offers concrete hope for change. These approaches have ancient roots. In recorded history Socrates and later Jesus both used them. In modern times they are best known as embodied by men like Gandhi and Martin Luther King, Jr.—whom androcracy handled by killing and canonizing. But by far their most extensive use has been by women. A notable example is how in the nineteenth and twentieth centuries women nonviolently fought against unjust laws. For access to family planning information, birth control technologies, and the right to vote, they permitted themselves to be arrested and chose to go on hunger strikes, rather than using force or the threat of force to gain their ends.

The concept of feminine deities has ample precedents. The ancient Greeks had Athena, the goddess of wisdom, whom the Romans called Minerva. The ancient gods of Hellenic civilization are not known for their exclusive masculinity, but for their jealousy of other gods. The ancient Semitic god Yahweh is not only jealous of other gods, but also seems to be the masculine element of Elohim. The Genesis 1:27 account of the creation of humanity exemplifies the Elohist tradition: "So God (Elohim) created man in his image, in the image of God (Elohim) he created them; male and female he created." The Hebrew original for God here is a plural word, which we would translate strictly as "gods," reflecting the plural ending of the name.

Eisler comments on this usage:

> But as the god of thunder, of the mountain, or of war, or later on as the more civilized god of the prophets, there is only one God: the "jealous" and inscrutable Jehovah who in later Christian mythology sends his only divine Son, Jesus Christ, to die and thereby atone for his human children's "sins." And although the Hebrew word, Elohim has both feminine and masculine roots (incidentally explaining how in the first creation story in Genesis both woman and man could be created in Elohim's image), all the other appellations of the deity, such as King, Lord, Father, and Shepherd, are specifically male.

So the record in canonical tradition contains a slight ambiguity in two characteristics of God, the plural number and the mixture of male and female genders. Feminist scholars contend that the female and the plural were edited out in the long and convoluted development of Judaic and Christian theology. So we can see the bare possibility of a remnant of two gods, one female and the other male, or of an androgynous single god. The rise of masculine domination of culture has clearly suppressed such concepts of female deity.

Some venerate Mary the wife of Joseph and the mother of Jesus in a manner not very far short of goddess worship. The serious barrier to her deification is not her gender, but the claim made for the utterly unassailable and exclusive deity by the surrogates of the Father God. The combination of maleness and solitariness of the Father God presents a formidable image for our civilization, steeped as we are in the image of God as both male and dominant. We perceive no way of expressing a higher reality in religious terms than "Father God."

However dominant the exclusive male deity has been and still is in official "out-loud" language, there is a definite undercurrent of thought and feeling for a different kind of divine other. The commentaries of mystically inclined Christian saints who were enraptured by the scene of the impregnation of the future mother of Jesus carry some of the most suggestive expressions of this kind. The Father God, in the guise of the Holy Spirit, impregnated her. Luke's Gospel says:

> And, behold, you will conceive in your womb and bear a son, and you will call his name Jesus... And Mary said to the angel, "How can this be, since I have no husband?" And the angel said to her, "The Holy Spirit will come upon you, and the power of the Most High will overshadow you; therefore, the child to be born will be called Holy, the Son of God." (Luke 1:31-35)

This story has come to us through Semitic, Greek, and Latin languages and cultures. We read it through the eyes of the Roman celibate priests and Euro-American Puritan sensibilities of many centuries past. How far does this story depart from the other stories in the world's mythologies that depict the intercourse of a god and a goddess in producing either the natural world, humanity, or an offspring who will have a mission among humanity?

In the High Middle Ages among the cloistered mystics of France, Saint Bernard of Clairvaux (1090-1163) wrote some poems that have come down to us as highly imaginative devotional hymns, among them, "Jesus, the very thought of Thee," and "O Sacred Head now wounded." In a provocative book entitled *Innocent Ecstasy*, a Roman Catholic scholar, Peter Gardella, has written about how Saint Bernard interprets the way the Father God greeted the maiden Mary:

> According to Bernard, the greeting...showed that God's "excessive desire in its flight" had "preceded His messenger to the Virgin, whom He had loved, whom He had chosen for Himself, whose comeliness He had desired." Bernard's word for "desired," *concupierat*, was the same term theologians used for the essence of original sin: concupiscence, the inordinate desire that caused humanity to prefer the flesh to the spirit....Bernard and his followers seized on these passages to support their attribution of concupiscence to God.

It is quite easy to see the potential transition from "the Father God and a Jewish maiden" to "the Father God and the Mother Goddess" within the canonical tradition. Mary as the "Mother of God" has already crossed the threshold into her own "Immaculate Conception." That is, Pope Pius XI in 1854 decreed that although she was naturally conceived by her parents, she was supernaturally prevented from receiving their inheritance of original sin. In this mythology, she, out of all offspring of fallen humanity, came into the world without the curse of sin in her "nature." So, was her humanity "fallen," or was she somehow a hybrid, a god-woman, even as her son was said to be a god-man? With all the ambivalences in the tradition about sanctity and sexuality, the fevered imagination of the religious enthusiast can create novel combinations. Can we not faintly hear from a long past century, a desert hermit, too long in the sun, crying out in frustration after he had glimpsed a maiden in a passing Bedouin caravan, "O God, you had your virgin. Why can't I have mine"? Suggesting that God had intercourse with a woman in historical time may strike some as blasphemy. How blasphemous is the claim the there is flesh in the wafer and blood in the cup? How blasphemous is it to claim that the charismatic Christian behavior of ecstatic jumping, shouting, and swooning is the outpouring of the Holy Spirit? Does such an outpouring account for similar behavior at sports events and rock concerts? Is it blasphemy only when an outsider to the canonical tradition inquires into the language of the ecclesiastical texts, and not when charismatic believers deny that the same human psychological process generates both their religious excitement and other human excitement?

The tradition tells us that this one single young woman crossed the chasm from God to humanity, that she so charmed God that he was fascinated with her and became her partner in bearing a human child. The myth of Incarnation tells us not only that the Word could become flesh, but also that the flesh could take on divinity. Much more than this has come down in the myth that reconciles humanity with God, nullifying the separation brought about by human sin and guilt. If that single step was enough to cross the chasm from God to man, with Mary as the intermediary, how nonhuman can Jesus be? This suggests that humanity has the capacity to do the work of God in reconciling humanity's divisions into a single family.

The humanity of Jesus is at the real heart of the most cherished Christian traditions. However, the human Jesus has too long been obscured by the theological Christ. The churches have portrayed this Christ as a conquering monarch who offers to make America the triumphant power among all the people of the earth. We have had centuries of aggression, dominance and defiance at home and abroad. We need a voice of reconciliation, relationship and partnership. The human Jesus has such a voice. The human Jesus called God "Father," and all of humanity his family. When the churches of America have learned to say "Brother Jesus" with their loudest and clearest voices, then they will have given America what they owe.

Reference Notes

All references cited are described in the Bibliography.

All Biblical quotations are from the Revised Standard Version.

page	**Chapter One**
7	"The American religion…": Bloom, p. 45f.
8	"There are qualities…": Gregory, p. 316–317.
11	Professor Trueblood expounded upon this phrase in lectures.
	Chapter Three
41	"If I have wrested…": Thoreau, p. 88 in Krutch's edition.
42	"In words that any…": Zinn, p. 69.
45	"Izanagi asked his spouse…": Earhart, p. 15.
	Chapter Four
57	"Man is only a reed…": Pascal, p. 200.
60	"When in our own time…": Malcolm, p. 164f.
61	"We need to recognize…": Sandmel, pp. 64–65.
63	"Chapter thirteen is a self-contained…": Meeks, p. 41n.
67	"The divided self…": James, p. 143f.
69	"Therefore do not seek…": Augustine, *Commentary on the Gospel of John*, p. 184.
70	"…you have made us…": Augustine, *Confessions*, p. 3.
71	"Aristotle gave more…": Kirk and Raven, p. 5.
74	"Man is the measure…": Zeller, p. 98.
76	"…Of one substance with the Father": Bettenson, pp. 24–25.
76	"the Son has a beginning": Bettenson, p. 39.
77	"…do not interfere…": Bettenson, p. 19.
77	"…137 left dead…": Bickerman, p. 243.

Chapter Five

89   "It seems the time": Odum, p. 263.

Chapter Six

108   "Democritus' theory…": Zeller, p. 82.

109   "In economics…": Lodge, p. 42ff.

111   "Possessive individualism…": MacPherson.

113   "God's role…": *Process and Reality,* p. 346.

114   "Religion is…": *Religion in the Making,* p. 47

115   "For his academic dissertation…": Schmidt, p. 1.

116   "Speaker, you speak too late.": Buber, *I and Thou,* pp. 97–8.

118   "The world is twofold": *I and Thou,* p. 53.

119   "Relation is reciprocity": *I and Thou,* p. 67.

120   "The basic word I-Thou…": *I and Thou,* p. 62.

121   "The unlimited sway…": *I and Thou,* p. 100.

Chapter Seven

125   Zinnbauer and Pargament, p. 549ff.

127   "My mistress…": Douglass, *Narrative,* pp. 39–40.

128   "He devised games…": *Narrative,* p 40.

129   "It is sometimes said…": *Narrative,* p 83.

129   "I had at one time…": *Narrative,* p 82.

130   "Helen and Annie…": *Helen and Teacher.* See especially Chapter Twenty-five, p. 440 ff.

Chapter Eight

148   "See our present condition…": Lincoln's *Speeches and Writings,* 1859–1865, p. 354.

149   "Yet the myth persists…": Kilpatrick, p. 31.

150   "The reality the South has had…": Kilpatrick, p. 35.

150   "The abolitionists who saw…": Lerner, p. 16.

152	"Almighty God hath...": quoted in Higginson, p. 6.
153	"May it be to the world...": Jefferson, *Writings*, p. 1517.
154	"[it] is not their condition...": Jefferson, p. 268.
156	"A Summary View...": Jefferson, p. 1433.

Chapter Nine

168	"The mass of men...": Thoreau, *Walden and Other Writings*, p. 111.
168	"...the cost of a thing...": Thoreau, p. 128.
170	"I learned this...": Thoreau, p. 343.
172	"For venture capitalists...": Rosenberg and Birdzell, p. 201.
175	"There are today...": Lodge, *The American Disease*, p. 40.
176	"As much as anyone...": Locke in Burtt, p. 415.
181	"Man cannot dispense...": *I and Thou*, p. 98.
184	"General Conception," Rawls, *A Theory of Justice*, p. 303.
186	"We find this...": *Property and Contract*, Ely, p. 96.

Chapter Ten

189	"What is the best religion?" Carver, p. 11.
189	"This church would be founded...": Carver, p. 14.
190	"Again, the Fellowship...": Carver, p. 133.
190	"If Christians make themselves...": Carver, p. 137.
190	"Those who heed...": Carver, p. 5.
195	"I must admit...": quoted in Reed, p. 68.
202	"After graduation from college...": Coughlan, p. 8.
205	"Eisenhower concluded...": quoted in Ambrose, p. 536.
205	"If it were possible...": Paine, p. 21.
208	"...a hard time for hope": McKibben, *Hope*, p. 1.
208	"The transformation...": *Hope*, p. 67.
208	Yuri Gagarin, *Hope*, p. 67.

209	Andre Mairaux, *Hope*, p. 65.
209	"But the most impressive…": *Hope*, p. 106
209	"Such awareness…": *Hope*, p. 155.
210	"Karela offers…": *Hope*, p. 169.
211	"Remember what…": *Hope*, p. 168.
212	"Although this…": Eisler, p. 92.
213	"But as the god of thunder…": Eisler, p. 94.
214	"According to Bernard…": Gardella, p. 120.

Bibliography

Ambrose, Stephen. *Eisenhower, Soldier and President.* New York: Simon and Schuster, 1990.

Augustine of Hippo. *Confessions.* Translated by Henry Chadwick. Oxford: Oxford University Press, 1991.

———. *The Works of St. Augustine.* In *Nicene and Post-Nicene Fathers.* Vol. 7. Edited by Philip Schaff. Peabody, Mass.: Hendrickson Publishers, Inc., 1999.

Bellah, Robert, et al. *Habits of the Heart.* Berkeley: University of California Press, 1985.

Bettenson, Henry. *Documents of the Christian Church.* 2d ed. London: The Oxford Press, 1981.

Bickerman, Elias. *Columbia History of the World.* New York: Harper and Row, 1972.

Bloom, Harold. *The American Religion.* New York: Simon and Schuster, 1992.

Bly, Carol. *Changing the Bully Who Rules the World.* Minneapolis: Milkweed Editions, 1996.

———. *The Passionate, Accurate Story.* Minneapolis: Milkweed Editions, 1990.

Boorstin, Daniel J. *The Americans: The Colonial Experience.* New York: Vintage Books, 1958.

Boyd, Gregory A. *God at War.* Downers Grove, Ill.: InterVarsity Press, 1997.

Buber, Martin. *I and Thou.* Translated by Walter Kaufmann. New York: Charles Scribner's Sons, 1970.

Burtt, Edwin A. *The English Philosophers from Bacon to Mill.* New York: The Modern Library, 1939.

Carver, Thomas N. *The Religion Worth Having.* Boston: The Houghton Mifflin Company, 1912.

Coughlan, Neil. *Young John Dewey.* Chicago: The University of Chicago Press, 1975.

Dewey, John. *The Quest for Certainty.* New York: Milton Balch and Company, 1929.

Douglass, Frederick. *Narrative of the Life of Frederick Douglass.* Edited by Benjamin Quarles. Cambridge: Harvard University Press, 1960.

Earhart, H. Byron. *Religion in the Japanese Experience.* Belmont, Calif.: Dickenson Publishing Company, 1982.

Eisler, Riane. *The Chalice and the Blade.* San Francisco: HarperSanFrancisco, 1987.

Ely, Richard T. *Property and Contract.* New York: The Macmillan Company, 1912.

Fanon, Frantz. *Black Skins, White Masks.* Translated by Charles L. Markham. New York: Grove Weidenfeld, 1967.

Farmer, James. *Lay Bare the Heart.* New York: Arbor House, 1985.

Fitzhugh, George. *Cannibals All.* Edited by C. Vann Woodward. Cambridge: The Harvard University Press, 1960.

Fredriksen, Paula. *From Jesus to Christ.* New Haven: Yale University Press, 1988.

Fry, John R. *The Great Apostolic Blunder Machine.* San Francisco: Harper & Row, Publishers, 1978.

Gardella, Peter. *Innocent Ecstacy.* New York: Oxford University Press, 1985.

Garrett, William R., ed. *Social Consequences of Religious Belief.* New York: Paragon House, 1989.

Goodenough, Ursula. *The Sacred Depths of Nature.* New York: Oxford University Press, 1998.

Gregory, Joel. *Too Great a Temptation.* Fort Worth: The Summit Group, 1994.

Hacker, Andrew. *Two Nations.* New York: Charles Scribner's Sons, 1992.

Herrmann, Dorothy. *Helen and Teacher.* New York: Alfred A. Knopf, 1998.

Higginson, Thomas W. *Anti-Slavery Pamphlets.* Vol. 2. New York: American Anti-Slavery Society, 1855.

James, William. *The Varieties of Religious Experience.* New York: Penguin Books, 1958.

Jefferson, Thomas. *Writings.* New York: Literary Classics of the United States, Inc., 1984.

Johnson, L. T. *The Real Jesus.* San Francisco: HarperCollins Publishers, 1996.

Kee, Howard Clark. *The Interpreter's One-Volume Commentary on the Bible.* Nashville: Abingdon Press, 1971.

Keller, Helen. *The Story of My Life.* New York: Grosset & Dunlap, 1902.

Kirk, G. S., and Raven, J. E. *The Presocratic Philosophers.* Cambridge: The University Press, 1957.

Kilpatrick, James J. *The Southern Case for Segregation.* New York: The Crowell-Collier Press, 1962.

Kosmin, Barry A., and Lachman, Seymore P. *One Nation Under God.* New York: Harmony Books, 1993.

Kozol, Jonathan. *Savage Inequalities.* New York: Crown Publishers, Inc., 1991.

Lash, Joseph P. *Helen and Teacher.* New York: Delacorte Press/Seymore Lawrence, 1980.

Lerner, Max. *America as a Civilization.* Vol. 1. New York: Simon and Schuster, 1957.

Lincoln, Abraham. *Speeches and Writings, 1859-1865.* New York: The Literary Classics of the United States, Inc., 1989.

Locke, John. *Philosophical Works.* Freeport, N.Y.: Books for Libraries Press, 1969.

Lodge, George C. *The American Disease.* New York: Alfred A. Knopf, 1984.

Macpherson, C. B. *The Political Theory of Possessive Individualism.* Oxford: Oxford University Press, 1962.

Malcolm X. *Autobiography.* As told to Alex Haley. New York: Ballantine Books, 1964.

McKibben, Bill. *Hope, Human and Wild.* Boston: Little, Brown and Company, 1995.

Malcolm X. *Autobiography,* as told to Alex Haley. New York: Ballantine Books, 1964.

Mangarella, Peter. *Human Materialism.* Gainesville, Fla.: University of Florida Press, 1993.

Meeks, Wayne A. *The Writings of St. Paul.* New York: W. W. Norton & Co., 1972.

Nevens, Winfield S. *The Witches of Salem.* Stamford, Conn.: Longmeadow Press, 1994.

Odum, E. P. *Ecology and Our Endangered Life-Support Systems.* Sunderland, Mass.: Sinauer Associates, 1989.

Pascal, Blaise. *Pensees.* Translated by A. J. Krailsheimer. Baltimore, Md.: Penguin Books, 1966.

Putnam, Robert. *Making Democracy Work.* Princeton: Princeton University Press, 1993.

Ranke-Heinemann, Uta. *Eunuchs for the Kingdom of God.* Translated by Peter Heinegg. New York: Penguin Group, 1991.

Rawls, John. *A Theory of Justice.* Cambridge: Harvard University Press, 1971.

Reed, Ralph. *Active Faith.* New York: The Free Press, 1996.

Renan, Ernest. *The Life of Jesus.* New York: The Modern Library, 1927.

Robertson, Pat. *The New World Order.* Dallas: Word Publishing, 1991.

Rosenberg, Nathan, and Birdzell, L. E., Jr. *How the West Grew Rich.* New York: Basic Books, Inc., Publishers, 1986.

Sandmel, Samuel. *The Genius of Paul.* Philadelphia: Fortress Press, 1979.

Schmidt, Gilya Gerda. *Martin Buber's Formative Years.* Tuscaloosa, Ala.: The University of Alabama Press, 1995.

Spong, John S. *Why Christianity Must Change or Die.* San Francisco: HarperCollins Publishers, 1998.

Stampp, Kenneth M. *The Peculiar Institution.* New York: Vintage Books, 1956.

Temple, William. *Christianity and the Social Order.* Baltimore: Penguin Books, 1942.

Thoreau, Henry David. *Walden and Other Writings.* New York: Bantam Books, Inc., 1962.

Turnbull, Colin M. *The Human Cycle.* New York: Simon and Schuster, 1983.

Wertengren, Thomas. *The Puritan Oligarchy.* New York: Scribner's Sons, 1947.

Whitehead, Alfred North. *Process and Reality.* New York: The Free Press, 1978.

Wildergren, George. *Mani and Manichaeism.* New York: Holt, Rinehart and Winston, 1965.

Windelband, Wilhelm. *A History of Philosophy.* Vol. 2. New York: Harper and Brothers, 1958.

Zeller, Eduard. *Outlines of the History of Greek Philosophy.* Thirteenth Edition. Revised by William Nestle. Translated by L. R. Palmer. New York: Meridian Books, Inc., 1955.

Zinn, Howard. *A People's History of the United States.* New York: Harper & Row Publishers, 1980.

Periodicals

Sokolov, Raymond. "Ancient Bioengineers." *Natural History,* October, 1933.

Paine, Thomas. "Protest Over Moon Shot." *New York Times,* July 17, 1969.

Weinstein, Myron M. "A Hebrew Qur'an Manuscript." *Studies in Bibliography and Booklore,* Winter, 1971/2.

Zinnbauer, S. J., and Pargament, K. I. *Journal for the Scientific Study of Religion* 36:549ff.

To order additional copies of this book, please send full amount plus $4.00 for postage and handling for the first book and 50¢ for each additional book.

Send orders to:

Galde Press, Inc.
PO Box 460
Lakeville, Minnesota 55044-0460

Credit card orders call 1–800–777–3454
Phone (952) 891–5991 • Fax (952) 891–6091
Visit our website at http://www.galdepress.com

Write for our free catalog.